MOBILIZING BOLIVIA'S DISPLACED

NICOLE FABRICANT

MOBILIZING BOLIVIA'S DISPLACED

INDIGENOUS POLITICS & THE STRUGGLE OVER LAND

FIRST PEOPLES New Directions in Indigenous Studies

The University of North Carolina Press CHAPEL HILL

*Publication of this book was made possible, in part, by a grant
from the Andrew W. Mellon Foundation.*

The University of North Carolina Press has been a member of
the Green Press Initiative since 2003.

Library of Congress Cataloging-in-Publication Data
Fabricant, Nicole.
Mobilizing Bolivia's displaced : indigenous politics and the struggle over land /
Nicole Fabricant.
    p. cm. — (First peoples : new directions in indigenous studies)
Includes bibliographical references and index.
ISBN 978-0-8078-3713-9 (cloth : alk. paper)
ISBN 978-0-8078-7249-9 (pbk. : alk. paper)
1. Movimiento Sin Tierra (Bolivia) 2. Land reform—Bolivia—History—21st
century. 3. Peasants—Political activity—Bolivia—History—21st century.
4. Indians of South America—Land tenure—Bolivia—History—21st century.
5. Indians of South America—Bolivia—Politics and government. I. Title.
HD1333.B5F33 2012
333.3'184—dc23   2012016634

cloth   16 15 14 13 12   5 4 3 2 1
paper   16 15 14 13 12   5 4 3 2 1

TO MY MOTHER AND FATHER, *who modeled fierce engagement and a deep commitment to a lived politics, and* TO MY HUSBAND, *who teaches, inspires, and challenges me to uphold these values on a daily basis.*

CONTENTS

MAPS AND FIGURES

ACKNOWLEDGMENTS

I would not have been able to complete this book without the warm and loving support of so many different people. In reality, like so many projects, this has been a collaborative effort. Thanking each and every person who contributed to the final product is the most humbling part of this long journey.

I am extremely thankful and indebted to the Landless Peasant Movement (MST-Bolivia) for letting me into their homes, communities, and intimate spaces of politics. I have learned so much from every organizer. First and foremost, my research assistant, Ademar Valda Vargas, provided stimulating conversations on many a trip to the *campo* and challenged me to think beyond one-dimensional academic models of production. In many ways, Ademar was my primary mentor and teacher in the field. I express my deepest gratitude to Silvestre Saisari, who trusted me and allowed me into the intimate circles of movement politics. Thanks are due to Ponciano Sulca (*mi compadre*) and his wife Gregoria Mamani for opening their lives to me in San Pedro and always pushing me to rethink the North/South divide. You have taught me so much! Eulogio Cortés, *mi cambinga de oro*, was my main comrade and friend. Thank you, Eulogio, for your contagious energy, political passions, and transnational friendship. I would also like to thank all the CEJIS lawyers, representatives who sat through hours of interviews and then provided critical documents and a safe place to study and read. It is often your lives that are put on the line for the movement, and I appreciate that kind of commitment.

My mentor Mary Weismantel has provided consistent support and guidance. She has challenged, inspired, and forced me to find my creative voice, and she always knew just what I needed during distinct moments in my career. Micaela di Leonardo, another wonderful mentor, has given me the gifts of theoretical rigor and intellectual stimulation and introduced me to all sorts of ideas that will forever define my scholarship and teaching. Josef Barton opened his office doors to me many years ago when I was in the depth of my despair and patiently guided and nurtured me back to life. I will be forever indebted to him for opening those doors and introducing me to his endless bibliographic resources. I would also like to thank Robert Albro, Jorge Coronado, and Brodie Fischer for their insights and rigorous comments, which helped turn this research into a book.

I am especially grateful for Emily Steinmetz and Kathryn Hicks, two of my closest *compañeras*, who tested, pushed, and radicalized me in recent years. We engaged in a struggle to change the academy, to remain politically committed, and to always *be* on the frontlines. Thanks also to Raquel Balcázar Soto, David Caballero, Umud Dalgic, Jose Muñoz, Juan Olmeda, Dawn Pankonien, Carlos Revilla, Tamara Roberts, and Ximena Soruco.

I could not have completed this book without the support of a cross-section of colleagues who in large and small ways sustained my spirit during difficult and trying moments. One of my closest *compañeros*, Bret Gustafson, challenged me intellectually, spiritually, and politically. I learned so much from him about empathy, long-term commitment, and pushing the bounds of engaged anthropology. Nancy Grey Postero also provided a combination of support and rigor as we exchanged ideas regarding Santa Cruz and the Bolivian Right. Other *Bolivianistas* who have paved a path for this work include Juan Arbona, Michelle Bigenho, Pamela Calla, Daniel Goldstein, Doug Hertzler, Ben Kohl, Brooke Larson, Andrew Orta, Tom Perreault, and so many others.

A big thank-you goes to my colleagues Matt Durington, Samuel Collins, and Dean Terry Cooney, who unconditionally supported me in my first few years at Towson University. Brett Williams has provided stimulation, political motivation, and much emotional support. Further, the students at Towson from two classes, "Revolution in Latin America" and "Resource Wars," influenced the rewriting and rethinking of this manuscript. Their smart insights, ability to connect their lived experience to theory, and passion for social justice forced me to rethink many chapters of this book. Special thanks to Alice Brierley, De Carlo Brown, Natalie Demyan, Antonio Hernandez, Kelly Mitchell, and David Reische. You *all* make teaching such a pleasure and have taught me so much about the dialogical relationship between theory and practice.

I am especially grateful to Andrew Canessa, who first introduced me to the First Peoples series and made this book possible. His mentorship has been invaluable. He has provided both personal and intellectual support, gentle guidance and nurturance, and unabated enthusiasm. His passionate relationship to ideas helped bring disparate themes together. His lasting mark remains on nearly every page of this book. Mark Simpson-Vos provided an initial entrée to the University of North Carolina Press and helped to tighten the manuscript through an acute sense of narrative structure and flow; he has been indispensable during the final stages of development. I extend deep gratitude to the editorial contributions of Ron

Maner, John Wilson, Zachary Read, Lauren Simpson, Whitney Goodwin, and Alejandro Figueroa. I also would like to extend a special thanks to a not-so-anonymous reviewer, Steve Striffler—it was a pleasant surprise to find out that someone I so respect and admire in the field challenged me to get rid of some theory and find my voice.

Several people important to this project have passed away during these last years. While they are no longer physically with me, their legacy continues to define my political and academic work. Joan Driscoll Kelly first introduced me to a lived politics through her work with the homeless, living in a hospitality house in Elizabeth, New Jersey, and shedding all material pleasures in life to provide unconditionally for others. There is not a day that goes by in which I do not think of her and how much my life and work has been influenced by her convictions. Kenneth Hale taught me how to build and nurture community and remain committed, despite the distance. His spirituality continues to feed me! The echoes of laughter of my grandmother, Harriet Fabricant, who passed away as this project came to fruition, will continue to sustain me. Finally, this work is a product of the risky research and pedagogical practice of Dwight Conquergood. His life was cut short, but he blazed a path and set a standard for engaged scholarship and activism.

Lastly, I would like to thank my family for their remarkable patience and gentle ways, even when I was quite neurotic. To my father, you transmitted to me your burning commitment to justice, intellectual quest, and fierce attachment over a lifetime. You always challenged me to "dig a little deeper" and "plug away a little harder." My work will forever be dedicated to you! To my mother, thanks for always keeping the balance, for the many nights on the phone, and for your calm and loving ways. You have given me the foundation to make something like this possible. Many thanks are due to the person who has perhaps endured the most, *mi compañero* Luico, who always allowed me to labor on nights and weekends. I wouldn't have completed this project without your consistent love, support, and nurturance. Finally, my daughter Amelia was born just as I completed the book. Her contagious smile and giggle have kept me grounded in what really matters.

A NOTE ON NAMES

Ethnographers often disguise the names of the people they work with in order to protect informants' rights and identities. However, in light of the fact that many of the MST leaders with whom I collaborated were, and continue to be, public figures, who have voiced their opinions on radio and television and in newspapers, I chose to use their real, complete names. Further, I have followed the same practice and used the real names of all the landowners and right-wing leaders who are mentioned in the text. All places and dates are true to history.

MOBILIZING BOLIVIA'S DISPLACED

INTRODUCTION

Indigeneity, Resources, and the Limitations of a Social Movement State

The election of Evo Morales and his political party MAS (Movimiento al Socialismo) to the presidency of Bolivia in 2005 represented a watershed victory for social movements and indigenous peoples worldwide. Morales, a coca farmer and peasant union leader, did not come out of one of the "ethnic" movements but rather emerged from a new social movement called the "Cocaleros," or coca growers.[1] Along with other resource-based movements, the Cocaleros mobilized the idea of "indigeneity" as a political tool to use against U.S. policies that militarily supported the eradication of coca. In their struggle to hold onto their lands and other critical resources, as well as their rights to cultivate this native crop, coca farmers politicized discourses centering on Indians as aboriginal peoples who had historically produced and consumed coca. This politicization of indigeneity has become an effective social movement strategy, which, with the election of Morales, has now come to define state-making in Bolivia.

Interestingly enough, Morales did not publicly self-identify as indigenous and there has even been much doubt as to whether or not he is fluent in Aymara, the language of the Aymara people who historically inhabited part of the Lake Titicaca basin in the highlands of Bolivia (Canessa 2007). Yet in the early 2000s—a period referred to as the "indigenous awakening" in Latin America—Morales began to embrace his indigenous roots and to employ highland indigenous culture as part of a broader MAS political campaign to undo a long history of colonial, and more recently neo-colonial, policies that once subjugated native peoples for slave labor and later exacerbated the already gross inequalities by privatizing state-owned industries and liberalizing markets. While indigeneity worked at a local level as a strategy to reclaim land and rights to cultivate coca, the political uses of indigeneity were suddenly scaled up to the state level, informing the reshaping of laws and the economy. Morales mobilized native philosophical tenets, cultural ideas, and social and reciprocal models of governance to reclaim national-level space from oligarchic elites, rewrite the

1

constitution to include indigenous peoples as citizens, and ultimately redefine the state as "plurinational." Plurinationality was the product of years of social movement organizing to incorporate Bolivia's nearly three dozen indigenous groups into one nation. At the same time, calls for a plurinational state transformed the idea of an exclusionary nation-state born of violence and conquest into a sovereign, democratic, and unified state that protects and respects the diversity of its people.

This was a quite remarkable time in Bolivian history. While indigenous peoples had been organizing for decades seeking cultural recognition and more inclusion in Bolivian society, this achievement represented a moment of radical cultural and structural transformation. For the first time, progressive social movements and indigenous peoples saw themselves as part of the state. In fact, when Morales was elected president he declared, "Indigenous Comrades, for the first time, we are Presidents!" (quoted in Postero 2007b), and on numerous occasions, when I asked various activists in both the highlands and the lowlands why they identified with Morales, many would reply with the same line, "He is one of us. *We* are now all part of the State." That expression suggests the capacity of social movement strategies not only to create change at the grassroots level, but to scale such practices up from local to regional and national levels. At first glance, Bolivia presents a kind of social movement victory, a David and Goliath story, whereby movement activists, who originally organized to reclaim water and gas from transnational corporations, ended their long resource battles by ousting neoliberal president Goni Sánchez de Lozada. They mobilized indigenous bases to elect someone of their own choosing and to initiate the process of rewriting the constitution and reconstructing a nation-state. Yet a closer look at contemporary Bolivian politics reveals a complicated and multifaceted tale of indigenous resistance, in which grassroots organizing has led to some shifts culturally and symbolically. However, a long history of global interconnectedness also limits the possibilities for radical economic transformations.

While many scholars and analysts have focused on Morales's Bolivia, few have looked in depth, over an extended period of time, at some of the movements that brought him to power. This book, then, seeks to understand, through a case study of the Movimiento sin Tierra (Landless Peasant Movement), better known as MST, how movement participants mobilized indigeneity to inform new ways of producing, living, and governing. MST also shaped both the arc of a national leader's success and reformed the state. The Landless Peasant Movement, like the Cocaleros, is one of the many new social movements in Bolivia, comprised mostly of displaced peoples from highland rural areas. Most of its members are not natives to this agriculturally rich Amazonian region, but rather are Quechua or Aymara Indians, who were once lured to the lowlands by contract laborers to work in the sugarcane plantations of Santa Cruz. At the time, Santa Cruz was merely a frontier town. However, international investment in agricultural improvements transformed it from a town of 43,000 people in the 1950s to one of 256,000 in 1976 and eventually into a booming economic center of nearly 1.4 million people in 2010. Historic government policies that denied migrant laborers access to land while favoring capitalist entrepreneurs with concessionary credit intensified a racialized hierarchy in places like Santa Cruz, whereby white and mestizo[2] elites held onto regional economic and political power and reinforced a strict labor code based upon race, class, and geography (being born in the lowlands versus the highlands). Many of these migrants, living on the periphery of a city, along with other lowland indigenous groups who felt threatened by the encroachment of private capital upon their native lands, realized that land was perhaps the single most important issue in the east.

LANDED INEQUALITY: THE OLD AND THE NEW

Land, then, was at the heart of one of the most important resource-based conflicts of the contemporary moment (particularly with the recent expansion of agribusiness and the global demand for soy). But landed inequality also represented one of those age-old battles that dated back to the Spanish conquest, when indigenous lands in the highlands called "ayllus"—Andean political and territorial units based on kinship groups and communally held lands—were broken up and Indians forced to work in the silver mines. In the eighteenth century, after independence from Spain, liberal and republican governments instituted various reforms that made communal property illegal, with the hope of turning all collective lands into private property. This paved the way for the massive expropriation of Indian lands and the creation of the latifundio system, in which Indians served as laborers for white or mestizo landowners, on large landed estates.

There have been several attempts to undo this long history of landed inequality. One was the 1952 revolution, in which a radical uprising of peasants sought to reverse historic injustices with a new agrarian reform act promising the redistribution of land across Bolivia. While the law largely eradicated latifundio lands in the west, the reforms never reached the east. Instead the law created the possibility for consolidating lands and productive resources in the hands of a few elite families (Friedsky 2005). By the mid-1970s, the reforms had been abandoned, although no one could say when it had concluded. It ended in the corners of a handful of offices as thousands of files remained both invisible and unconcluded. Over time, all subsequent government offices and administrations were negligent in directing this process. Bolivia's military dictatorships distributed large portions of land as political patronage to single families in eastern Bolivia, exacerbating existing inequality (Urioste 2003, 2006; Soruco, Plata, and Medeiros 2008; Soruco 2011).

To correct the shortcomings of the original Agrarian Reform Law, new reforms were established in the 1990s. The law creating the Instituto Nacional de Reforma Agraria (National Institute for Agrarian Reform), or INRA, sought to redistribute land more equitably and to rationalize land markets and property titles in the east. However, such legislation provided merely symbolic rights without massive material or structural changes to the highly unequal agrarian system. The INRA Law promised to provide juridical security over property, recognize the rights of indigenous peoples to their ancestral lands, establish principles of sustainability to secure access to land, and create a new set of institutions through which to manage land issues in a transparent manner (Valdivia 2011). In addition, it was supposed to introduce three principles. The first had to do with the function of the property in question: property that did not fulfill a social function should be expropriated by the state and redistributed to the landless. The second principle focused on the best uses of the land and included a land-use plan for each department devised by the Ministry of Sustainable Development with the overarching goal of sustainability. Lastly, *saneamiento*, or a clarification of land rights, involved the production of cadastral surveys to map the boundaries of properly functioning property. Altogether it was conceptualized as a "healing process" to end the irregular granting of land for undisclosed purposes by binding together geographic location, surface delimitations, and fulfillment of function into a legal land title (Valdivia 2010).

The 1990s witnessed a wave of reforms that signified at least a partial end to the corruption of prior military dictatorships, which had siphoned resources and gifted lands to elite families, often friends of dictators. Most significantly, however, indigenous peoples were legislatively deceived into believing they would receive land rights through this process of surveying and redistributing land and eventually would become full-fledged citizens. As Benjamin Kohl (2003) points out, although this neoliberal land legislation symbolically gave rights to indigenous communities, those responsible for carrying out the law materially failed to follow through on its promises. Exact figures are hard to come by, but even the most generous statistics document that between 1996 and 2003, 79 million acres were distributed (or redistributed) to 40,000 people in large parcels, while only 10 million acres were awarded to 550,000 campesinos. More to the point, most campesinos were forced to live on plots of less than five acres (Friedsky 2005).

This unequal land legislation, coupled with shifts in agriculture, created an increasingly difficult landscape for small-scale farmers. The liberalization of trade and international investment in export-oriented agriculture favored a small group of industrial farmers in the east. Elites in Santa Cruz who had once invested in sugarcane plantations quickly shifted to soy production,[3] accelerating the consolidation of landownership, deforestation, and the expansion of monocultures—in this case, the production of soy for biofuels to feed the global demand for energy resources. Importantly, small-scale farmers could not compete with this wholesale transformation of land use and production processes; some took out loans with very high interest rates in order to find a niche in this new market, but in many cases they fell deep into debt and had to sell off their land, property, and machinery.

This devastating geography of expansive capitalism and consolidation of productive resources led to new forms of displacement and socioeconomic dispossessions. Many farmers lost their landholdings and migrated to city centers in search of work in the expanding informal sector as small-scale vendors or bus or taxi drivers. While some found jobs in the informal economy, many joined the ranks of the unemployed and dispossessed, becoming what Mike Davis (2006) has referred to as "refugees of neoliberalism" (see also Harvey 2006). As their numbers swelled, these displaced peoples began to think about long-term, sustainable strategies to confront the problems of landlessness and unemployment.

It is within this context that the Landless Peasant Movement emerged as one of the most important social movements of the decade of the 2000s, not as an ethnic or indigenous movement, but rather a heterogeneous movement of displaced laborers, agricultural workers, and both highland and lowland Indians. They adopted a militant structure and strategy from the better-known Brazilian Landless Movement, whereby hundreds of displaced peoples would seize or occupy latifundio land as an act of resistance, squat on the hacienda (using their physical bodies as visible signs and symbols of the stark inequality), and begin to farm in collective ways. This strategy brought attention to the problem of landed inequality in the east and also placed a certain amount of pressure upon the state to begin to investigate whether or not the property served a social and economic function (which was required under the Bolivian constitution) and begin a process of reclamation and redistribution.

MOBILIZING INDIGENEITY: PRE-COLUMBIAN CULTURAL FORMS ACROSS TIME, SPACE, AND SCALE

In order to understand the cultural strategies of this new social movement in the east and how they, in turn, informed the shaping of a new state, I traveled with MST activists on their daily rounds, observed and participated in meetings, and lived for an extended period of time in two key agricultural zones, considered the northern regions of Santa Cruz: Obispo Santiesteban and Ichilo. Along with my research partner and friend, Ademar Vargas, a young student from the University of San Simon in Cochabamba, I traversed regional spaces on the backs of agricultural trailers, microbuses, and mopeds and followed leaders across regional, national, and global spaces to transnational arenas of MST organizing. From 2005 to 2007, I witnessed, alongside MST representatives, the inauguration of the New Agrarian Reform Law, the nationalization of Bolivia's gas and oil, and the beginning phases of the rewriting of the constitution. I took part in spectacular symbolic celebrations, protest marches, and agrarian events as indigenous peoples listened attentively to Morales. This mobile research strategy informed my understanding of the flexibility and adaptability of indigenous ways and customs, as distinct activists grabbed onto them to negotiate change in contemporary Bolivia. Because the idea of indigeneity is no longer grounded to national or territorial space, or rooted in language or birthplace, landless activists can use it, perform it, dress it up, and claim ownership over it as a critical organizing tool.

Mobility, or motion, then serves as a central trope throughout this book, informing the development of several key analytic themes: how the past influences the present, or rather how historical memory defined contemporary movement organizing, and the use of these cultural forms as they travel from community to community and inform the reconstruction and rebuilding of small-scale communities and local governance in Santa Cruz. The imagined ayllu, the fundamental unit of social organization of ancient Andean communities based on kinship groups and communally held territory, has been crucial in shaping the form of the movement's resistance. This cultural construct served as a powerful ideological framework for rebuilding community, productive units, and democratic structures. These imagined alternative lifeways (in which individuals are tied to communal land and property) become sediments of history that redefine contemporary politics and link past struggles to present forms of landed economic inequality. While the landless might mobilize the ayllu to restructure agrarian social and landed relations, they also use it to organize settlements democratically. It becomes a model of participatory democracy and ensures a form of protection against violent threats from outside and within these agrarian settlements.

I follow in the engaged anthropological tradition of Joanne Rappaport (1994), an anthropologist who, rather than dismissing such historical and cultural practices as "strategic essentialism," sought to understand why ancient Colombian narratives carry such weight in contemporary Cumbal performances. She notes, "These are not experiences-turned-stories, . . . they are not yarns of long-gone and forgotten disasters, but reflections on events that still impinge upon everyday life. In this sense, they are much more than stories, although they have certainly grown and changed with the years since the original events. . . . [T]hey are palimpsests, whose multiple presents overlay the pasts they seek to represent, pasts conveyed through careful selection of words and images" (2).

On one hand, culture becomes a political force, a vehicle through which historic understandings serve particular purposes for organizations in the present. Therefore, I ask questions about the strategic use and mobility of cultural narratives of the ayllu: Why have historical memories of pre-Columbian communities become particularly important in the contemporary period? Why and how do these excavated histories serve as both model and blueprint for alternative forms of living, working the land, and redistributing resources? Further, in what ways have these narratives informed state-building?

As cultural forms travel on marches and demonstrations, from the grassroots to regional to national spaces, practices become mobile and malleable and inform nation-state building and rebuilding. Morales has used and manipulated particular grassroots cultural strategies of "imagined community" (Anderson 1983), tales of indigenous resistance, and symbolic reclamations of space in order to forge a new kind of state structure. In part, the mobility of grassroots strategies and performances of indigeneity have contributed significantly to the solidification of support for the MAS project. Cultural, historical, and territorial performances deeply linked distinct groups of people to the idea of decolonizing a state. It was on this basis that they often saw collective reflections of themselves—of their own daily struggles and histories—informing the practice of state-making. As Morales continued to mobilize indigenous history and struggle in his public reclamations of land/territory, national industries, and spaces of governance, that created a more intense partnering of sorts between movements and the state.

Much recent scholarship has focused on the leftward shift in Latin American politics (Postero 2007a; Kozloff 2008; Lazar 2008; Petras and Vetmeyer 2009; Escobar 2010). However, few works have explored ways in which grassroots organizers, through cultural forms, have contributed to a remapping of power structures in Latin America. As well, the subsequent challenges and tensions of transforming a state that now claims to represent all indigenous peoples is underexplored. Recent work by Gustafson (2009b, 2010) does query what it means for social movements to be a part of the state; he even coins the term "social movement state," in which the state relies upon the social, cultural, and performative mechanisms of movements, but also on the mobilization of diverse sectors to sustain the regime. He warns that these relationships complicate ethnographic inquiries of power relations, since sovereignty-making practices have now been instrumentalized in and through the production of new alliances between subaltern peoples and those in power.

I conceptualize these tensions as the new frictions between grassroots organizations and the state, which can halt all forms of progressive or forward movement. Anna Tsing's (2005) insightful work on friction among environmental activists in Indonesia informed my thinking about tensions between global actors and local activists, individual and collective desires, as well as between indigenous "cosmovisions" and a broad-based capitalist logic, which defines everyday life in contemporary Santa Cruz. This, then, is not a simple tale of landless using indigenous ways to implement a fairer and more egalitarian agrarian structure, but rather a story that also exposes how long histories of exploitation and extraction have defined contemporary forms of organizing and even reproduced similar structures of inequality, fear, and violence at a local level, which can also scale up to other spaces of governing. Nor is this a tale that romanticizes all things indigenous; rather, I look at this new, complicated, and murky terrain of the political uses of indigeneity. While the indigenous *usos y costumbres* (ways and customs) can be quite radical and can present redistributive possibilities, they also prove dangerous and problematic, particularly when right-wing businessmen in the east used them for the distinct purpose of maintaining their historic racial and economic privilege and to hold onto their rights to lands, resources, and region.

By mapping the limitations of the use of culture at the local and regional levels in MST politics, I attempt to shed light on the dangers of culture's use at the state level, with regard to Morales's cooptation and use of indigenous history as a means of transforming law, economy, and the state and of reinforcing an alliance between movements and the current administration. Morales performed Andean rituals at the famous site of Puerta del Sol in Tiwanaku as he was inaugurated into the presidency, and he recited the final words of Tupac Katari in the place where that martyr suffered his brutal death at the hands of the Spanish as he strove to initiate his agrarian revolution. Yet these indigenous performances remain separate and severed from real structural change, as Morales has been unable to fulfill many of his promises. The MST had a particular agenda with regard to land reform, including a proposal to eliminate the unproductive latifundio landholdings, when they came to the seat of power in La Paz. Yet even now the very same agrarian structure exists and Bolivia remains trapped in webs of debt and dependency. This limits the MAS proposals for reviving small-scale agriculture. While Morales might provide some monetary benefits to small-scale producers, most cannot compete in this broader marketplace. Proposals for food sovereignty—which promote the idea that food is first and foremost a right of all people and only secondarily an item of trade—remain limited when export-oriented industries continue to define food production. These frictions become ever more apparent as the MST story unfolds.

However, the most recent case of tensions between indigenous peoples and the new state centered on the proposal to run a major highway through the TIPNIS (Territorio Indígena Parque Nacional Isiboro-Sécure), the Isiboro National Park and Secure Territory, in lowland Bolivia. The indigenous communities who live in the TIPNIS park believe that a massive road construction project would lead to environmental destruction and disruption of a particular way of life for native communities. Despite Morales's discourses of respect for native peoples and the need to protect and preserve the environment, this case crystallized the weaknesses and confines of this reformed government, while simultaneously illustrating the complicated and tense relationship between indigenous peoples and the state.

THE ONGOING FRICTIONS BETWEEN MOVEMENTS AND MORALES

In 2009, the Morales government granted indigenous territory status to the Moxeño, Yuracaré, and Chimán peoples living in or around the TIP-NIS, where they held common legal title to the land. This meant that Morales recognized these lowland indigenous groups as the first peoples, natives of this land, and recognized their rights to hold land communally, as a community, and to work the land in alternative ways.

Shortly thereafter, in the fall of 2011, Morales signed a pact with Brazil's national development bank to help pay for the costs associated with a massive road project that would produce deforestation, the disruption of natural flows and ecosystems, and eventual displacement of communities dependent upon local resources. More to the point, Morales (who speaks often of collective or co-governance) failed to consult with the lowland indigenous communities most affected by this road construction,[4] thus creating much resentment and backlash. In turn, the mounting resistance threatened to break the alliance between some social movements—among them the Consejo Nacional de Ayllus y Marcas del Qullasuyu (CONAMAQ; a confederation of traditional governing bodies of Quechua- and Aymara-speaking highland communities in the departments of La Paz, Oruro, Potosí, and Tarija) and La Confederación de Pueblos Indígenas de Bolivia (CIDOB; the Confederation of Lowland Indigenous Peoples of Bolivia)—and this left-leaning government. In the words of Adolfo Chavez, head of CIDOB: "Each Bolivian has the right to freedom . . . we have tried many times to contact the President and to meet with him to discuss the TIPNIS case, but they never listen to us. It was when they heard the President say 'whether they want it or not, we are going to build this road,' that the brothers [indigenous brothers] demanded this march" (Kenner 2011b).

After several months of waiting for an answer from Morales, Amazonian lowland indigenous groups, deeply disappointed by both the proposed road project and his undemocratic practices, organized a massive protest march. This classic land march, which began in September of 2011, took the form of a sacrificial thirty-day walk from the lowland regions of eastern Bolivia, through the valleys to the highlands of western Bolivia, and eventually wound up in La Paz. It was to climax at the seat of governance, in Plaza Murillo before the Presidential Palace, with a rally intended both to place significant pressure on the administration and to make the demonstrators' demands visible. The march started solely as a form of resistance to the construction of the highway; over time, however, indigenous marchers added several demands, including an end to hydrocarbon exploitation in the area, respect for indigenous peoples and territories, development and implementation of the right to be consulted, legislation that protects "forests and natural parks," access to health care for indigenous peoples, higher education and indigenous universities in the lowlands, housing plans, cleaning up contaminated rivers, and more. These protests became a symbolic battle in which Bolivia's indigenous peoples—from both the highlands and lowlands—defended their historic rights to land and territories. In addition, they publicly denounced a government with which they had identified, but which had reneged on its promises and promoted a model of development contrary to the values and needs of indigenous peoples.

On September 28, 2011, Morales, who was fearful that there would be serious confrontations between distinct indigenous groups along the march, sent 450 federal police just outside of Yucumo, in the Beni department of Bolivia, where several hundred MAS-affiliated *colonos* (colonists)—highland Indians who migrated to the lowlands in search of land and labor—blocked the roads, limiting the forward movement of the protestors. The conflict erupted into aggressive police violence against indigenous marchers, with 152 protestors treated for injuries in San Borja (Bjork-James 2011). The police repression received national and international attention, eventually impelling Morales to negotiate with the protestors. On the night of October 8, 2011 the Chamber of Deputies passed a modified MAS proposal, which required Senate approval and the president's signature. The modified proposal suspended construction on Segment 2 (the primary zone of conflict running directly through indigenous communal lands) pending free, prior, and informed consultation of the TIPNIS indigenous peoples, respecting their own norms and procedures in the framework of the Constitution, International Labour Organization (ILO) Convention 169, and the UN Declaration on the Rights of Indigenous Peoples. It also authorized a study of the alternatives for the

Villa Tunari–San Ignacio de Moxos highway, with alternatives required to guarantee the rights of indigenous peoples in their territory and the ecological equilibrium of TIPNIS. The consultation process, however, was not binding. That is, the repeated indigenous opposition to the project may be ignored by the government in the future under the new law.[5]

The tension between TIPNIS protestors and Morales powerfully demonstrates how complicated these identifications and de-identifications can become when a "friendly" state uses the same repressive, militaristic strategies of previous regimes, particularly mobilizing armed police forces to quell resistance. The following questions, emerging from these contradictory relations between the state and social movements, will inform this analysis: How do these tensions influence indigenous forms of governance? How and in what ways has Morales used culture to legitimize particular reform agendas, yet contradictorily reproduced the same unequal relations of power and repressive state apparatuses? How has this reproduction of power and wealth been influenced by global and regional capital?

What has also been crystallized through the TIPNIS case and will be developed in the remainder of the book is that public demonstrations and performances of indigenous culture, linked to a history of oppression and dispossession, do not assure intended outcomes. Indigenous movements have focused on mobilizing indigeneity as a political tool for constitutional reforms and concrete legislative shifts regarding land rights and so on; however, what has become much more apparent is the fragility of national-level legislation as a singular or primary tool to protect the most vulnerable citizens. Indigenous peoples and movements place much faith in laws as a primary medium for remedying their long histories of subjugation and racism. However, the power of these laws remains murky—as we saw in the TIPNIS case, written right into the law was the possibility to override indigenous communities once again. So where do laws or shifting legal frameworks leave us in terms of understanding these complex new dynamics and tensions between indigenous peoples and the state? Will these new laws actually protect the environment and preserve natural ecosystems even when transnational forces override state power? How do historically dominant economic interests degrade and ultimately attempt to override such legislation? What power can a movement mobilize to resist not in a single moment but over time these reactive forces? Where does this leave us in terms of the cultural politics of state-making? How can culture be deployed to build movements and not only resist the global marketplace of extractive industries and displacement but offer viable economic and political alternatives to present discourse and practice?

I answer these questions in three parts. The first addresses the history of resource struggles in Bolivia and the new culture- and knowledge-centered challenge to neoliberal reforms. I explore shifting modes of production, displacement, and forms of resistance in both the western and eastern parts of the country, locating land struggles in a longer history of interconnected global forces, extractive industries, and subjugation of indigenous peoples. The narrative progresses to tell the story of uneven regional agricultural development and modernization in Santa Cruz and the birth of MST in two key areas. While agrarian unions served as the main political tool in these areas, this section hones in on the distinctive and diffuse organizational structure of the movement, which borrows from Andean ideals of the ayllu. Culture, then, becomes deeply embedded in a new spatial and territorial politics, which has the capacity to reach into new arenas, politicize distinct communities, and spread across national terrain. All of this sets a context for understanding the background and history of MST.

The second part explores the creative cultural and political strategies and the mobility of "invented traditions" (Hobshawm and Ranger 1983), how migrants transport and reassemble history and symbolic forms and, in turn, manufacture new hybrid political identities that serve as a direct response and grassroots solution to the problems of market liberalization, dispossession, and export-oriented production. These invented and reconstructed cultural forms, which ensure a new model of governance, food security, and environmental sustainability, form various layers of indigenous and grassroots citizenship, which can be reassembled and scaled up to inform state-building.

The last part connects these movement-based cultural strategies and performances to new mechanisms of state-making and the highly charged and reactionary regionalist response. This section looks at how Morales has made use of MST tactics, such as mobilizing cultural forms, narratives, and performances, to legitimize reforms. Yet, the constant resistance from regionalist elites, particularly around land tenure, has led to a compromised constitution. This then opens a space for interrogating the limitations of Morales's symbolic performances of Andean history and culture. At the very end, I return to the possibility and potential of radical social movements that work in collaboration with a left-leaning state. While the Morales administration created much hope and expectation for a new constitution and the radical redistribution of wealth and resources, we have come to see how little power it has, compared to multinationals and regional agribusiness elites, in negotiating contracts and reclaiming national-level governance. However, greater social, economic, and ecological issues loom in the background of this compromised state, and I query at the end of the analysis what possibilities might emerge in a moment of crisis for real social, economic, and governmental transformation.

PART I

HISTORY OF RESOURCE STRUGGLES IN BOLIVIA

SEDIMENTS OF HISTORY

Resources, Rights, and Indigenous Politics

[MST] is a conglomeration of Bolivians who have come from
distinct parts of Bolivia. Over the course of the last twenty years,
we have come to understand one fundamental right, and that is
access to land. We are an organization composed of peasant women
and men, and we have one critical objective: to obtain land for
ourselves and our children, to be able to produce for our families.
This is the Landless Peasant Movement: We are a social movement
of the masses, with some *sindicalista*[1] traditions and with some new
popular forms of organizing. We are seeking a just redistribution of
land and fair and equitable rural economic development.

—ANGEL DURÁN, president of MST-Bolivia at the first national-level
MST congress in 2000

I first met Silvestre Saisari, one of the original members and founders
of MST–Santa Cruz, in the Centro de Estudios Jurídicos e Investigación
Social, or Center for Legal and Social Science Research (CEJIS), offices in
February 2006. He was a short, stocky man in his thirties with an uneven
beard and a Chicago Cubs hat perched backwards on his long, black
hair. At first, he stared at me suspiciously, interrogating me with his eyes.
Then, after studying me, he asked what I was doing in Bolivia and why I
was studying the movement.

Four months later, Saisari invited me to a karaoke bar in the outer ring
of Santa Cruz. These *anillos* (ringlike circles) illustrate the uneven geographies of race and class: the closer to the core or center of the city, the
more affluent the neighborhood (see Map 1).[2] Several plastic refreshment
tables and white lawn chairs had been set up around a tiny room. Our
waiter brought us five bottles of Paceña, the Bolivian beer of choice. We
sat close to a small jukebox in the corner of the room, where we listened to

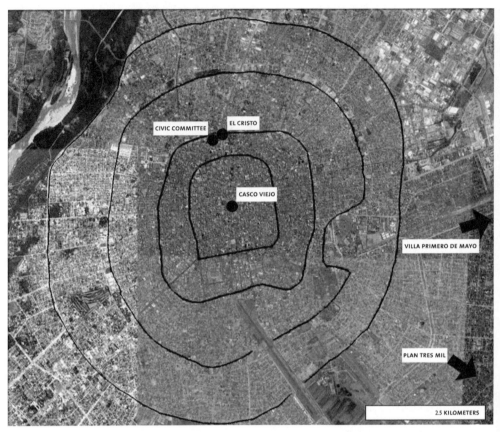

MAP 1. The City of Santa Cruz, illustrating concentric ring roads and key communities. Map by Shannon Stone.

some popular Spanish hip-hop tunes interspersed with musical sounds from the Andes. With the music serving as a rhythmic backdrop to his story, Saisari proceeded with great enthusiasm to describe his early family history and his hometown of Potosí—a city in the highland region of western Bolivia with one of the highest elevations in the world and the center of silver mining production.

> My parents still live in a small mining village outside of the city of Potosí. They are incredibly poor. My whole family once depended upon the mines for daily survival. Potosí used to be a very rich town; in the time of my great-grandparents, they said that you could build a bridge from Bolivia to Spain with all the silver that was taken out

of our country. Working in the mines was always tough physical labor—many of our friends and family died of diseases from the mines. But the miners always had their rich indigenous history and traditions to rely upon to get through those long days.

When I was growing up, it was tough times. Sometimes there wasn't enough food for the entire family. I had ten brothers and sisters. At the age of eight, I began working all kinds of odd jobs to survive, like shining shoes or selling newspapers. About the time I was a teenager, the mines suddenly became privatized and things radically changed. Many miners left our town to find other jobs, while some remained employed by the private mining companies. My first job . . . I remember, I earned ten cents. But I was so happy to come home to my mother with ten cents.

At the age of seventeen, I traveled first to Santa Cruz to work as an agricultural laborer in the fields. Then I heard of opportunities in Argentina. They worked us like slaves. People used to call us "negro," "*colla*," "*bolita*,"[3] and all sorts of other insults. Some of the Bolivians worked in factories . . . and others worked as slaves for the Argentinean agribusinesses. They really exploited us. . . . It was incredible how they exploited us. A wealthy Argentinean family practically adopted me—I worked for them, while they provided food, shelter, and all sorts of support. They were large-scale landowners who owned lots of large machines and taught me a lot about agriculture. I loved it initially. It was incredible. I had breakfast: They served me milk, yogurt, fruit, and breads. I was accustomed to eating only a piece of bread and a cup of coffee. And sometimes, in Potosí, we didn't even have that. So at first it was like heaven for me. I was so lost in my dreams. I never wanted to return to Bolivia. I was so comfortable! However, when the father of the family got sick and told me that he wanted to leave me a part of his inheritance, I felt incredibly uncomfortable. For the first time, I realized that this was not my life. I refused the inheritance and began to feel incredibly depressed. Then, I remembered how little my family had in Bolivia—the daily struggles for bread, food, and shelter. I could no longer live in such a contradiction. I had to return to Bolivia and I had to begin to organize the landless.

Saisari's comrade and friend from MST, Eulogio Cortés Arauz, also a veteran member, articulated a very different life history and motivation for joining the movement. Unlike Saisari, he grew up in the tropical low-lands of Bolivia and had little or no connection to life in the mines. When I first met Cortés, he was dressed in white cotton pants with an old t-shirt and baseball cap. We usually met to talk about politics in his home, several miles outside the city of Santa Cruz. While Saisari rented a temporary room on the outskirts of the city, Cortés and his family managed to purchase their plot in El Plan Tres Mil and built a three-room house where he, his children, and some grandchildren live. "El Plan," as the migrants call it, is one of the poorest districts in Santa Cruz. With a high proportion of recent migrants and rapid growth, the district has far exceeded the capacity of urban planners to build adequate infrastructure: houses lack running water, streets are rutted and unpaved, and sewage drainage is problematic. Many farmers who lost small plots of land migrated in the 1980s and 1990s to these peripheral areas of the city, where they constructed their own homes on a rented plot of land.

One chilly day in April, we sat in Cortés's front yard, surrounded by chickens and other animals, and drank warm tea at a rickety wooden table. He began to tell me about his early life, born into slave-labor conditions on a plantation in Santa Cruz.

> When I was born in 1958, my father was a slave, then he became a laborer, and then a worker. Because of this, when I was born, I had this gift, which was to be born in a public hospital. . . . Cortés, my father's last name, is not my father's last name, but the last name of my father's master. Before, all indigenous peoples were taken away from their communities; they were taken away from their towns and were sold in the city, and the men bought the native, or Camba, as they were called—because they didn't call them Native Americans, they called them "Indians" or "Cambas"—so the master would buy the Camba and give him his last name. My dad changed his name three times during the course of his life. He changed it three times because he tried to escape three times from the hacienda where he was working. . . . Even today, what is known as the Social Club, in the main plaza, the 24 de Septiembre, there the masters threw big parties where they would purchase a Camba and take him to work. What was the purchase? Those who threw the party played the drum, and all the Cambas would go to drink in the big social hall. They would set up a table full of bags of silver—a quarter-kilo, half a kilo, etc. When a Camba grabbed a small bag of a quarter-kilo,

he had to work for six months, a bigger bag, he had to work for a year . . . so all these Cambas would leave through the main plaza and they would go by foot to the haciendas in Beni, Pando, etc. . . . It was a game of life and death—whoever didn't want to walk was killed, whoever wanted to run away was killed.

Cortés, like Saisari, spends most of his life in transit between rural and urban areas, organizing landless peasants and negotiating with the world of nongovernmental organizations (NGOs) in search of funding for his many agricultural projects. What is interesting about these two tales is that despite such motion, both organizers recollect their early life as being grounded in the spatialized logic of the mines or plantation system and the subsequent slave-labor regimes. Cortés often refers to his family history as a critical frame of reference for understanding contemporary forms of poverty, inequality, and violence against Andean migrants and lowland Indians. Saisari, on the other hand, uses his family narrative in the mines and the Leftist tradition of the miners as powerful historical memories shaping and informing the need to revive a radical politics in the contemporary period.

At first glance, these two histories appear quite different. They traverse geographical space: the Andean region is a rough and rugged mountainous terrain rising almost ten thousand feet to mark its western limit, whereas the lowland region is comprised of the dry savannah of the Gran Chaco in the south and the subtropical region of Santa Cruz. Quechua and Aymara Indians come from the west, which was originally part of the Inca empire, while the Guaraní, Guarayo, and Ayoreo Indians of the east were a part of the Cordillera region. Native peoples of the highlands and the lowlands had distinct understandings of and connections to the land and the organization of work prior to the conquest. Even their laboring lives, postconquest, seem opposed: in the west, Indians were turned into slaves through practices such as the mandatory service known as *mit'a* (a kind of tribute in the form of corvée labor to the Inca empire), while in the Amazon, the *enganche* system (a form of labor through a system of credit and debt) tangled indigenous populations in cycles of debt and dependency (Soruco 2011).

These histories are not often narrated side by side since many scholars become experts of either the lowland region of the Amazon or the highland region (see Map 2). In academia, Bolivia has long been positioned in an Andean slot, such that those who work and study there are assumed to be Andeanists. This often reflects the demographic imbalance, for there are well over 2 million Quechua and Aymara Indians compared to 180,000 Chiquitano and 125,000 Guaraní. Further, the Andean political and historical centrality—the strength of their resistance movements—has been critical in shaping the Bolivian state. Yet Andeanism also reflects a longer tradition of ethnological area studies that sought to understand peoples in relation to ecologies, often in quite deterministic ways. Such work deemphasized how the dynamics of wider political and economic shifts influence and transform cultural forms, ways of being, and even livelihood. Though much of Bolivia is in fact Amazonian—and a good part is in the Chaco—this Andeanization of Bolivia has left a lasting mark on internal cultural politics and academic frameworks and continues to influence policy-making (Gustafson and Fabricant 2011).

But if throughout history populations have continually moved from place to place and have been forced to transition from one mode of production to another, and if more recently they have experienced new forms of displacement and life in urban areas, why do we continue to analyze culture and ethnic identity as fixed in geographical space? People have always been in motion. As Bolivia's populations shift from one mode of production to another and migrate from the highlands to the lowlands, partly in response to the infusion of international dollars building an agroindustrial complex, the transfer and mobility of cultural forms across time and space force us to think about these distinctive geographic, historical, and political-economic tales as intimately connected, particularly in today's globalized economy. Highland migrations to the lowlands have influenced lowland indigenous understandings of community, production, labor, and even political organizing. At the same time, the natural landscape and environment of the lowlands have contributed to changes in the ways highland migrants work and live off the lands.

MST is one of these new heterogeneous movements, comprising highland indigenous peasants, lowland Indians, mestizos, and urban informal laborers. Its members might share the common vision of reclaiming productive land for small-scale farmers, but their regional, ethnic, cultural, and even class backgrounds differ radically. How does an ethnographer narrate a history of this kind of movement, which is in constant motion?

Since I locate MST's politics in contemporary social movement struggles to reclaim means of production and resource wealth, I choose to tell a tale of early global interconnections, dislocation, and resistance, of shifting lenses or foci from the Andean highlands to the eastern lowlands

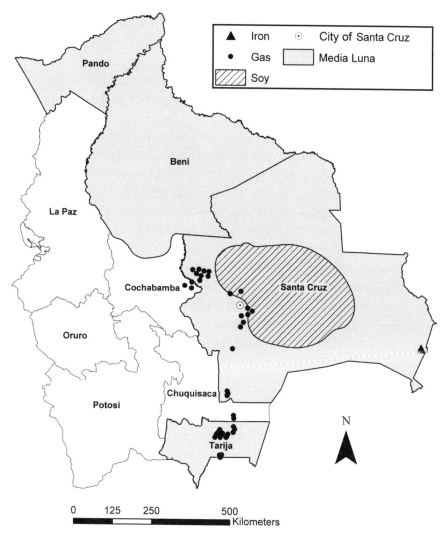

MAP 2. Bolivia, showing its nine departments—four of which make up the lowland "half moon" (Media Luna) of opposition to President Evo Morales—and significant resources. Map by Shannon Stone.

in Bolivia. This chapter, then, narrates histories in motion, or rather the importance of historical memory to contemporary social movement activists: the tales of Andean forms of dislocation and resistance and eastern forms of plantation labor and violence prove critical to building a pluriethnic political body. Yet as people moved across geographic locales, there was also a mixing and remapping of histories, only partially grounded in particular communities of origin. As people moved, they brought with them their rich cultural histories through narrative, tales, and performances, which they told and retold, reshaping these classic myths. Despite these flows, new forms of inequality eerily resembled older forms, and movement activists put their stories into motion in order to inform a new kind of politics in the 2000s, reclaiming rights, resources, and territorial identities.

In narrating these dual histories, I follow in the tradition of Marxist geographers such as David Harvey (2006), who conceptualizes new forms of "accumulation by dispossession" as part of a longer historical trajectory of uneven geographical development, which, he states, began with primitive accumulation. The European conquest transformed indigenous ways of life, livelihood, cultural norms, and traditions. Ellwood (2007) describes this as the intimate relationship between "old globalization" and "new globalization" (12–13). He traces direct connections between early colonial pillaging of lands and resources and neocolonial policies of privatization and commoditization of the most basic elements.

Drawing these economic and political connections between past and present is imperative for understanding how neoliberal policies have exacerbated age-old global antipathies, uneven forms of development, and debt and dependency. Yet what proves critical is understanding how and why these highland and lowland colonial tales of displacement and resistance matter to the newly displaced and dispossessed. Just as colonialism and now neocolonial policies have fragmented old ways of life, social relations, and even forms of resistance, movements today creatively reconnect (through historical memory and embodied performance) earlier ways of life, transport them to new arenas, and actively remake their histories.[4]

Saisari's life history tracks that of many MST members who have faint memories of their lives in the mining towns of Potosí or Oruro and who migrated to new areas of Bolivia in search of employment after privatization. Their stories often reveal fragments of this slave-labor history in their daily forms of organizing. These colonial legacies of the Spanish "stealing their ancestral lands and turning Indians into laborers" permeate historical memory and tale-telling in contemporary politics in the east, where a few agrarian families have monopolized control over most of the productive resources. Saisari, while living in the lowlands of Bolivia for more than half of his life, uses the Spanish conquest and destruction of the ayllu system as an ongoing motivation for reclaiming land and territory, particularly in a new geographic space. Surrounded by hundreds of new landless recruits in April 2006, who work as day laborers in the fields of Santa Cruz, he declared:

> We have lost our land historically to outside forces. [The Spaniards] lived off our land, our mines, and our money; they were able to collect taxes, and with this we acquired a huge debt, just because we were indigenous. We didn't know how to read or write. We lived or continued to live through the labor they provided for us, and then later, we decided to go to other countries to search for work. . . . We are an underdeveloped country. . . . We pay daily for this horrible mark that the Spanish have left upon this country. For five hundred years, comrades, and now we have an indigenous government that speaks Quechua and Aymara, that has the capacity to govern. Last year, [the agroindustrial powers] beat us down, and I haven't run away, and after they beat me, *caramba* [a mild curse, like "darn"], two weeks later, I was denouncing this violence. If we don't fight for what we don't have, who is going to fight for us?

MST members narrate this early colonial history as justification for the contemporary struggle over land and territory. This history of "conquest" continues to define everyday life, tracing land struggles through multiple sources, shifting geographic terrains, and creating new spaces for a reconquest of sorts. Though listeners often have very different ancestral histories in the lowlands, they too grab onto these tales and claim them as their own, as we will see more clearly in the following chapters.

While regimes of power and control have shifted through time and space, each regime has left its mark on Bolivian protestors' imaginary. What will prove important for the remainder of this analysis is not so much how these regimes left their footprints socially, culturally, and ecologically but rather how movement organizers in distinct periods interpret and understand this history as intimately related to present-day conditions of subjugation and oppression. Grassroots organizers in Santa Cruz narrate their own ancestral history and that of other indigenous groups in the lowlands. Diana Taylor (2003), a performance studies scholar, describes this narration as a repertoire, specific acts of transfer that transmit social knowledge, memory, and a sense of identity through reiterated, or twice-lived, behavior. While historians might rely upon an archive to trace and map cultural, regional, and geographical differences, movement activists rely upon these repertoires of memory. Through these kinds of embodied performances of their past or other people's pasts, Bolivians link contemporary forms of inequality to an age-old system of uneven distribution of land and resources. These stories and oral tales, then, travel and take on meaning as social activists narrate them in distinct circumstances, spaces, and places. The mobility of these narratives and tales is dependent on who picks up the story, when, and how they use it.

Since activists rely upon both their own history of subjugation in the west and the plantation system of violence in the east, I begin by narrating the power of colonial forces in both regions, the quest for critical commodities and resources, and the transformation of lifestyles to suit the needs of broad-based extractive industries. I turn first toward the west in order to sketch European interests in the highlands for silver extraction and early forms of creative destruction[5] left in their wake, which in turn led to distinctive forms of resistance.

GLOBAL INTERCONNECTIONS, SHIFTING MODES OF PRODUCTION, AND RESISTANCE IN THE WEST

From the sixteenth century to the end of the eighteenth, European colonial powers were in search of new lands from which to exploit fresh raw materials as well as cheap labor. The prime motivation in Bolivia was first gold and then silver, which quickly eclipsed gold in the mid-1500s. Latin America offered a huge mine, with Potosí as its chief center. This extraction of silver stimulated Europe's economic development: "Spain is like a mouth that receives the food, chews it, and passes it on to other organs, retaining no more than a fleeting taste of the particles that happen to stick in its teeth" (Galeano 1973: 34). The impact of Potosí on Europe and its trade with Asia was staggering. For Europe, Potosí silver contributed to inflationary pressure and a longer-term trend toward rising prices. At the same time, Europe was able to greatly increase its importation of Asian goods and correct its ongoing negative trade balance with the Far East through the payment of Potosí silver (H. Klein 2003: 54). Early on, it became apparent that the extraction of raw materials from the south led to the consolidation of wealth and power in the north.

The arrival of the Spaniards and silver mining disrupted an entire way of life for indigenous communities by displacing families and forcing them into new laboring relationships. Indian ayllu communities were divided into *encomiendas*, or grants, which were large parcels of land given to the Spanish. The ayllus were once based upon fictive kin configurations that organized work and distributed land and productive resources among their members. While some classes existed outside the ayllu structure, the overwhelming majority of commoners, nobles, and rulers were members of an ayllu. This transformation of the ayllu, which essentially marked the breakup of collective and communal agricultural structures into private property holdings, illustrates Marx's original primitive accumulation as a process by which large swaths of the population are violently divorced from their traditional means of self-sufficiency (H. Klein 1982). These narrative threads of disruption of way of life, violent displacement, and loss of self-sufficiency carry through from old colonial relations to new neocolonial ones.

Although they once lived off the land as independent agriculturalists, indigenous peoples in the highlands were quickly turned into wage laborers, as the need for labor increased with the growing silver mining industry. The Spanish Crown set up two systems: one republic for the Spaniards and another for the Indians. Indians were allowed to hold and use communal property and to maintain rights to self-governance, but they had to contribute their labor to the Crown and pay tribute taxes (H. Klein 1982).

Despite a semblance of protection from the Crown, the system was essentially exploitative (Postero 2007b: 27–28). Viceroy Francisco de Toledo instituted a pre-Columbian corvee system, the so-called mit'a,[6] to extract forced labor for the mines in Potosí. Some sixteen districts stretching from Potosí to Cuzco were designated as mit'a supply areas and provided an annual labor force of some 13,500 men, which fueled a continuous supply of workers. While miners received a small wage, the surrounding communities were required to provide food for the workers, maintain their families, and pay for their transportation.[7] Silver production reached extraordinary levels: 45,000 short tons (41,000 metric tons) of pure silver were mined from Cerro Rico from 1556 to 1783. Of this total, 9,000 short tons (8,200 metric tons) went to Spain (H. Klein 1982, 2003). The mitayos (conscripted laborers) produced enough silver to triple the total European returns and turned Potosí into the richest city in the Americas. The tremendous human cost of such economic transformations: brutal servitude, displacement, poisoning, and death (Galeano 1973).

THE AGE OF INSURRECTION AND OCCUPYING CITY CENTERS

Historian Sinclair Thomson (2002) has described how major transformations that occurred throughout the eighteenth century led to indigenous forms of resistance. The traditional system of authority, or cacicazgo (chieftainship), entered into crisis and gave way to a new and distinctive arrangement of community political power. Thomson argues that structural forces and regional dynamics set changes in motion at a local level, and he chronicles how Tupac Katari emerged as a great leader at a moment of crisis and raised an army of some forty thousand indigenous peoples, eventually laying siege to La Paz in 1781:

> From their camps in El Alto, on the rim of the Andean plateau, tens of thousands of Aymara peasant warriors looked out over an impressive scene. Below them opened up a wide basin created by the drainage, over tens of thousands of years, of an ancient sea, whose waters had flowed down from the highland elevation of thirteen thousand feet through the highland valley and lowland foothills. . . . La Paz served as an important commercial nexus between Cuzco and Potosí. It was the main point of Spanish settlement and colonial political control. . . . Yet after two and one-half centuries of colonial rule, the city was under full siege and Spanish power was on the verge of destruction. . . . The siege of La Paz had two phases, and lasted a total of 184 days. . . . Tupac Katari was captured and quartered in a brutal ceremony, held in the name of God and the king, before a massive assembly of stunned Indians from around the lake district. (4–5)

Tupac Katari had roused his followers with the prospect that "they would be left as the ultimate owners of this place, and of its wealth" (10). Thomson asserts that the crucial connection between Aymara community transformation and insurgency in the eighteenth-century Andes was essentially the issue of self-rule, which continues to be present in Aymara political culture today. But he would likely not have predicted, when he did his historical work in the 1990s, that the powerful sign and symbol of the ayllu in its pre-Columbian existence or the tale of Katari would travel from highland to lowlands and inform new kinds of resource politicking in the 2000s.

THE LEGACY OF THE PRE-COLUMBIAN AYLLU AND KATARI IN HIGHLAND MOVEMENTS

Pre-Columbian histories—particularly accounts of the ayllus as the basic communal units that existed well before European colonization (Lucero

2006)—and anticolonial resistance continue to define contemporary indigenous politics. The 1980s represented a critical period for the rebirth and revival of these kinds of stories, focusing on Indian rights within the new multicultural context of Bolivia. The "return of the Indian," as Xavier Albó (1991) once called it, has taken place in a moment of what Charles Hale (2002, 2004) refers to as neoliberal multiculturalism: the use of a cultural identity politics that urges citizens to monitor or survey themselves within the logic of globalized capitalism. Those who conduct themselves within this logic are considered "modern" and "rational" and are rewarded and empowered. Hale calls these Indians "*Indios Permitidos*" (permitted Indians), and they represent less of a political challenge to those in power. On the other side of the coin are those who do not abide by the logic of rational capitalism and are considered to be conflict-prone Indians. Activists in Bolivia, however, fell outside this dichotomy. They did not see neoliberal multiculturalism as encouraging individual citizenship rights and a "do it yourself" attitude, but they took full advantage of the spaces opened by the multicultural turn, accepting international dollars that supported projects for cultural revival. The activist Aymara intellectuals of the Taller de Historia Oral Andina, or Andean Oral History Workshop (THOA), worked steadily to reconstitute the ayllu among indigenous peoples. The THOA movement, headed by Aymara sociologist Silvia Rivera Cusicanqui, calls for the recognition of colonial territorial boundaries between communities and the reestablishment of traditional Andean forms of governance.[8]

North American anthropologists have written about the work of the THOA, arguing that indigenous activists used the concept of the ayllu discursively to create an alternative counterpublic and oppositional consciousness, and they consequently stood against prevailing intellectual practices, which historically relegated indigenous peoples and their communities to the category of premodern other. Andrew Orta (2001) suggests, for example, that indigenous activists and intellectuals appropriated the ayllu as an opportunity for reinventing the nation-state as a pluriethnic space. The use of the ayllu in contemporary political discourse, he argues, hinges less upon a romantic recuperation of an indigenous past than on an insistent alignment with that past, thus rendering a complex present as part of a meaningful future-oriented historical process.

It is important to note that this ayllu discourse is not solely an autonomous or grassroots phenomenon, but rather partly due to the influence of international organizations, such as Oxfam International and the

Inter-American Development Bank. John Gledhill (2005) notes that the 1980s and 1990s brought increasingly powerful NGOs that funded grass-roots efforts with a focus on cultural heritage and revitalization. The transition to neoliberal regimes and the new modes of "governmental-ity" also brought with it a "rights-based approach," which, says Gledhill, was not solely about organic grassroots initiatives but rather emphasizes the increasingly influential role of international actors who create ideas about "active citizenship" (2). Oxfam called the ayllu "an ancient form of community organization that predates the Inca empire," and supported THOA because it interprets the structure of the ayllu as a beneficial device of empowerment to articulate disparate claims and defend rights (Andolina 1999, 2001; Albro 2005). For international funders, then, the significance of the ayllu is a worthy subject in the ongoing discussion of indigenous global rights.[9]

Besides THOA and the ayllu movement, other indigenous movements like the Kataristas have used the legacy of Tupac Katari in order to link rural and urban Aymaras in a struggle to reclaim cultural rights. While this movement might have started as a cultural project, it developed into a strong trade union political platform that attempted to connect issues of ethnic identity to questions of class (Canessa 2000; Gustafson 2002; Lucero 2006; Postero 2007b). In 1978, the movement split into two factions: the Movimiento Revolucionario Tupac Katari de Liberación (MRTKL), led by Víctor Hugo Cárdenas, which attempted to bridge the question of urban and rural Aymaras (especially addressing the exploited working classes and the ethnic identity question), and the Movimiento Revolucionario Tupac Katari (MRTK), led by Felipe Quispe, which focused solely on promoting Indian issues at the national level. The more radi-cal proposals for Aymara nationalism and self-determination expanded and developed in the 1980s. Government officials jailed many leaders for guerrilla activity, and in order to "reclaim their ancestral culture," these leaders called for the building of an indigenous nation, Kollasuyo, adopt-ing the original name of the Inca empire.

In the highlands, the use of historical memory of the pre-Columbian ayllu system and Tupac Katari's resistance to Spanish colonialism in-formed contemporary issues of ethnic revivalism, self-determination, and new forms of nationalism, but the lowlands had its own history of global interconnections, exploitative labor regimes, and indigenous resistance. Still, despite the uprisings of the Mojeño and Guaraní, An-dean pre-Columbian ideals of production, reciprocity, and redistribution continue to define and inform the cultural politics of the lowlands, particularly in regard to new social movements like the *Cocaleros* and MST. The following are some of the questions that inform the remainder of the analysis: How do these symbols (stories, narratives, ways of organizing politics) travel from highland ethnic revitalization movements to landless politics of reclamation in the lowland? Moreover, why would an Andean cultural history inform lowland organizations in their daily battles to reclaim land and productive resources?

GLOBAL INTERCONNECTIONS, DISRUPTIONS, AND RESISTANCE IN THE LOWLANDS

In order to understand the power of these tales of Tupac Katari and the communal structure of the ayllu in the geographically and environmentally distinct space of the lowlands, I now shift focus from the west to the east, where instead of mines, it was the hacienda that held particular social, political, and economic power and that continues to define contemporary struggles today. As Ximena Soruco, a Bolivian sociologist, explains it, "The *Cruceño* identity[10] was built around the image of their economic activity: the private extraction of raw materials, ostensibly opposed to any kind of state intervention and strongly linked to the international market. . . . The haciendas were symbols of civilization and progress . . . just as the mines represented to the elites from the Andean highlands of western Bolivia their source of accumulation and their vital space of reproduction" (2011: 80).

Lowland indigenous communities came to national attention along a distinct trajectory: Indians were not part of the "tributary pact" that colonial powers built with Andean peoples; rather they were considered savages and forced into labor on the haciendas (Postero 2007b; Gustafson 2009b). A small number of Spaniards gained control over local indigenous groups and organized settlements on cleared jungle land for growing sugarcane, rice, and cotton and for raising cattle (Gill 1987). By 1621, there were twenty-five centers that produced sugar for local consumption and sale in highland markets. A constant shortage of laborers, however, led to the practice of capturing indigenous people in the northern Moxos regions and forcing them to work on these agricultural operations.

The hacienda represented the dream of conquering virgin land and controlling Indians through the suppression of a labor force. If in the Andes an entire system of labor exploitation was built around the mit'a, in the Amazon, the structure of forced labor was the enganche system, first established during the rubber era,[11] and still used for chestnut collection in the Amazonian north, the harvesting of sugarcane in Santa Cruz, and cattle farming in the ranches of the southern Chaco (Soruco 2011). Willem Assies (2002) argues that both the enganche system, which subjugated the worker to the boss through an intricate system of debt dependency, and the *habilitación*, a credit system established by the rubber industry in exchange for food, utensils, and cash, depopulated indigenous communities and nearly obliterated older ways of life that had remained intact since the colonial period and persist in distinct forms today. Swedish anthropologist Erland Nordenskiöld, writing in 1917, stated, "During the good times, what was most needed in the rubber forests were men. Naturally, many of them went of their own free will to look for work; however most of them were tricked with false promises or taken by force. . . . Savage natives were captured to work in the collection of rubber and many died due to hardships and fever" (2001: 340).

INDIGENOUS REBELLIONS OF 1887 AND 1892

Ximena Soruco, Wilfredo Plata, and Gustavo Medeiros (2008) explain that the 1887 rebellion by the Mojeño (lowland indigenous group originally found around the Beni region), led by Andres Guayocho, had everything to do with the conquest of their lands and subjugation of indigenous peoples. The rebellion was in reaction to the fierce repression by hacendado Ruceno Saavedra, who set fire to houses and plantations, gunned down many people, and raped women. Guayocho stood up to these colonial forces and was eventually captured and murdered.

Several years later, in 1892, the killing of Kuruyuki in the province of Santa Cruz also marked and shaped memories of resistance to the Cruceño occupation of eastern Bolivia, the region known as the Oriente.[12] Guaraní, desperate to protect their lands, were brutally put down by the army. Bret Gustafson (2009b) recounts a horrific tale of two Guaraní warriors who escaped the battle and sought refuge in the bush. Captured by Bolivian troops, the two were taken to Monteagudo, where they were whipped to extract information about the general plans of the rebels, but when they refused to give up their brothers, these two Cambas were executed by a firing squad. A turncoat Guaraní warrior lured an escaped brother right to enemy lines but was also tortured and killed, and his body was displayed for twenty-four hours. Gustafson writes, "Unruly bodies and tongues, as well as claims to epistemic and territorial authority, were silenced, destroyed and dispersed" (38).

These sediments of violence and trails of horror shape our understandings of landless politics today and the desperate attempts of regional elites to hold onto their historic claims to land, productive resources, and territory in the Oriente. This new geography of colonial forms of violence in both rural and urban areas continues to define and constrain the movement of landless organizers. Gustafson (2010) describes recent violence over land tenure in Alto Parapetí: "The spectacular form of punitive violence was explicitly characterized by the Guaraní and government officials in terms of historical colonial relations (rape, captivity, massacre, humiliation and punishment). A lawyer even said, 'I felt in my own flesh what indigenous peoples in the hacienda suffer'" (61). This violence, the marks (both symbolic and material) on indigenous peoples' bodies, and their fears of traveling through parts of the city often define their cultural politics and their use of narrative and stories as well.

What is interesting about the contemporary use and value of these tales of indigenous resistance is how such narratives can become easily appropriated, adopted, and reinvented. Just as MST organizers might grab onto the tale of Tupac Katari, NGO workers and indigenous organizations in the lowlands might use Guaraní narratives of resistance as "allegory for the resurgence of a different kind of Guarani struggle, that of bilingual education" (Gustafson 2009b: 38). At the same time, regional elites who imagine themselves as victims of new conquerors, specifically the indigenous highlanders who have been migrating east since the second half of the twentieth century, might also adopt such tales as their own in order to support and legitimize a different kind of self-determination and territorial autonomy.

While the previous section illustrated colonial regimes and shifting modes of production and resistance, this next section charts present-day cycles of accumulation by dispossession and contemporary forms of indigenous mobilization. Before analyzing the neoliberal shifts that led to new kinds of disruptions, however, we must understand the shifting political-economic landscape of the lowlands in the mid-twentieth century. Foreign investment in the lowland region of Bolivia exacerbated age-old inequalities and forced highlanders to move to lowland regions to fill a new need for low-wage laborers on sugarcane plantations, which led to many current tensions between the European elite and the indigenous landless population.

THE OPENING UP OF THE ORIENTE AND DISLOCATION
OF HIGHLAND INDIANS FROM WEST TO EAST

Beginning in the 1950s, Santa Cruz in particular benefited from international investment in agroindustrial development and the opening up of the lowlands to global trade. The United States was quick to assist the economic expansion of places like Santa Cruz because it considered the Movimiento Nacionalista Revolucionario (Revolutionary Nationalist Movement, MNR) to be reformist and wanted to maintain Bolivia within its sphere of influence (Gill 1987). Thus, the United States provided millions of dollars in aid to stimulate large-scale agroindustrial development in Santa Cruz and create an entrepreneurial-minded class of capitalist farmers. The highway linking important highland and lowland regions was completed, while feeder roads between sugar mills and important sugarcane-producing properties were developed with U.S. funds. Further, the United States provided credit and technical assistance to the large-scale producers, especially sugar mill owners, to purchase new equipment and expand processing capacity. A state-owned mill, Guabira, was built with U.S. capital in 1956. Most importantly, large-scale sugarcane producers received easy access to credit, which peasants were unable to obtain.[13]

As the United States funneled large sums of money into the development of the regional economy, there was a sudden need for a steady supply of laborers. International dollars and the expansion of sugar in the northern regions contributed to the "spontaneous" and "forced" migrations of highland Indians to work on these plantations, once again displacing whole communities from places of origin to new geographical terrains in the lowlands. Many MST members first migrated to the area during the 1960s as part of state-sponsored colonization programs, where they worked as sugarcane laborers. These colonization programs were intended to redistribute the population more evenly throughout the country; however, they were also a preemptive response to fears of a more radical agrarian reform in the highlands. In part, people's histories, cultural forms, and understandings of community and labor were now transported in their migratory patterns from the highlands to lowlands. Quechua-speaking and Aymara-speaking immigrants experienced a radically different geographic and ecological zone; they suffered from physical ailments due to dramatic shifts in climate and diet and ruptures in communal, social, and kin relations. Yet many of these communities relied upon Andean ways of living and political organizing in these newly colonized zones, forming agrarian syndicates modeled after their high-land counterparts. These syndicates directed and participated in a wide range of activities, including the distribution of land, initiation of infrastructural development, and the resolution of internal debates.

Once again, however, in the late 1970s and 1980s, global political-economic forces disrupted Andean migrant lives. Although they had survived as wage laborers or small-scale farmers for many years, their lives and livelihoods were about to change again. The lowland region had always been targeted as an agroindustrial center, where the consolidation of wealth and power remained in the hands of a few. State-led capitalism furthered class struggles, and the uneven distribution of fiscal incentives, agricultural credit, road building, and foreign aid promoted the growth of large agro-export enterprises. Hugo Banzer, a military dictator in the 1970s, working in partnership with Cruceño agroindustrialists, allowed agrarian capitalists to secure credit and land for growth of their individual enterprises, while small-scale farmers often went into debt taking out loans with high interest rates to try to survive. Shifts in land and agricultural policy in the 1980s exacerbated already existing inequalities, forcing whole populations yet again to move from rural to urban spaces and shift from one mode of production to another.

FROM OLD GLOBALIZATION TO NEW FORMS OF "ACCUMULATION BY DISPOSSESSION"

Wayne Ellwood (2007) connects old globalization—colonial powers in search of raw materials and cheap slave labor across the globe—to what he calls "new globalization," or the post–World War II governing institutions that have refined and exacerbated these forms of unevenness through debt and loans with particular conditions. While many scholars would argue that the world has changed in the last century in ways that have altered the character of the global economy and its impact on people and the natural world, what we continue to see is a dominant belief in the magic of the marketplace as a solution to the problems of poverty and inequality.

Major political-economic shifts in the 1970s and 1980s opened the door for the neoliberal order, which proposed that human well-being can best be advanced by liberating individual entrepreneurial freedoms and skills within a framework characterized by strong private property rights and free trade (D. Harvey 2005: 2). Neoliberalism can actually be traced back to the classic nineteenth-century liberalism of Adam Smith, James

Mill, John Stuart Mill, and others who argued that allowing markets to function without government interference would bring about the best social ends most efficiently (Collins, di Leonardo, and Williams 2008: 4).[14] What is new, however, about this "magic of the market" discourse today is the increasing influence and power of multinational conglomerates to define national policy, particularly as countries in the global South have fallen deeper into debt.[15] Free trade, unfettered investment, deregulation, and the privatization of publicly owned enterprises became the remedy to ailing national economies across the globe. After forty-plus years of neoliberal reforms—which cut back on social programs, privatized state-owned industries, and opened borders to the free flow of capital and goods—we are seeing the great human, social, environmental, and ecological costs, which in part are driving new social movements to come up with radical alternatives to challenge this neoliberal model.

NEOLIBERAL REFORMS IN BOLIVIA AND NEW URBAN AND AGRARIAN STRUGGLES

Bolivia, deep in debt in the 1980s, asked the International Monetary Fund for loans in order to pull itself out of crisis. The first round of reforms was packaged as the "New Economic Policy" (NEP), which was an ideological and philosophical framework intended to redefine the country's future economic, social, and political choices through particular prescriptions (Connaghan, Malloy, and Abugattas 1990; Spronk 2007). The NEP cut government spending and imposed a rigid monetary policy, which succeeded in bringing hyperinflation under control. It allowed the currency to float against the U.S. dollar, privatized state-owned industries, opened the country to direct foreign investment, and ended protectionist policies.

The first round had destabilizing, deterritorializing effects, however, as the privatization of state-owned mines displaced whole populations of laborers, forcing them to search for work elsewhere. Simultaneously, small-scale peasant farmers could no longer keep up with the newly liberalized market, which opened borders, allowed surplus goods to flood local markets, and eventually put the farmers out of work.[16] Both ex-miners and unemployed peasants migrated to cities, searching for housing and work on the outskirts, because the cities could not absorb the massive flows of displaced laborers (Goldstein and Castro 2006; Lazar 2008; Revilla 2011). Migrants looked for jobs in the expanding informal economy as domestic servants and street vendors and frequently moved in search of employment. The social and economic fragmentation and intensified poverty produced by the reterritorialization of miners and peasants created a difficult environment for union-based organizing,[17] which had been the backbone of the mining and agrarian sectors. These groups began to form their own neighborhood organizational structures, borrowing from Marxian mining history and agrarian unions. Marginalized urban spaces on the outskirts of cities, such as El Alto, became the epicenters of a new kind of politics. Distinct from the struggles of some indigenous movements to defend and recover traditional and ancestral spaces, entities such as the Neighborhood Boards in El Alto became hybrid spaces of displaced and dispossessed peoples, collective organizations through which people with differently positioned experiences forged political identities around territorializing logics and agendas.[18]

A second round of neoliberal reforms came in the 1990s, and Gonzalo Sánchez de Lozada's *Plan de Todos* (Plan for All) had seven key components that aligned with this project: (1) constitutional reforms; (2) privatization through the law of capitalization; (3) the law of decentralization; (4) agrarian reform under the National Institute of Agrarian Reform Law; (5) judicial reforms; (6) educational reforms; and (7) restructuring of the pension system (Kohl 2003). The centerpiece of this proposal was an ambitious plan that combined administrative decentralization with privatization, placing a special emphasis on popular participation. Under this plan, 50 percent of publicly owned shares in various enterprises were to be transferred to transnational corporations. For example, the publicly controlled water system in Cochabamba was privatized, which led to massive uprisings, as did the proposed privatization of gas in 2003. The focus of this book, however, is not water or gas, but land and agriculture. Neoliberal land and agrarian reforms greatly affected rural landscapes, peasant livelihoods, and self-sufficiency in Bolivia.

In the eastern lowlands, neoliberal reforms not only contributed to the collapse of small-scale farming, but also accelerated the expropriation of productive resources, such as land and forests. As part of his Plan de Todos, Sánchez de Lozada passed a second agrarian reform bill called the National Institute of Agrarian Reform Law (INRA Law) in 1996. Two critical events precipitated the development and passage of this legislation. The first was the illegal transfer of 100,000 hectares (almost 250,000 acres) of land by Jaime Paz Zamora—the president of Bolivia in 1989–93, who opposed the complete eradication of coca, as proposed by President George Bush, yet cooperated with the main thrust of the War on

Drugs—to a member of his cabinet with the suspicious name of "Boli-Bras."[19] The scandal forced Paz Zamora to suspend all land titling and land grants by the National Agrarian Reform Council in 1993 until an investigation could be completed (Hertzler 2008). The second event was the 1990 March for Territory and Dignity to La Paz,[20] organized by indigenous groups in the Beni and Santa Cruz regions with substantial NGO support, to protest timber exploitation in their territories and draw attention to their demands for new land rights. These groups were the most marginalized of Bolivia's citizens, having been completely left out of the agrarian reform of 1953. The march garnered much support from labor unions and indigenous highland peasant unions, as well as international solidarity.

Sánchez de Lozada's INRA Law was intended to protect campesinos and indigenous landholdings[21] while promoting the redistribution of agricultural land through the creation of efficient land markets (Kohl 2003). Multilateral organizations such as the Inter-American Development Bank (IDB) and the World Bank operate under the assumption that the most cost-effective way to combat hunger and reduce poverty is through the creation of markets. The World Bank, for example, has followed a neoliberal agenda, emphasizing the privatization of land and the creation of speculative land markets by providing funds for cadastres, titling, and market-assisted redistribution in which land is purchased at established prices and credit is extended to farmers to help them purchase it from a land bank. This approach has made little difference in situations of major social inequality and has actually benefited large-scale landowners (Hertzler 2008).[22]

Despite the fact that the INRA Law institutionalized a process of reclaiming unproductive lands, the pace of redistribution was so slow that many social organizations became increasingly frustrated. By May 2005, nearly ten years after the passage of the law, only 15 million hectares (out of some 107 million) had been effectively clarified in favor of campesino claims. Redistribution was severely limited as a result of pressures from large landholders, who circumvented the spirit of the law by claiming fictitious subdivisions of their property, or by moving herds from one place to another to convince inspectors that the land was in full use. Under the Bolivian constitution, it is illegal to hold large plots of land that do not serve an agricultural function. These market forces and the political exercise of power by elites to extend their holdings exacerbated highly unequal landholding patterns in Santa Cruz: a mere 7 percent of the population benefited from the land reform programs, owning 87 percent of this new cultivable land, while the remaining 13 percent is shared by the other 93 percent of the population—the campesinos.

This neoliberal land legislation, combined with intensified global competition, the opening of markets, and the slashing of state subsidies, created greater problems for small-scale farmers. The INRA Law resulted in the consolidation of wealth and power in the hands of a few; cattle ranching, soy production (for export), and speculative landholding patterns left few possibilities for the poor. Small-scale farmers continued to take out loans from private banks with high interest rates in order to compete in this new export-oriented agricultural economy, but many simply fell deeper into debt. Cattle ranching and soy production take up large expanses of land, demand lots of capital and machinery, and in the case of soy, heavy use of pesticides. This new model of agrarian practices preys on small farmers; a common end result is that small farmers are dispossessed of their lands and must abandon their livelihoods. Just as primitive accumulation forced people off their lands and imposed new governing structures, private property laws, and distinct modes of production, these forms of "accumulation by dispossession" had a similar effect. In the past, indigenous communities invented creative mechanisms of standing against colonial forces by occupying their centers of power, but these new heterogeneous movements of landless peasants search for ways to disrupt flows of capital, to unsettle oligarchic landholding patterns, and to push the bounds of legality.

THE BIRTH OF A NEW PEASANT MOVEMENT IN THE EAST

The Movimiento Sin Tierra (Landless Peasant Movement, or MST), was born in the Gran Chaco Region, an extensive area of more than 100,000 square miles of plains spread across parts of northern Argentina, northwestern Paraguay, southwestern Brazil, and southeastern Bolivia. It covers a large part of the Bolivian department of Santa Cruz, bordering Paraguay to the south and Brazil to the east. Gran Chaco was the site of the Chaco War, in which Bolivia lost a large portion of territory to Paraguay.[23] More recently, parts of the Gran Chaco have become a fierce battleground for big oil companies seeking to exploit the resource wealth unevenly distributed under Guaraní territory in these geographic domains (Gustafson 2011).

While perhaps these other resource battles are better known, inequalities in agriculture and landholding are a daily backdrop to conflicts over gas and oil extraction. In a region where more than 80 percent of the area's campesinos have no title or rights to land, many of the MST members spoke of working as employees in the city centers, like Yacuiba. Juan Sala Sala described it as follows: "A few families owned all the land. There weren't any places to work. They hired us to work on their land. But many times, they didn't want to pay us. When we would charge them, they would say that they had no money. They worked us hard. . . . Even at night, we continued working. They treated us like children. It was like returning to an era of the *patrón* [boss] and the slave. There was a great need to organize, to take over these lands. So we started studying the situation" (Interview, August 10, 2007).

Many of the landless in the Gran Chaco who were interviewed for this book described their lives as "being in constant motion," in search of work in the cities as domestic workers during the day and returning at night to the rural spaces where they lived. Many were part of agrarian unions but had grown increasingly frustrated that unions were no longer effectively negotiating their needs.[24] As one MST-Chaco member described the situation, "As [this was] the most desperate of times, something had to be done in order to change this highly unequal structure."

While there were no direct contacts between Bolivia and Brazil, landless peasants began to think about occupying unused land as a strategy for reterritorializing it. Since the Bolivian constitution stated that land that did not serve a social or economic function should be taken back by the state and redistributed to poor campesinos, some of them began to think about how they could pressure state agents to begin to enforce agrarian reform. Occupations seemed to be the most logical way to bring attention to the problem of landlessness, to take matters into their own hands and begin to restructure agrarian relations.

MST-Bolivia was founded in 2000 through a land occupation on the hacienda known as Panantí in the Gran Chaco region of Tarija. In the words of Angel Durán, former president of MST-Bolivia, "MST has achieved incredible success in these past four years. We were born occupying land on February 20, 2000, we were born in the public light with an already established structure by June 9, 2000, and it was through this that we built such a strong organization."

On June 23, 2000, 200 migrant campesino families entered this private property, making it the first official MST occupation. The estate was an archetype of what would become the norm for MST takeovers. "We don't just take whatever piece of land there is," says Raul Machicado, member of the rank and file. Rather, he explains that MST's takeovers are calculated grabs at "available" land, often belonging to known enemies of the Bolivian Left. Prior to every occupation, MST identifies large estates that are unused and therefore in violation of the constitutional amendment. Some Panantí residents began communally farming and raising animals on their new 7,500 acres, while a small group of residents embarked on a long march to Tarija to solidify the validity of this new movement as a means to negotiate land title. As one representative from Tarija declared, "It was necessary to reunite with the governor of the department in order to declare ourselves an official organization and begin the legal and bureaucratic process of petitioning for rights" (Mendoza 2003: 74). Ermelinda Fernández, the first regional coordinator of MST, explained that during this meeting with the governor, "We had to declare that this was an official movement that would last many years and pressure the government because we do not want free land handouts; we wanted many other things, like citizenship rights and productive resources" (Mendoza 2003: 74).

In order to define a political identity for the movement, regional leaders moved from the site of occupation to a national forum to launch the first MST congress, Land and Agrarian Reform from Below,[25] held in October 2001 in Yapacaní, Santa Cruz, Their public position was increasingly militant; the mission statements indicated that MST would democratize the distribution of land and enter into a massive campaign to end the unproductive latifundio while pushing for agrarian reform from below. Further, the members would begin to rewrite the INRA Law. They also stressed the need to reorganize agriculture toward independent, small-scale development and to defend natural resources.[26] Lastly, the movement promised to develop legal challenges for the titles of lands occupied by MST and continue to bring attention to unproductive land through an expansion of militant occupations. MST members' unity at the national level in elaborating and sharpening movement ideology was reinforced through the brutal and intensifying struggle for land in Panantí.

The deadly assault that came to be known as the "massacre of Panantí" was the first systematic attempt of elite businessmen aligned with the regional government to demobilize MST. Cattle ranchers launched the massacre on November 9, 2001. "At 6 A.M., about forty heavily armed paramilitaries entered the encampment, showering bullets on [and killing] six campesinos, wounding twenty-one others," recalled a community member (quoted in Friedsky 2005). The attacks began less than three months after the initial takeover, when a group of assailants hired by estate owners entered the settlement of Los Sotos and burned MST houses, destroyed everything inside the houses, and injured several people. In response, the landless farmers killed a leader of the paramilitary organization. Police arrested five landowners linked to the violence and nine landless farmers. Juana Ortega, who had given birth just three days before, was one of those arrested, explaining, "I decided to do it for my children, for the land they will need to survive" (quoted in Dangl 2007: 93).

Instead of diminishing MST's organizational strength and capacity, however, this horrific incident led to the consolidation of a number of campesino unions into a movement. The Panantí massacre mobilized many families, especially women, to march from Tarija to La Paz to pressure the federal government to hold the perpetrators of violence accountable and put land reform back on the national agenda. Out of tragedy, MST decided to step up its occupations, bringing attention, both nationally and internationally, to the problem of land inequities. Land occupations quickly spread from the Gran Chaco region to Santa Cruz. At this point, the organization began to think about the rich cultural heritage of the highlands and how to incorporate ideas regarding democratic organizational structures modeled on the ayllu—how to reconnect people to one another, to the land, and to a collective work project.

This chapter has charted the dual histories of the highlands and lowlands: common themes of global interconnections and shifting modes of productions created much displacement and a disassembling of communal and social relations for indigenous communities. Yet both highland Indians and lowlanders seized and occupied centers of power in order to resist regimes of violence and control. What is important for this analysis is how narratives of pre-Columbian forms of living and tales of anticolonial resistance travel as people migrate to new locales. Andeans carried with them tales of self-sufficiency, independence, and resistant political cultures in order to survive in new geographic terrain, and once again as slave laborers on sugarcane plantations. These narratives also took on new meanings in and through new landscapes of inequality and new racialized and spatialized regimes of control. The use of indigeneity as an overarching political weapon to reclaim rights to land and territory emerged in and through new resource battles. This language of indigeneity, once linked to the territorial, the geographic, the material, and the socioeconomic, had to become increasingly flexible, mobile, and generalizable. This flexibility and mobile language of justice and rights has led to new possibilities for organizing across class, race, and ethnicity and remarkable success in transforming age-old colonial structures and spaces of governance. At the same time, this language of indigeneity as generalizable and flexible has also led to all sorts of dangers, which will be explored in the following chapters.

The use of indigeneity as a political language paralleled that of other resource-based movements, like the coca-grower unions in the Chapare. The expansion of agribusiness, conceptualized by landless peasants as new attacks upon their land and livelihood, has politicized and Andeanized territorial battles in the Oriente, just as the War on Drugs and zero-coca policies have led to the ethnicization of coca. Much like MST, coca growers initially migrated to the Chapare region as part of the broader push to the east[27] or the state-based plan to develop and expand agribusiness in the lowlands. Coca became a critical domestic and export-oriented crop, bringing lucrative business to this underdeveloped region. More highlanders migrated to the region as they lost their jobs in the mining industry due to neoliberal privatization schemes. Just like other regions of Bolivia in the 1980s, such as the peripheral neighborhoods of Cochabamba and El Alto, MST territories in northern Santa Cruz and coca-growing areas have become important centers of a new hybrid politics, mixing agricultural *sindicato* (union) traditions with ex-miners' class-based discourses and anti-imperialist stance.

The turn toward culture or indigenous identity as a powerful language of protest, then, was about both displacement and new attacks on land, community, and livelihood. Anthropologist Thomas Grisaffi (2009) describes how the neoliberal state made efforts to eradicate coca production under the rubric of the War on Drugs, whereby peasants in the region were forced to eliminate the production of coca, and their homes and communities became sites of attack. As Grisaffi explains, "The military's efforts to forcibly uproot coca plantations have not only been ineffective but have resulted in violent confrontations with peasants. The troops responsible for coca eradication have been implicated in the torture, robbery, murder, and rape of civilians"(430). Within this context of increasing violence and militaristic attack, coca growers have fought to maintain their right to grow coca in the region and legitimize their political actions through a discourse of historic "indigenous," ancestral, territorial, and even sociocultural practices of chewing and sharing coca leaves. While these coca-sharing rituals do not exist in the Chapare in any pure way, the discourses of Andean Indians as the "original peoples" have become important as imagined or invented cultural frames that can be made mobile and flexible in a moment in which distinct groups struggle to hold on to a way of life.

Just as the coca growers use the coca leaf as a sign and symbol of sovereignty and indigeneity, MST mobilized anticolonial myths and narratives of the ayllu as a platform for the reclamation of land, rights, and new communal identities. Land, like the coca leaf, is linked to some primordial sense of indigeneity, and is also becoming a more generic "indigenous" issue. Unlike distinct indigenous groups in the lowlands that are fighting for their TCOS, or *tierras comunitarias de origen* (traditional communal lands), this heterogeneous group of landless and displaced peasants mobilizes a generalizable idea of "indigeneity" as inherently connected to land, territory, and alternative forms of production and exchange. They justify their need to reclaim or seize lands—notably, lands that are not their ancestral lands—as part of their response to the long dureé of colonial and neocolonial forces violently usurping and destroying their lands and socioeconomic structures and eventually displacing them. While the northern regions of Santa Cruz are not their TCOS, MST activists centralize their efforts on the belly of the beast, the center of elite power where several oligarchical families have complete control of land and resource wealth.

These battles over land, then, did not emerge in the neoliberal era but rather are sediments of a history that is deeply etched in people's minds, environmental surroundings, and ways of organizing. While this chapter charted unequal regimes of power from west to east and through time and space, the next chapter will hone in on the region of Santa Cruz, looking at the expansion of agroindustrial development in two key areas, Ichilo and Obispo Santiesteban, and narrating the birth and organizational structure of the movement in that region. MST's language of indigeneity as political engagement has in many ways shaped the agrarian landscape of Santa Cruz, where regional elites, seeking to hold on to their historic rights to land, resources, and privileges, have to come up with novel ways of controlling new movement power in the region, which poses a great threat to their investments. In order to maintain their money, wealth, and power, which are intimately tied to free market capitalism and resource extraction, agrarian elites have mobilized their own discourses, language, and performances of regionalism as linked to global agribusiness and transnational wealth.

THE MAKING OF A MOVEMENT IN SANTA CRUZ

Uneven Regional Agrarian Development in Obispo Santiesteban and Ichilo

In order to travel to the Yuquises hacienda, the site of a well-known occupation in the region of Santa Cruz, which received international recognition and now represents an officially titled MST collective called Pueblos Unidos (United Peoples), one must catch a bus early in the morning in the third anillo. The bus stop is diagonally across from the Hypermaxi, a rather large American-style supermarket, which flashes orange fluorescent lights in the wee hours of the morning onto the Avenida Banzer. The bus drivers line their micros up in single-file fashion, waiting for the seats to fill in order to embark on their journey to Montero, a small migrant city about fifty kilometers north of the city of Santa Cruz (see Map 3).

On an unusually sunny day in April, I wait at 6:00 A.M. for the first Montero-bound bus to fill up. People squeeze into these minibuses, leaving very little room for movement on the 45-minute journey. The seats are bright red, covered with plastic, and many are ripped at the seams. The bus's dashboard is decorated with adornments: "La Virgin de Urkupina" or "Jesús es mi dios" and other sorts of stickers. The music is a mixture of pop, salsa, and merengue. Occasionally, the music fades and switches to screechy political commentary. Finally, the bus pulls out of the Santa Cruz station around 6:30, passing through the desolate streets. At a later hour, these streets will be bustling with congested traffic, shoppers moving into and out of the marketplace, and students gathering to drink at the little kiosks along the way; but at this hour of the morning, they are silent. The cobblestone streets, lined with well-built concrete homes and small *bodegas* (grocery stores), quickly become a blurry memory as we head directly toward the Santa Cruz–Montero Highway. The last of the advertisements for Paceña beer, featuring perfectly tanned, slender mestiza women in string bikinis, mark this territorial, racial, and ethnic divide—here, the city of Santa Cruz de la Sierra gives way to its rural and agricultural peripheries.

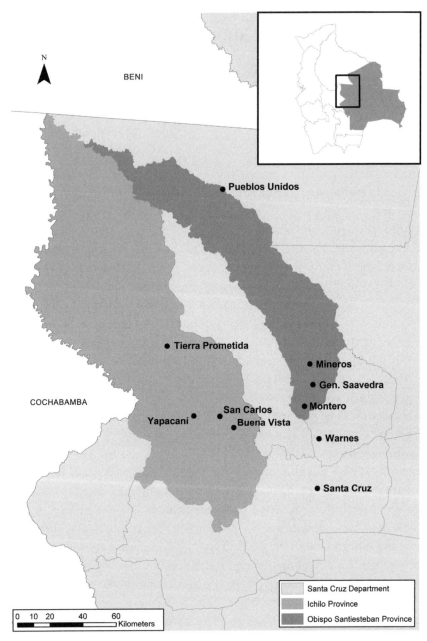

MAP 3. The Department of Santa Cruz and its rural provinces, showing key locations.
Map by Shannon Stone.

The small microbus speeds along the paved highway, and we suddenly pass a strip of factories along Aceite Fino and Aceite Rico, which manufacture and export soy oils. Soy represents the new green gold in the region: agrarian elites have built corporations and consolidated wealth and power through it, particularly the manufacture and export of soy oil. There are two factories here owned by IOL-SA, the largest domestically owned exporter of soy and sunflower oils, with soy second only to hydrocarbons in the broader export-oriented market of Santa Cruz. IOL-SA is currently owned by the well-known Marinkovic family,[1] an elite European-descended family in Santa Cruz, whose quick rise to power models the path of other oligarchical families in the region. They built their businesses from the bottom up, enjoying state credits, protection, and subsidies. They also invested in large expanses of speculative land and accrued great wealth.

The physical borders between the city of Santa Cruz and the end of the North-South Highway, which extends deep into agricultural towns and to the pueblos of San Pedro and Harderman, are also economic, social, political, and spatial divides between soy entrepreneurs and the people trying to survive in soy-producing zones. It is apparent, as we head backward through the commodity chain from the site of processing and exportation to the places of production, that the landscapes radically shift from industrialized and highly developed to deeply impoverished. Even Montero, the closest small town to Santa Cruz, presents a poorer and less developed urban center than its neighbor, with congested open-air markets and the constant ebb and flow of highland Andean migrants in search of informal jobs. The housing structures range from well-constructed to self-constructed, and sometimes even makeshift, as we move further away from the center of Montero.

This bus does not travel directly to Pueblos Unidos. To get there, one must transfer to a second bus, which loads passengers at Montero and continues on to the pueblos of the north (including Mineros, Chané, San Pedro, and Harderman). This bus, rather different than the small white micro, is a larger vehicle with oversized wheels prepared to travel across the rugged dirt terrain. Andean migrants fill every crevasse of the bus with foodstuffs, fruits, vegetables, animals, and packaged goods, which they buy in Montero. Women carry nylon potato sacks packed to the brim from the market and stuff them into small holes on the bus, while others squeeze huge cardboard boxes stocked with toilet paper, potato chips, and other cheap goods, which they cart back to their markets. Even though people buy their seats, many passengers push and shove, trying to win out in this highly competitive marketplace of limited transportation. This constant pushing, pulling, shoving, and squeezing are part of the daily rhythm of movement toward the rural northern periphery. As soon as the bus is packed tightly, the driver pulls out of his spot and continues along the North-South Highway.

The long stretches of agricultural land from Montero to Chané appear endless. As we pass each town, the people, their homes, and their schools seem poorer and poorer. Most of the women are dressed *de pollera* (in a layered or gathered skirt typical of Andean indigenous women) with rubber flip-flops, while their children run through the streets with mud-streaked legs and feet. Eventually, we pass through Chané, one of the places where MST members landed and set up makeshift homes after the military displaced them from Yuquises, the initial *toma* (occupation) of land in 2004. As they waited for the saneamiento of the land, many had no homes or places to which they could return, and so they lived in this town's parks and plazas for months, camping with their sleeping bags and blankets, finding spaces on the concrete floors of public parks or schools. They bathed and washed in the river in Chané—a river that runs black, contaminated with chemicals.

It is a few hours from Chané to San Pedro, and the vast fields of soy along the route indicate the crop's centrality in the local economy. In order to get from Harderman to Pueblos Unidos, one looks for a large trailer or agricultural truck headed that way. Once you are aboard, the fields of soy are no longer visible from the windows, as the trailer often blocks all sense of movement and unfolding landscapes. A ride in the back of these trucks is painful, often accompanied by bumps and bruises along the way—someone once described it to me as a full-body horseback ride. Finally, after about seven more hours, one arrives at Pueblos Unidos. There is a large sign reading, "Welcome to Pueblos Unidos," where a narrow, dark, black river cuts across the terrain separating the road from the MST settlement. A small, makeshift, and rather rickety canoe takes visitors and their belongings across to the encampment. The boat often shakes lightly with the weight of sleeping bags, books, and other goods, but Pueblos Unidos residents always wait to greet visitors on the other side.

While the last chapter narrated a longer history of global interconnectedness and the transformation of life in Bolivia's west and east, this chapter tells the regional history of Ichilo and Obispo Santiesteban, two centrally important areas of rice and soy production, respectively, which have now become centers of MST organizing in Santa Cruz. New forms of extractivism—which funnel resources from the periphery to the center— have led to a model of development based on a form of urban-centered regionalism. Elites in Santa Cruz have historically relied upon frontier expansionism, constantly searching for new markets and reliant upon export-oriented production and resource extraction. Large-scale agriculture and its dependence on transnational capital reinforce the opposition to both redistributive land reform and to policies that could establish protection over natural resource exploitation. This extractive economic model, then, has become critical to elite performances of a regional and modern identity linked to transnational capital and agrarian development. As some of these private interests and possibilities for resource expansion have come under attack by progressive movements like MST and the Morales administration, which threatened to take back latifundio land and nationalize natural resource wealth, elites have built a broad-based movement in urban centers that focuses on promoting an idea of a decentralized form of autonomy linked to their "modern agricultural development" model. While the progressive movements have become savvy at using culture and indigeneity as a language of historic rights to land and resources, in their response agrarian elites have had to invent counterpropaganda or alternative discourses to defend their model of free market capitalism and extractivism. They were particularly threatened by the new mobility of indigenous actors, who now obtain powerful positions in the government. In a desperate attempt to hold on to the status quo, elites claimed autonomy for their region by promoting a campaign of departmental decentralization that would provide them with control over natural resource wealth within their territorial domain.[2]

In order to protect their region and cityscape from Andean and indigenous "invaders" who represented a threat to their regional project, elites created fictive and real borders between sites of production and sites of consumption, forging distinctions between who can and cannot participate in and celebrate the splendors of agrarian modernity. These borders are patrolled, reinforced, and maintained through a spatialized and racialized logic: poor and rural Andean migrants should remain on the outskirts of a city,[3] and walls designate who belongs and who does not with graffitied phrases like "Passports for Collas" (see Figure 1) that powerfully indicate how conflicts over space, place, and resources have become citizenship battles writ small. Indigenous activists, as they

FIGURE 1. Anti-indigenous graffiti, "Passports for Collas," on the wall of the Gabriel René Moreno public university, Santa Cruz, 2006. Photograph by the author.

transgress key city spaces like the central plaza, face daily threats of violence, abuse, and harassment from youth groups protecting spaces of capitalist development.

All the while, this economic model of frontier expansion, resource extraction, and systematic denial of citizenship rights has created backlash in some of the impoverished areas of the northern region. In Ichilo, the struggles of rice producers, in conjunction with illegal logging and timber extraction, led to their occupation of governmental land called El Cuchirón in 2000. In Obispo Santiesteban, the transformation of rich productive land from sugar production to soy created highly uneven geographical development and new forms of displacement, which led to the well-known occupation of the hacienda of Rafael Paz, popularly referred to as the Yuquises occupation, in 2004.

While the previous chapter mapped the destruction of indigenous lands and communities and the subsequent movement of people from west to east, this chapter charts the movement of resources and people from the regional periphery to urban centers. This transport of critical resources, like timber from the forests of Ichilo or soybeans from Obispo

Santiesteban, challenges various groups of peasants to rethink the uneven logic of extraction. Indigeneity was initially reinvented, remapped, and reconceptualized with the migrations of highlanders to the lowlands, and indigeneity here becomes tied to a politics of reclamation and revitalization, to remapping organizational structures and forms of governance capable of resource redistribution. This is not unlike what Michael Watts (2004) describes in terms of the Ogoni people of the Niger Delta, who linked territory and oil to indigenous rights. Despite ethnic fragmentation, they manufactured a sort of Ogoni unity in the face of local opposition by using international organizations, such as the ILO Convention 169 on indigenous peoples, and transnational environmental groups like Greenpeace to legitimize the use of ethnic identity as a platform for building a mass movement for resource control and self-determination. Similarly in the Bolivian context, resources become critical to rethinking the power of ethnic or indigenous identity as a rationale for why and how alternative political-economic and governing structures need to be in place. Displacement, migrations, disassembly, and reassembly of life and livelihood link disparate groups in a common struggle to claim territory, framing the present moment as a continuation of an age-old ethnic battle to hold on to historic rights to land, community, and ways of governing—in essence, autonomy.

The Gran Chaco might have been the birthplace of MST, but Santa Cruz has perhaps received the most attention for its fierce land occupations and battles after the initial seizure of Pananti. Since I spent most of my time observing landless politics in the two regions of Ichilo and Obispo Santiesteban, this chapter provides a brief history of these zones of production. Most of the work on extractive industries has focused on the global North's hunger for resource wealth and the paradoxical curse of having these critical, nonrenewable resources on or below rich agricultural lands in the global South. For instance, Humphreys, Sachs, and Stiglitz (2007) offer insight into the natural resource curse: unlike other sources of wealth, natural resource wealth does not need to be produced, merely extracted. Since it is not a result of a production process, the generation of natural resource wealth can occur independently of other economic processes that take place in a country; for example, it can take place without major linkages to other industrial sectors. Moreover, many natural resources—oil and gas in particular—are nonrenewable, and as such, they are less like a source of income and more like an asset. As Bebbington (2009) and Farthing (2009) both note, indigenous activists are now struggling to escape this "resource curse" to even the playing field between the global South and North.

While this kind of work proves essential to understanding new global landscapes of inequality as a result of resource extractivism, it is also necessary to illustrate how extractive industries like the illegal timber trade and export-oriented production like soy form new nodes of regional power and influence, creating a highly unequal landscape between rural peripheries and urban areas. I borrow from Neil Brenner (2004) to engage some contemporary debates regarding international political economy and the restructuring of urban and regional power. Brenner's argument, in essence, is that there has been a kind of reterritorialization of state power under contemporary globalizing capitalism.[4] In the case of Bolivia, processes like decentralization relegated more responsibility to departmental structures and regional elites and in turn debilitated state power. Whereas most analyses have focused on supranational and national institutional shifts, Brenner shows that strategic spaces such as cities and city-regions are representing new arenas of state restructuring and new nodes of power. This proves indispensable for understanding resource extractivism writ small—within the space of Santa Cruz, the peripheral areas literally support and feed the center, fueling new forms of regional influence as important players like Branko Marinkovic and others insert themselves into global fields. In this regional landscape of inequality, Andean migrant farmers have grown desperate, have lost land and jobs, and have become newly displaced and mobile as they search for new forms of employment. As they traverse these landscapes on a daily basis in search of work and livelihood, moving between urban and rural centers, they become highly aware of the divisions between "haves" and "have nots" and the importance of this new peasant politics of reclamation.

THE NEW REGIONAL LANDSCAPE OF
POLITICAL AND ECONOMIC POWER

Santa Cruz began as a frontier town, but it now occupies a central position in the national economy, accounting for more than 42 percent of Bolivia's marketed agricultural output (PNUD 2004). Beginning in the 1950s, Santa Cruz benefited from international and national investment in opening up the lowland region. From 1992 through 2001, the department of Santa Cruz contributed 30 percent on average to Bolivia's GDP, with growth rates consistently higher than those of the national GDP (INE 2001a, 2001b).

The regions of Obispo Santiesteban and Ichilo were important centers of colonization and production. Initially, through the Instituto Nacional de Colonización (National Institute of Colonization, INC) highland farmers marched to the east to make the lowlands productive. Some were directed toward Ichilo, others toward Obispo Santiesteban, where life was difficult in the early days. Some highlanders maintained multiple land-holdings in both their departments of origin and the lowlands to support household economies; others brought their practice of coca cultivation with them from the highlands to the lowlands. During this early period, MNR channeled resources to help highland settlers and provided subsidies and support to secure food sovereignty.

In the northern Obispo region, highland migrants worked as sugarcane producers. Many members of MST also had small plots and continued to find wage-labor positions in these regions. The initial spread of sugarcane cultivation centered in an area of 1,500 square kilometers between Warnes and Santa Cruz (Gill 1987). Sandy soils proved ideal for the production of this new and important crop, which served the San Aurelio, La Esperanza, and La Bélgica sugar mills during the 1950s. By the 1970s, the province of Obispo Santiesteban was the central location for sugarcane cultivation. The completion of a paved highway created openings for the transportation of sugarcane from peripheral spaces to regional centers, to the global marketplace.

The massive migrations of highlanders to lowlands and new forms of organizing in sindicato structures, which provided a certain amount of leverage for small-scale sugarcane producers, created insecurity among regional elites and large-scale producers who wanted to protect their economic and agricultural interests. Elites in Santa Cruz founded the Federation of Cane Producers in Santa Cruz, which represented the largest and most well-established cane growers in the region. Soon thereafter, they created an umbrella agency called the Cámara Agropecuaria del Oriente (Agricultural Congress of the East, CAO) which was supposed to formulate a coherent agricultural plan for the entire region and articulate the demands of large-scale growers at the national level (Gill 1987). CAO has become an important agricultural and political umbrella agency, linked to other civic groups that are now promoting regional autonomy. In its initial days, CAO and its affiliates negotiated policy concessions concerning credit allocations and government price levels. Eventually, however, they influenced government decisions and acquired benefits for their members.

Free market economics, which brought the liberalization of trade and the opening of borders to private capital in the 1970s and 1980s, led to what Gabriela Valdivia (2011) calls the "internationalization of the low-lands," where international NGOs and development projects sponsored all sorts of extensive deforestation and land-grabbing in the name of development. The most significant of these in Bolivia was the World Bank's Lowlands Project, which financed new areas of expansion to the north and east and began to clear lands for the international trade in soy. As Valdivia points out, USAID-funded extensions, seed programs, and technological improvements allowed for more than one harvest per year and reduced labor requirements.

Simultaneously, neoliberal policies also created opportunities for large-scale production of export-oriented crops like soy. Private investment in new, highly mechanized equipment and expensive pesticide packages combined with the subsidies and tax breaks for large-scale soy producers, which created an ideal environment for this kind of production. Soy reshaped agricultural areas of the north like Obispo Santies-teban, creating new environmental and health hazards associated with heavy pesticide use, while legitimizing Santa Cruz's reputation as the "engine of production." While soy covered 70,000 hectares in 1988, by 1994, it had grown to 307,000 hectares, and Santa Cruz accounted for 97 percent of the total production of soy in Bolivia. The manufacturing and commerce sectors also flourished with the influx of capital. By the mid-1990s, Brazilian, Argentine, and Peruvian industrial conglomerates and trading houses dominated the agricultural complex, financing loans for soy production and providing agricultural inputs to producers, such as fertilizers, pesticides, and seeds (Valdivia 2011).

Today's soy producers recognize that success in commercial agriculture resulted from this greater international investment, increased productivity, and above-normal international prices. Valdivia describes the ways in which the profit generated by soy—"the golden bean"—consolidated a kind of model of private investment that contributed to unprecedented economic growth, leading many to conclude that modernity was best achieved through private and transnational, not state, investment (71). At the same time, small and medium-sized producers were left out of this mode of production. Unable to secure any kind of loans because they represented risky investments for lenders, small and medium-sized producers would have had to pay higher interest rates for the money to purchase the same kinds of products as their larger competitors. Many sold their land and property because it lost its fertility or because they could not afford to cover the costs of production or repay their debts. Some joined the ranks of landless workers or moved to urban areas in search of new possibilities in the expanding informal sector.

These forms of displacement and dispossession led Andean migrants to occupy or squat informally on rural or peripheral city lands. In rural areas, some landless began squatting on open lands and eking out a living, while in the urban areas, they often found cheap housing on the outskirts of the city and constructed makeshift settlements. In many ways, agroindustrial elites began to view this influx of highlanders as an *avasallamiento* (invasion) and the discourse of assault, usurpation, and subjugation began to characterize the talk of both urban and rural Andean migrants (see Gustafson 2006). In the city, regional elites characterize the presence of informal laborers in city spaces as a "flood" or a "hemorrhage." When laborers set up small shops in markets or sell products on the streets, they can be described as "disrupting, cluttering, littering" city spaces. In reference to their squatting on or invading Cruceño territory in the periphery, elites often describe them as "peasant hordes" breaking laws and norms of private property rights.

To protect their model of large-scale economic development and to calm their new fears of crisis provoked by spatial, racial, and political-economic fragmentation (Gustafson 2006; Fabricant 2010), elites have consolidated their interests and come together under broader umbrella groups like the CAO, the Cámara de Industria, Comercio, Servicios y Turismo de Santa Cruz (Chamber of Industry, Commerce, Services, and Tourism of Santa Cruz, CAINCO), and Civic Committees—self-elected entities made up of business and agroindustrial elites, with a long history of controlling and demanding subsidization by the central government. A parallel entity for women is the Comité Cívico Femenino (Feminine Civic Committee) and young men enter regional politics through the Unión Juvenil Cruceñista (Santa Cruz Youth Union, UJC), which has been described as the shock troops of the Civic Committees. Recently, in order to deal with fears of Andean migrations and the increasing presence of highland Indians in redefining statehood and the national political scene, elites have intensified their efforts to foster a political project of autonomy or decentralization. Their agenda promotes a private and neoliberal model of agroindustrial development, which is reinforced through the celebration of their agrarian history—paying a kind of homage to the periphery. Yet this celebration of the agrarian traditions of Santa Cruz supports a private development model, thereby constructing a regional-global model of citizenship rights based upon a European ideal of progress, development, and modernity—in essence, positing that large-scale and extractive industries will bring fruitful regional and urban-centered development to the city of Santa Cruz.

EXPOCRUZ: CELEBRATING AND PERFORMING AGRARIAN "TRANSNATIONAL" MODERNITY

Agrarian elites have promoted a form of regional citizenship through celebrations of a modern, neoliberal, and transnational identity as rooted in an agro-export industrial model that brings wealth, privilege, and mobility to a certain group of people. Aihwa Ong's (1999) model of citizenship as flexible and malleable crystallizes elite understandings of a region linked to global neoliberal capitalism: identity, once tied to a small and dusty pueblo, has now shifted toward being part of a regional Camba identity, which itself is deeply embedded in a broader landscape shaped by the national and global ebb and flow of capital, technologies, and populations. As one representative from CAO explained to me, "We believe in the free market, in the world market. We believe in work and dignity. Why? Because we were once a small and dusty town with only 50,000 inhabitants. Now, we are well over a million. We used to only grow or cultivate 500,000 hectares, and now we have more than 2 million hectares under cultivation. We know how to progress. We grew into an agroindustrial center on our own" (Interview, August 15, 2007).

This globalized agrarian identity is reinforced and celebrated through transnational trade shows like Bolivia's Feria Internacional de Santa Cruz (International Industrial and Agricultural Trade Show, EXPOCRUZ), held in large convention centers and attracting international guests from a variety of industries. This kind of trade show becomes a middle-class social event, as well as a site for deal-making, networking, and advertising. EXPOCRUZ is a spectacular celebration of Cruceño economic power, with over half a million visitors from Bolivia and beyond, and over forty blocks of pavilions, stands, booths, and restaurants. Such fairs occur once a year and temporarily employ more than 50,000 people—often slender, fair-skinned, female models who stand as symbols of advancement and progress. These women perform as hostesses, bringing agricultural goods and products on plates to the guests, serving both products and Cruceña sexuality[5] in one swoop. The event moves more than $112 million with the intention of selling agroindustrial products and creating a new regional-global network.

EXPOCRUZ also promotes the new regionalist platform, which celebrates Santa Cruz's modernity through genetically modified products and agricultural wonders, allowing people to escape into a consumer's paradise of commodity fetishism that hides the processes and side effects of production: poverty, displacement, and dispossession. With fluorescent lights beaming down from the ceiling, as in some kind of disco, visitors walk past booths where they can taste and try out all kinds of products: they can sip on a hot cup of Nescafé from the Nestle booth, or even drive the latest and most stylish car. As David Harvey (1990) describes it, the interweaving of simulacra in daily life brings together different worlds of commodities in the same space and time. The latest fashions mix and mingle with all sorts of high-end agricultural toys, concealing any trace of the original labor process that produced them, or any social relations implicated in their production. One can travel, be transported to another world, and experience all the wonders of this Disneyland of consumerist capitalism, while leaving behind any economic worries. By merely experiencing, tasting, and touching the wonders of globalized capitalism, visitors to the show see that it is achievable here.

These kinds of trade shows also serve as propaganda for the regional autonomy movement. For example, in the mix of agroindustrial and daily consumerist products are also T-shirts reading "*Autonomía*" (Autonomy), bracelets engraved with the saying "*Autonomía Sí o Sí* (Autonomy Yes or Yes)," and other wares illustrating the possibilities of departmental or regional autonomy for the advancement of free market capitalism. The beautiful models employed at the trade shows often promote, extend, and expand a platform of autonomy by wearing green and white uniforms, the colors of the region. Gendered inequality mixes with a platform for autonomy based upon commoditized celebration of a modern and advanced agrarian reality.

Another reality came to light against the backdrop of the EXPOCRUZ in 2006, however, as Andean migrants constructed roadblocks in the center of Santa Cruz, pulling large objects onto the street to paralyze the flow of traffic and stand against Civic Committee efforts to celebrate neoliberalism as the impetus for universal growth and prosperity. The intention was to block the routes leading directly into the event. Two understandings of neoliberalism, based on the starkly different lived experiences of two distinct classes, came into conflict in Santa Cruz that day—one of celebratory cheer, pride in the neoliberal development model, and the hypersexuality of the perfectly manicured and constructed Cruceñas who serve agriculture; the other accusatory, voiced by indigenous communities and MST agricultural workers dressed in sandals and ripped clothes, present to create havoc in the roads surrounding the convention center. The laborers refused to play into capitalist class illusions that denied their immiseration.

Like an amusement park funhouse, the trade show displays alternative realities through distorted mirrors. The gifts and goods served to the middle classes on platters are the "talismans of progress and fetishes of modernity" (Sawyer 2004: 80), while outside, landless campesinos used their bodies and squatted in the streets,[6] screaming, "This is not *our* autonomy, no to the oligarchs of Santa Cruz!" Their very presence represented a different kind of agrarian reality. As a result, they were described as "violent outsiders" and "unlawful blockaders" who attacked the norms of "peace and democracy." To a certain extent, their very political bodies were described as polluting, dirtying, and cluttering this urban environment (Douglas 1966; Weismantel 2001), and discourses of illegal citizenship circulated in city spaces.

ON THE OTHER SIDE: PROVINCIAL REALITIES IN ICHILO AND OBISPO SANTIESTEBAN

The following questions inform the rest of this analysis: How can we trace outwards (from the center to the periphery) the movement of resources? How has this "new extractivism"—celebrated as "cosmopolitan modernity" in the center and understood by agrarian farmers as "accumulation by dispossession" in the periphery—forced peasants to rethink their organizational structures and launch a new politics in the provinces? The MST settlements, whether with or without titles, represent an alternative model of citizenship—not a model that celebrates the transnational, agroindustrial process that uses modern-looking mestiza women to promote genetically modified products, but rather uses historical memory and experiences from the highlands to shape small-scale, sustainable agriculture and promote food sovereignty. The term "food sovereignty" was coined in 1996 by the Vía Campesina,[7] an international conglomeration of peasant movements, urban-based activists, NGOs, and indigenous peoples from 148 organizations representing 69 countries. Food sovereignty refers to the position that food is a basic human right, which is at the core of the platform for reclaiming rights to land, territory, and community.

The journey toward understanding new forms of peasant politics begins along the roads to MST settlements, where we can piece together the movement of resources, shifts in modes of production, and the nature of debt and dependency. For on the other side of the border of agrarian capitalism and modernity is a form of agrarian struggle, a lifestyle lived out by small-scale farmers who are no longer able to produce off the land, which has led to new cycles of debt and dependency, the destruction of environmental surroundings, and the depletion of resources. The journey to these MST settlements provides images that illustrate these transformations environmentally, socioculturally, and productively, making even starker the celebrations of agrarian modernity in the city centers when these peripheries remain hollowed out and devastated by such economic endeavors.

TRAVELING THROUGH BUENA VISTA, SANTA FE, LA ENCONADA, AND AYACUCHO

One starts the journey to Tierra Prometida in a taxi from the headquarters of MAS in Santa Cruz,[8] close to Los Pozos Market and the Ex Terminal. This part of the city is one of the poorest: rundown buildings line the cityscape; sex workers hang out in front of hotels, luring working men in for an hour or a night; and small-scale vendors set up shop alongside the Ex Terminal, which used to be the main bus station, but now contains city governing structures, including the *prefectura* (mayor's office). As our taxi, now displaying a "Santa Fe" sign, leaves the urban space of Santa Cruz, the road it follows seems to be headed for Obispo, but instead of heading north from Montero, it veers northwest through the beautiful tourist destination of Buena Vista, a small pueblo that hosts many regional fairs and festivals. The landscape of the region is diverse, containing hills, mountains, and prairies. This lush vegetation is starkly different from the dry, hard soil in the northern areas that has resulted from many years of monocultural soy production. Buena Vista was initially founded as a Jesuit mission and now is part of Amboró National Park; it contains great biodiversity and is known for its eco-tourism and sustainable development projects.

A few hours outside of Buena Vista, we arrive at the small migrant town of Santa Fe, where the taxi ride ends. To reach the smaller provincial areas, one must continue in another vehicle, sometimes a four-passenger car or a motorcycle. We arrive at Santa Fe around 9:00 A.M. that day, and Samuel, an MST organizer from the region, offers us a drink of milk with bananas at a small kiosk in the plaza. A skinny man dressed in ripped jeans and a button-down shirt, Samuel was a part of the initial occupation of El Cuchirón nearly eleven years ago. He is warm and embraces us with a smile and a chainsaw-like laugh that cuts into and reverberates through the open walls of the kiosk. Samuel always carries a small briefcase filled with legal papers, which he often totes diagonally across his back. He, along with Eulogio Cortés Arauz, will continue with us along the journey toward Ayacucho.

Heading toward Ayacucho, one notices a combination of large-scale rice production mixed with plots of large-scale soy. Ichilo is the oldest and the largest rice-producing center in Bolivia, accounting for 49.7 percent of the national rice production. The scale of rice production is determined by the size of landholding cultivated: small-scale producers have between 0.5 and 20 hectares, while medium- and large-scale producers cultivate between 21 and 100 hectares. This division of productive landholding is not accidental: land granting and agrarian colonization programs in the mid-1950s, followed in the 1990s by national and international investors' support for large-scale farming and land allocation policies that favored export-oriented rice and soy over other products, resulted in a highly uneven pattern of land distribution. Foreign investment and national policy also produced racialized divisions, as both investors and state officials favored whites and mestizos over indigenous Andean farmers. Of the twelve thousand rice farmers in the lowlands, about 97 percent are small-scale producers of indigenous origin, while 3 percent, mostly mestizos and whites, are medium- and large-scale producers.

Despite Ichilos's status as the rice capital of Bolivia, farmers describe rice production in the province as an enterprise that diminishes economic security (Valdivia 2011). Rice farming requires substantial capital investment in order to cover basic production costs, such as labor and technology. Since the Bolivian government did not contribute significant financial resources to small-scale rice production, farmers relied heavily on high-interest loans (ranging between 18 and 30 percent, depending on the farmer's repayment history) from private lenders (such as trading houses, agroindustries, or large producers) to cover production costs. In a year with favorable climate and prices, a farmer paid off his debts and maintained his household, but conditions were often less than favorable, and farmers were frequently unable to pay back annual loans. On top of this, many of these small-scale farmers had no choice: they had little control over the price of rice, because they lacked the storage capacity and the equipment necessary for drying and hulling large amounts of their crop. Instead, once harvested, the rice they had grown was sold to intermediaries and mill owners for further processing and commercialization. By contrast, medium- and large-scale farmers typically have greater access to capital through private bank loans or through their exclusive grower associations, which they can invest in expensive, large-scale machinery for production and commercialization. All of this weighs in favor of the large-scale producer.

On the journey toward Ayacucho, many MST members from the zone describe the high interest rates and lack of autonomy[9] as "feeling imprisoned." The story of one such member, Don Wilford Choque, Doña Delia's husband, clearly illustrated this theme of dependency and loss.

Once we arrive in Ayacucho, we proceed to Delia's little *chichería*, a kind of bar where people drink *chicha* (a traditional fermented beverage found in the highlands),[10] which provides an interesting spot in the small pueblo. Delia is a rather robust woman, and that evening, she is dressed in an apron like those that most market women wear, with two long braids hanging down her back. Church music plays in the background as we sit and converse, and a wooden table laden with leftover food and dirty dishes completes the room. Small children pass on makeshift bicycles, some without handlebars and brakes. Many neighbors gather around in the front area, drinking *chicha camba* (a nonfermented beverage common in the lowlands), eating a warm meal, and watching the large color TV from wooden benches. Campesinos returning from a hard day of work, their pants ripped at the seams, their shirts filled with holes, and their faces streaked with dirt, sit side by side, mesmerized by the images on the television. Often the program is a *telenovela*, a Brazilian soap opera dubbed into Spanish, where all the characters resembled the elites of Santa Cruz, far from the realities of the daily lives of debt and dependency of agricultural workers. Still, despite (or perhaps because of) the dissimilarities, the drama provides an escape from the everyday grind.

As Delia tidies up the chichería, prepares a quick meal, and sets up two mattresses and blankets on the cold cement floor for the night, her husband speaks of his deep sense of despair and of the enormous debt that he has accrued through private loans from the banks to keep his plot of land and rice crop. "I have about 10 million bolivianos of debt," he tells us. "I'm not sure how I'm going to pay off this debt . . . I will be paying this for the rest of my life." While much has been written on debt and dependency on the international level (Williams 2004; D. Harvey 2010; Peebles 2010), these feelings of deep insecurity and fear, associated with high interest rates, permeate the regional and intimately personal level. Delia's husband travels back and forth to Santa Cruz in search of work in the informal sector in order to supplement some of his agricultural labor, with the hopes that he could just pay back the interest on his loan. But he says, "Eventually, I will have to sell this house and parts of my land in order to just survive."

We go to sleep with the faded drama of the telenovelas, and wake at 6:00 A.M. to the alarm clock of roosters crowing, then say our good-byes to Delia and her husband. A large agricultural truck will transport us to the last stop, MST's settlement of Tierra Prometida, or "Promised Land." Chubi, the main MST guide, opens the wooden door of the truck and we throw our bags inside. We all position ourselves for a long journey. I grab onto the wooden frame of the truck for support since I know the bumps and jerks are often exaggerated in the back of the trailer. However, my legs are like Jell-O—they move from one direction to the other, slipping and sliding as the truck bounces about like a ping-pong ball. Then suddenly my shoulders start jumping up and down, and I hold onto a metal ring for dear life. My *compañero* (comrade) Ademar is standing like Jesus Christ on the cross, his arms spread out against the frame of the truck, and his head bowed in a kind of prayer.

We travel through a mist of dirt and *polvo* (dust), a light brown cloud above the truck. It is like a kind of tear gas that settles first on your hair, then drips slowly down from your hair into your eyes and nose, and gets caught in your throat. We feel the dust setting deep into our lungs and try to cough, but coughing it up is nearly impossible. I tell Ademar, "I'm going to throw up . . . I'm about to throw up." Before I can do so, however, we come to a complete stop alongside the road, and someone decides that it would be best for me to ride in the main *cabina* (cabin) for a while.

Once I am situated inside the truck, Renee, the driver, turns to me with a thick wad of coca in the side of his mouth, exposing his green-stained teeth as he exclaims, "Can't take it, huh? The dust is pretty bad out there." He asks me where I am from: "España? Argentina?" I tell him the United States, and he asks how we treat Bolivians there, and whether there are jobs.

As I talk to Renee about migrant labor in the United States, he tells me about his life. "I've been driving these huge agricultural trucks since I was a kid," he begins. "It's tough work, but I love it. I work six days a week. Sometimes, I travel deep into these areas, pick up the rice, and then travel back out again all in the same day. I've never gotten in an accident either. I know these roads very well." I look at the dashboard of the truck, which holds three bags of coca, Casino cigarettes, pliers, screw drivers, a huge bottle of water, a flashlight, and some other gadgets. Behind the seat is a bed for the long nights in the woods.

From my new high-perched angle in the cabina, I am able to watch large trucks passing along the road filled with neatly stacked timber. I ask Renee about this wood coming out of the forests, and he says, "Oh, this kind of deforestation has been happening for a long time. People are getting rich off of these beautiful lands." I sit mesmerized by the movement of these trucks with logs piled up so neatly in the back.

The main cause of deforestation in the northern regions has been the rapid growth of mechanized soybean production. In this particular area of Santa Cruz, however, there has been a great deal of illegal logging in unmanaged forests. Commercial logging became important in Bolivia in the 1970s and has expanded rapidly in recent years. In 1994, Bolivia exported over $112 million in primary and processed forest products. Four species—mahogany, cedar, oak, and ochoo—account for 60 percent of the wood produced between 1985 and 1994. Regarding timber, short-term economic benefits have been quite remarkable, generating $80 million in export earnings in 1994. But logging these timber species for ten or twenty years can hardly be a basis for sustainable and long-term economic growth. Bolivia has already depleted much of its mahogany reserves, and similar problems may be emerging with other tree species (Kaimowitz, Thiele, and Pacheco 1999).

As we arrive at Tierra Prometida, this stark history of commercial logging looms conspicuously in the impoverished forests of the area. The initial MST occupation in the region, called El Cuchirón, was a response to the illegal trade of lumber; as Wilford Colque, a longtime member of MST-Ichilo, described it:

Most of the land in Ichilo is designated as forestry reserves. Many landowners have acquired concessions on forest land, depriving small farmers and the indigenous of access to land. Some of this land was up for sale on the Internet in 2000, when everyone knew that the land could not legally be sold. Businessmen and livestock ranchers have accumulated large tracts of land, and the INRA has given them legal titles. The law is routinely overturned by those with access to power at the national level. Because land was lying idle, we decided to set up the MST and to give land to those who didn't have it. . . . The important thing is that this first occupation happened on land that was being used for the illegal lumber trade.

The El Cuchirón occupation was carried out by five hundred highland migrant families, both *colonizadores* (colonizers) and campesinos without land. Watching the events unfold in the Gran Chaco, these groups consulted with their bases, and instead of joining the *colonos*, they decided to form a section of MST. In an act of defiance against the illegal timber trade, they set up their first occupation, which was carried out by families fed up with the illegal sale of land for extractive purposes. One MST organizer described the occupation:

For two or three months, our activists visit the villages and communities in an area where there are lots of landless farmers and start raising awareness—proselytizing, if you like. As far as land occupations are concerned, we know our business—not everything, but a lot. Everyone has to go, all the families together. It has to be done at night to avoid the police. Those who want to join have to organize themselves into committees. Then, each committee—there may be twenty or so of them—has to hire a truck and set up a kitty to buy a canvas and stock up on provisions. One day, there's a meeting of representatives from each of the fifteen-person committees to decide when the occupation will take place. The decision has to be kept a secret. One night, the hired truck arrives, well before daybreak, and goes 'round the communities, picks up all it can carry, and then sets off for the property. The families have one night to take possession of the area and build their shelters, so that the next morning, when the proprietor realizes what's happened, the encampment is already set up. By morning, the settlement is established, and the basis for conflict is sprung.

For MST, the act of occupying the land, which members call "cutting the wire," is the cornerstone of the movement. It is the baptism of fire for the

MST *militantes*, an essential part of their identity. As a famous MST-Brazilian poet wrote, "When the pliers cut the wire and it snaps like the string in a violin and the fence tumbles down, the Sin Tierras lose their innocence" (Branford and Rocha 2002: 65).

The occupation, then, represents an alternative model of citizenship by invading private property in order to obtain collective land rights. Since the formal laws bend in favor of a few large-scale producers and landowners who manage to accumulate and consolidate vast landholdings and power through favorable treatment, MST cuts the wire on private property, reclaiming justice through the act of breaking the law. In this sense, the occupation can be thought of as a form of insurgent citizenship, conceptualized by anthropologist James Holston (2008) as resistance to state-building that aims to control populations by imposing a particular idea of order upon city planning, development, law, and government. By "insurgent," Holston refers to practices through which people problematize such projects—practices that work against the established and structural conditions of inequality and provide alternatives for including citizens and redistributing rights. In this particular case, MST occupiers—who, as politicized Andean highlanders, are already considered outlaws and out of place by elites in city centers—use their bodies to respatialize agricultural production and regain territorial control.

Once the occupation and encampment have occurred, the landless enter into a formal legal process. The conflict invariably results in the proprietor petitioning authorities to have the squatters evicted. Shortly thereafter, CEJIS lawyers arrive on the scene to document that the property is unproductive and therefore breaches the constitution. They subsequently assemble a *carpeta* (file) petitioning the land reform office (INRA) to evaluate, expropriate, and redistribute the unproductive land to the poor. INRA eventually makes an inspection of the property and either decides to reclaim the land or file for an eviction and return the property to the landowner. Oftentimes, if the squatters refuse to leave, landowners hire paramilitary troops to displace them, including violence. This does not mean that the struggle ends, however; MST members simply set up a new encampment farther down the road or come back to the same location until the land dispute is legally settled.

Today, after more than eleven years of squatting on the land, MST still does not have official title to Tierra Prometida because of complicated land politics—the land is considered to be part of a state-protected forest reserve and therefore cannot be collectively titled to the movement.

Nevertheless, MST has set up several communities called Tesoro, Primero de Agosto, and Quince de Agosto, where members practice agroecology and implement all sorts of strategies for sustainable development, like reforesting parts of the property.

When we arrive at Tierra Prometida, the sky is a deep shade of blue, the clouds white and fluffy. The land occupied and being made productive by MST is on the other side of the forest. I hear Wilford's voice coming from a small hut of made of *motacu*,[11] echoing through the trees. After our nearly twelve-hour journey, we have finally arrived at this most spectacular physical landscape, surrounded by a lush ecosystem built out of the rainforest. As we walk through the community, one organizer says, "Our hope is to connect all three communities. Right now, we have three *núcleos*, and through a kind of urbanization plan, we hope to have a plaza, water tanks, soccer fields, and so on. We will begin some of our collective farming projects once all the MST organizers move permanently to this area."

The politics of Tierra Prometida and the Ichilo region form crucial parts of my analysis, particularly in reference to large-scale rice production, debt dependency, and new forms of extractivism. I will examine peoples' daily struggles to maintain their livelihood, farming without holding title to the land; and look at the debate over dissolving MST and returning to a peasant union structure that defines regional politics.

YUQUISES OCCUPATION: SEIZING AND OCCUPYING SOY TERRITORY

I turn now to another MST occupation story in the region that is a rather heroic tale of landless peasants winning out against a large-scale soy producer, a kind of David and Goliath story. The protagonists in this story, unlike their comrades in Tierra Prometida, received international attention and support, governmental intervention in the form of machines, seeds, and infrastructure, and even title to the land. Much of this outcome had to do with the nature of the occupation site, which was not on a protected forest reserve like Tierra Prometida; but perhaps even more because it was a story quintessentially about attacking illegal landownership and latifundio power.

What links the two occupations and tales in this region are themes of debt and dependency and increasing levels of poverty and displacement caused by this agroindustrial model of development. Yet the reality of not receiving support from the government defines MST politics in these distinct geographic landscapes today. This is similar to Wendy Wolford's (2011) findings that regional differences between the northeast and the south defined membership in MST-Brazil. In the south of Brazil, farmers joined the movement in order to continue the way of life that they had practiced for generations, deeply embedding themselves in the collective model of the movement. In the northeast, however, the original MST members were pushed into the movement by their desperate situation and their lack of alternatives. These regional differences—not necessarily the differences between rice and soy production, but between settlements being located in a forestry reserve or in the middle of soy territory—define how and in what ways members develop their political organization and their model of production in Bolivia.

Whether in Ichilo or Obispo Santiesteban, the majority of MST members were highland Andean migrants who had worked as wage laborers in sugar or rice production; many now form the ranks of the landless and displaced peasantry. They had seen and experienced the limitations of this agroindustrial model but were also frustrated by the failure of union-based organizing to redefine agrarian production in an era when indigenous needs, ideas, and language became particularly powerful in demanding political, economic, and social rights. MST-Bolivia began to think about how indigenous ways and customs could redefine their political organization, from democratic forms of governance to plans for rebuilding farming communities. Indigeneity had to be linked to ideas about territoriality: reclaiming land and territory was critical to defining a new kind of agrarian citizenship and reterritorializing power through a highly flexible and mobile organizational structure that would move platforms and demands from the local level to the regional and state levels.

As mentioned earlier, parallel organizations like the Movement for the Survival of Ogoni People (MOSOP), in places as far away as the Niger Delta, show indigenous communities responding to a history of neglect and local misery to call for self-determination. The Ogoni, for example, demanded "political control of Ogoni affairs by Ogoni people, . . . the right to control and use a fair proportion of Ogoni economic resources, . . . [and] adequate representation of rights in all Nigerian national institutions" (Watts 2004: 71). Saro-Wiwa, a Nigerian author and environmental activist, emerged as a critical figure who advocated for the rights of the Ogoni people and called for Ogoni unity, despite ethnic conflicts and fractionalizing, in an era of increased resource conflict. Oil was key to this process of reunification, as it was the basis on which claims could be made and rights talk could be instigated; oil served as a ground on which the Ogoni could demand corporate compensation, accountability, and resource control. It was precisely linked to indigenous claims on the state, which requires ethnic identification to be discursively and politically produced in relationship to a history of marginalization.

The Ogoni case, like MST-Bolivia, illustrates that indigeneity is not fixed—there are no predetermined, deep historic or territorial ties—but rather, ethnic identity is fluid, heterogeneous, and can be contested. It is malleable and can be shaped in relationship to new landscapes of inequality and resource control; "Ogoniness" or "Andeanness" can be recreated to manufacture and accommodate new identities.

In the case of MST–Pueblos Unidos, the idiom that unified the protestors was not oil, but soy. Soy was the key export-oriented crop through which regional elites had consolidated wealth, power, and control. Soy was eating away at available farmland, and because it relies heavily upon chemicals and fertilizers, it affected both the environment and communal health, in addition to leading to new forms of displacement through debt and dependency. In June 2003, a group of two hundred landless men and women occupied a region known as San Cayetano in order to claim their rights to land and resources. Three hundred families without land occupied the property controlled by Brazilian Francisco Marchetty, an agribusinessman in the region. They were violently removed, but in September 2003, the same group occupied the zone called "La Luna," situated in the province of Guarayos, in northern Santa Cruz. This property was controlled by Juan Guillén, who was also a member of the agribusiness elite investing in soy production. In this case, there were verbal negotiations with the landowner and state bureaucrats, and in time, MST decided to remove the settlers from the contested zone. Finally, on August 8, 2004, several families from MST–Santa Cruz occupied Los Yuquises, a hacienda owned by the well-known agribusinessman Rafael Paz Hurtado, situated in the province of Obispo Santiesteban, approximately 260 kilometers from the city of Santa Cruz.

Before analyzing this occupation from the point of view of MST members, it is important to shift the lens back to the center of power to understand how Paz Hurtado, a longtime landowner in the region, understood this occupation as a violation of private property rights and ultimately a failure of the democratic institutions that should protect its citizens from land "invasions."

On a crisp day in August 2007, I traveled to the home of Rafael Paz Hurtado in the wealthy neighborhood of Equipetrol. The house was hidden behind several security walls, and a call-in box greeted any outsiders. Several SUVs were parked in the outside lot. Paz Hurtado was in his mid-sixties, with a fully gray head of hair and a bit of a comb-over. He wore wire-rim spectacles, a perfectly ironed striped Kenneth Cole shirt, and khaki pants. Once he opened the door to his spacious home, we traveled through a long foyer with marble floors and glass tables and wound up in an open living room. Paz Hurtado took a seat on a soft, off-white couch behind a glass table with a ceramic flower pot placed carefully in the middle. While Paz Hurtado was strikingly nervous about the interview, he regaled me with charming stories of his family, in particular his oldest son, who worked hard in the United States to earn a business degree. He was quite hospitable, offering several large glasses of ice-cold lemonade.

Everything in his house was immaculate: there were no streaks on the glass table, the floors had been recently cleaned, and the oak furniture showed no sign of dust. A large glass door led to the kitchen, revealing the silhouette of an indigenous woman sweeping in a highly mechanistic fashion in the other room—a sight that hung over our interview space. She moved by rote, back and forth, as Paz Hurtado jumped into a history of his life as an agricultural entrepreneur in Santa Cruz. "My name is Rafael Paz Hurtado. I am a large-scale agricultural laborer. I have always worked in agriculture. I started out in the 1980s in the zone called Peta Grande. The problem of land comes from a much earlier era. It's not just about the government of Evo Morales. In the late 1990s, people from the western highlands started coming down to the lowlands in truckloads and invading our lands. . . . We were always fighting them" (Rafael Paz Hurtado, personal communication, August 2007).

While Paz Hurtado might start with the 1980s, Lesley Gill (1987) actually traces the history of the family's landowning in the region to the rubber era in Santa Cruz, where elite Cruceños owned import-export houses, initially founded by German immigrants between 1898 and 1910. These families received large government land concessions and were thus able to control important rubber reserves in various provinces of Santa Cruz. The houses exported rubber to Europe and imported high-priced manufactured goods to Bolivia, but primarily acted as credit lenders. When the rubber boom collapsed, they extended their activities, bought land, and invested in large-scale cattle production or exploitation of timber concessions. The Paz family owned one of these import-export houses and retained numerous properties after the agrarian reform of 1953. The total number of hectares claimed by the Paz brothers was 14,350, but in 1954, the firm cultivated only 212. It possessed agricultural machinery valued at $20,582, and its assets were divided among the heirs upon the death of the two owners—Roberto Paz in 1954, and Rosendo Paz in 1956. So while Rafael Paz Hurtado might only date his landowning to the 1980s, his family has old ties to systems and structures of power and unproductive landholding in the region. These rotating regimes of resource control and power continue to influence unequal landholding, while the passing on of power from one generation to the next keeps these old colonial systems and structures in place. Similar mechanisms of violence and control as that seen in the first chapter in plantation-style economies continue to suppress the labor force.

In part, Paz Hurtado shapes his narrative in such a way that he can tell a story of a hardworking and productive soy entrepreneur, a kind of "productive citizen" who has been a victim of theft and invasion. He is not alone in shaping this discourse. Members of a much broader agricultural community, like those represented by CAO and CAINCO, also frame themselves as a "successful class of producers"—hardworking, productive, organized, and responsible[12]—whereas the others, the Andean Collas, come "in truckloads" and invade their lands. When I asked Luis Valdemar, a representative from CAO, about recent peasant invasions in the north, he described it in a similar way: "These Andeans occupy other people's land. In other words, they rob. Well, if you rob, you actually take something with you. In the case of land, these invaders cannot take the land with them. However, they are violating our fundamental right to private property" (Luis Valdemar, personal communication, August 2007). This imaginary construction of the "rural Indian hordes" invading, usurping, and subjugating frames a regionalist discourse of autonomy that is essential to promoting ideas of modernity, agricultural productivity, and regional citizenship. In keeping with this theme, Paz Hurtado ended our conversation with these words:

It's when these people come and take over private property and abuse people that it becomes a big problem. They take hostages. For instance, that's what happened in my zone, Yuquises. They invaded my property. We built everything with our own hands. We built the roads, the public roads, and that's when the invasions intensified. The government of Evo Morales enters [into power] and MST invaded Yuquises. This land invasion received international attention. There were many hostages; MST members took people hostage and there was one dead guy. . . . That's when lots of people got involved and MST put marijuana in my soy production plants. They put twelve plants of marijuana and they made it seem like I was a narco-trafficker. Where you plant soya, you use lots of chemicals, so there is no way I could be growing marijuana in the middle of that. I contacted lawyers and spoke to the press. You see, this land in the north is the best land in all of Bolivia. They invade the lands, and once they are encamped there, they sell it, and go farther north to seize more land. They are what we call "traffickers of land." This is the reality of these social movements. (Rafael Paz Hurtado, personal communication, August 2007)

While Paz Hurtado might tell the story of the invasion in a way that reflects his social, economic, and political—not to mention, personal— view of the history of land ownership, when the analytic lens shifts, we see and hear a very different tale of this invasion. MST–Santa Cruz entered the property of Los Yuquises in August of 2004 and squatted with about five hundred occupiers. They began to work the land collectively, setting up productive work groups and advancing a model of agroecology and sustainable development. A few days after the occupation, the Paz Hurtado family demanded the evacuation of the MST settlement on their property. After a month or so of very little government intervention, the CAO decided to intervene and publicly supported the Paz Hurtado family. On September 15, the CAO published an open letter in *La Razón*, demanding that Bolivia's interim president, Carlos Mesa, take measures to defend private property in Santa Cruz. In the same letter, the CAO warned that in the event there was no government reaction, the property owners "would defend their property rights with their own measures" (Quiroga and Núñez 2005). Even more surprisingly, exactly two weeks later, the prefect of Santa Cruz, Ruben Costas, signed an authorization, without approval of the national government, for a military intervention in order to clear MST–Santa Cruz from the private property of the Paz Hurtado family. Even though the meddling of third parties provoked rising tensions, no official action was undertaken by the prefect or INRA. In the following months, however, several clashes between MST members and armed men allegedly hired by Paz Hurtado took place.

On May 8, 2005, nearly eight months after the initial occupation, Rafael Paz Hurtado allegedly hired *sicarios* (assassins) from a peripheral community in Santa Cruz to violently displace the landless workers from his hacienda. Two days later, these armed hitmen looted homes, burned pineapple and rice fields, beat and abused women, and even took several MST members hostage. One of these hostages was Luis Salvatierra, who was reluctant to speak with me in the aftermath of the Yuquises incident. Salvatierra was not a part of the movement—a landless leader had convinced him to take part in the occupation in order to find work that he desperately needed, and he got caught up in the chaos of the *enfrentamiento* (confrontation) between the sicarios and MST. He describes the events as follows:

> The police arrived at Yuquises and said that a man, one of the sicarios, had disappeared. I had this old coat and I never thought or imagined that the coat belonged to the "disappeared man." They grabbed me because of the coat. . . . I had no idea that the coat belonged to this disappeared man. I just put it on because it looked better than my coat and it was pretty cold. They took me away to a little prison in Montero. I wasn't allowed to have contact with anyone. They tortured me in prison. They said, "We don't care about your feelings. They paid us to hit you, to beat you, and to torture you to give up names of the MST members."[13] This went on for a very long time, and finally, the CEJIS lawyers got me out. I do not want to hear about MST again. I am now working in a factory [Aceite Fino]. The work is hard, but it's better than life in Yuquises. I don't want to ever be involved with this kind of politics again.[14] (Luis Salvatierra, personal communication, April 2006)

Several days after the attack on the community, after a press conference in Santa Cruz's main square concerning the "disappeared" inhabitants of Pueblos Unidos, MST–Santa Cruz leader Silvestre Saisari was beaten and kicked unconscious by several members of UJC. He describes it as follows: "I was just walking through the plaza, when all of the sudden these kids start beating the shit out of me. They were screaming, 'So you are the *machito* [little tough guy] who is stopping traffic and organizing people. You are the big guy, heh? You're nothing more than a *colla de mierda*

[Indian piece of shit]! Your life is worthless!'" (Silvestre Saisari, personal communication, April 2006)

After this attack, Saisari had to go into hiding. CEJIS lawyers indicated that the attackers took his bag and his mobile phone, which they had allegedly been using to make threatening phone calls to MST–Santa Cruz members. Documents that were in the bag were allegedly shown during an interview with the landowner on the nationwide Red 1 de Bolivia TV station the following day.[15]

This daytime attack on the MST–Santa Cruz leader by UJC created much backlash. After several months of waiting, on July 1, 2005, despite their eviction, MST members presented their case to INRA, demanding the 16,686 hectares of land that they had occupied. This plot of land had already been declared clear of title, public, available, and accessible. On August 1, the national director of INRA granted the demand for special endowment of title presented by the Comunidad Campesina Agroecoló-gica Pueblos Unidos (PU). On September 7, the new president, Eduardo Rodriguez, and members of his cabinet entered into a dialogue with a number of indigenous and campesino organizations, including MST. The conversation ended with the signature of a memorandum, which was an unofficial special endowment of title to the Pueblos Unidos community. After several delays in transmission, INRA sent the file to the Departmental Agrarian Commission in Santa Cruz for their consideration. However, their proposal was rejected on November 15 (Diemel 2010).

As illustrated earlier, while citizenship rights within the city of Santa Cruz might be displayed through spectacular trade shows and illusions of development, real agricultural laborers are denied access to land and productive resources. Regionalists, in order to defend "rights to private property" and a form of civic democracy, hired sicarios to displace or "disappear" MST members. When this strategy proved ineffective, they used outright violence, abuse, and torture. Finally, since the Agrarian Commission had to approve the special endowment, they used their legal power to deny MST leaders any procedural guarantees and their right to due process of law, personal liberty, and a fair defense. A number of evictions subsequently occurred, and MST members filed several criminal complaints, which never went to court. The governor instead ordered that the "ringleaders" of the movement be arrested. There were great fears developing around this "militant movement" and the possibility that it could disrupt the agroindustrial model of development and progress. After all, the wealthy citizens of Santa Cruz represented a particular form of agrarian democracy and transnational modernity, while these rural laborers represented undemocratic practices of militantly seizing land, blockading roads, and operating outside of the legal frame of private property ownership.

The movement did not receive official title to the land until Evo Morales passed his New Agrarian Reform Law in November 2006, which sought to significantly transform the INRA Law. He made a point to publicly present the movement with its official title at a regional agrarian celebration in the community of Pueblos Unidos. The movement received 16,686 hectares of agrarian land in the form of two expropriated estates previously owned by the Paz Hurtado family. Pueblos Unidos is the first officially titled and legal "communally owned land" in the Santa Cruz region.

This chapter has looked at the new regional borders between the rural periphery and urban centers of consumption and accumulation of wealth. The borders divide producers from consumers and create fictive and real ethnic, racialized, and gendered bounds, where the threat and use of violence sustain an age-old colonial structure dependent upon extractive industries. Elites perpetrate a model of violence, torture, and disappearance intended to pacify "resistant peasants" into a submissive state to advance their own agenda for regional autonomy, but the landless have rejected this model of global, cosmopolitan citizenship. Instead of searching for transnational agrarian links to private capital, genetically modified organisms (GMOS), and external markets, landless peasants extend their networks to other displaced and dispossessed workers, nationally and transnationally. Their discourse and platform centers not on progress and advancement through an agroindustrial complex, but on an idea of "peasant" culture, using and mobilizing indigeneity in order to reclaim rights to land, productive resources, and means of production.

Yet as we will see, there is no purity to this model of indigenous politicking—after all, MST–Pueblos Unidos, while experimenting with some agroecology, has not abandoned the model of large-scale soy production. Rather, the community wants to promote an idea of "development" by which they too might reap some of the benefits of this model. How do we capture ethnographically the contradictions inherent in this not-so-pure model of "indigenous development," built upon the premises of large-scale agrarian capitalism?

The next chapters will chart the use and mobility of indigeneity as a discourse and practice of grassroots citizenship, a form of governance and organization that remains deeply embedded and grounded in communal self-determination, producing food for national consumption, and rethinking sustainability. But as Suzana Sawyer (2004) and others have argued, "there was nothing inevitable about an indigenous politics of opposition; it had to be produced" (87). Indigeneity, then, constituted a language of reclamation, a language that was malleable, sometimes used for the benefit of small-scale and peasant-based agriculture, while at other times simply evoking native histories of subjugation to justify receiving a more adequate piece of the pie.

PART II

MANUFACTURING IDENTITY AND TERRITORIALIZING RIGHTS

CHAPTER THREE

AYLLU DEMOCRACY
Indigenous Law and Collective Governance as Territorial Protection

The Yuquises occupation, which is now the community of Pueblos Unidos, is located about fifty kilometers north of a small migrant town called San Pedro, in the fifth section of the department of Santa Cruz. With about 14,644 inhabitants, mostly Andean migrants, San Pedro is one of the most productive zones of Santa Cruz and Bolivia for soya.[1] It looks like any other small rural pueblo in the north, dotted with makeshift huts with thatched roofs of motacu branches, small shops and bodegas, and roosters and hens roaming the streets. Kids run through the plazas, barefoot, streaked with mud and crusted with dirt.

Many of the residents of Pueblos Unidos did not officially move to the community until the fall of 2007 due to complications with land tenure and title, and many of their meetings and political events continued to take place in the provincial areas where they lived. We spent most of our time observing meetings in the San Pedro municipality since the majority of the Pueblos Unidos community meetings took place in this centralized location. One *dirigente* (leader) and active member of the Yuquises occupation named Ponciano Sulca became a vital component of the project. Although he was initially skeptical of our interest in the organization, asking if we might be spies for North America or for the Bolivian government, he slowly came to trust us and fold us into his everyday life. Constantly interested in U.S. foreign relations, he would ask questions about the wars in Iraq and Afghanistan or about increasing levels of poverty in North America, trying to understand a territory, place, and space so radically different from his own. He always offered us a place of rest, food, and great conversation during our frequent treks from Santa Cruz to Guarayos, and he often asked to accompany us in the back of a truck or trailer to his settlement, Pueblos Unidos.

Sulca is about five foot four, with sun-streaked brown skin, and always dresses in a ripped T-shirt and a pair of brown cotton pants with unraveling seams. His eyes hang low, deep wrinkles form under his lids, and small gray hairs poke up at random on his face, not forming a full mustache or beard. He migrated to the city of Santa Cruz from Potosí in the 1960s to find work on the sugarcane plantations. As sugar rapidly gave way to cotton, however, Sulca searched for other forms of employment and was able to find work as a day laborer building the international airport, Viru Viru, located eighteen kilometers from Plaza 24 de Septiembre. He met his wife, Gregoria Mamani, in Villa Cochabamba, a peripheral neighborhood of Montero. They moved to San Pedro in the 1970s, just as agribusiness accelerated both its economic reach and political influence in the region, and he found weekly work with the transnational corporations that were first establishing themselves there.

As soon as Sulca realized that steady employment was available, he built a small house behind the main plaza in San Pedro and started a family. In 2006, when I visited his home, the names of his three grandchildren were written in colorful lettering on the wooden planks. There were a few lawn chairs in the yard, a small, unstable wooden table, and lots of animals—chickens, dogs, including some puppies, and two horses. The kitchen was a makeshift hut with a wood-burning stove. Every day, Sulca cut wood with a huge machete and carried the logs back to the house from the surrounding woods. There was no bathroom, only an outhouse composed of a few planks, with a curtain pieced together from bright Andean blankets serving as a door. Clothes were piled high on the line running from the house to the outhouse.

Sulca was never home for long, however. Like other MST organizers, he lived his life in transit—moving from the rural periphery to the city of Santa Cruz to meet with lawyers from CEJIS, keep INRA appointments, and more. He often carried a small briefcase or book bag with critical papers from the Yuquises occupation; he camped out for days in the MAS offices in Santa Cruz, then caught up on sleep in the back of a bus or while hitching a ride on an agricultural truck. In his worn and broken sandals, which rubbed against his blistered feet, he also walked long distances to find a cheap means of transportation. This constant motion, the traveling between the periphery and center, was often marked by violence. Sulca spoke about how he was kidnapped and imprisoned for five months after the Yuquises occupation.[2] For two of those weeks, the guards tortured him in jail, and he was refused the medical attention he needed for a urinary infection aggravated by bladder cancer. This experience of torture and fears of unknown enemies shaped his travel and movement through rural and urban space. Sulca often repeated, almost like a mantra, "There is no fear . . . the fear is gone . . . we must not live our lives in fear." He spoke publicly about letting go of fears, but privately, he expressed great concerns about his own security and that of his family. Members of the violent youth group UJC frequently circled his house in SUVs and threatened to "disappear" or kill his family members.

One day in May 2006, we were traveling from San Pedro to Montero with Sulca and a group of MST organizers. We squeezed into a small taxi in San Pedro, heading through the main pueblos that whizzed past our windows. The images faded so quickly that scenes blurred together. Suddenly, from the back of the taxi, we heard some commotion coming from a hut in Chané, and at the edge of my vision, I saw a large man on a motorcycle bolt off his vehicle with a huge rifle. Then the sound of shots filled the air, mixed with a cacophony of high-pitched yelps and screams. We were not sure what had happened or why the shots were fired, but we were mesmerized by the horrific scene of the rifle, the fallen body, the cries for help. The motorcycle screeched into our lane, cutting us off, as we held on to the side paneling for dear life. The blasts from the rifle continued to ring in our ears, and the image of the wave of people rushing to the victim played over and over like a silent movie. In this moment, however, Sulca and the taxi driver appeared undisturbed; they explained that the man on the motorcycle probably wanted to steal something and the campesino arrived too early, and it was his bad luck that day. Sulca in particular seemed numb to this kind of violence.

For Sulca, life was, in part, about negotiating a multilayered terrain of violence: the daily struggles of loss of work and poverty; his son occasionally coming home with wounds and scars from his wife, who often beats him for drinking and infidelity; his daughter, who had several misdemeanors and was often held in jail for a few nights; and his constant fears of mestizo youth aggressively taunting him in city centers. Helen Risor (2010a), who has conducted extensive ethnographic work in the migrant neighborhoods of El Alto, narrates a similar terrain where her interlocutors must navigate a complicated environment of state and nonstate violence. *Vecinos* living in El Alto begin to identify and read signs of dangerousness, often fixing dangerousness onto specific criminal bodies. In this case, too, MST organizers and rank-and-file members identify groups of people based on race, class, and political alliances that they consider "dangerous," and attempt to avoid daily contact with them. Like Risor's (2010a) analysis, the complicated landscape of violence in rural peripheries of Santa Cruz includes that of agribusiness elites and constant threats from mestizo youth who might displace and dispossess them, yet there is also a daily social violence that occurs among family members, *vecinos*, neighbors, and even political comrades. This kind of social violence—which MST members might identify as infidelity, cheating, stealing, and ultimately as a form of betrayal—manifests itself as racisms and classisms, as daily suspicions and fears of distinct groups of people.

The last chapter charted resource extraction from the periphery to urban centers, which fueled the regional economy and promoted new performances of a globalized, transnational agrarian citizenship, but also hollowed out communities and created ever-greater insecurity. As a result, in agroindustrial centers like Santa Cruz, small groups of mestizo elites have come to dominate resources, flows of capital, and spaces and places of governance. Within this context of extraction and consumption, new borderlands have created territorial, racial, and gendered divides between producing rural peripheries and modern city centers. These borderlands are surveilled and controlled through subversion, intimidation, and violence. While the last chapter honed in on the movement of resources and people from the periphery to urban areas, this chapter's analysis turns inward toward agricultural communities like Pueblos Unidos, which are located far from the urban centers, far even from the rural provinces like San Pedro. There is great insecurity and fear as politicized Indians cross into sites of consumption, but there is greater insecurity and fear in remote rural areas. These geographical locales of MST organizing are often left unprotected by the state or even formal security forces and are under constant threat from agribusiness and extralegal violence.

This idea of "insecurity" parallels recent work in anthropology that has centered on the relationship between neoliberalism, the retreat of the state, and the emergence of autonomous, decentralized governing structures in new urban squatter settlements like Cochabamba and El Alto, where residents have come up with their own solutions to structural problems of poverty. Primarily, however, this work has focused on urban and peripheral squatter settlements. For example, the state's retreat has forced community residents in Villa Pagador, a migrant community on the outskirts of Cochabamba, to come up with a system of governance and punishment involving lynching criminals (Goldstein 2004). Goldstein analyzes these lynchings as spectacular and performative ways for marginalized groups to bring attention to the insufficient authority of the state and to demand citizenship rights. These marginalized citizens could be considered "insurgent" (Holston 1999: 157), for their actions of enforcing law independent of the state indicate that the basis of citizenship may be derived outside of or on the margins of the state (Das and Poole 2004). Risor (2010b) also looks at the phenomenon of self-help justice, as urban residents of El Alto inhabit a space of violence and danger that fills their lives with fear. Since this danger is elusive and mutable, residents engage in actions to manage the inherent anxiety, ranging from identifying criminals or dangerous individuals to providing communal forms of surveillance and spreading vague rumors of torturing and lynching. Risor argues that these attempts to manage insecurity are not taken in defiance of the state, but rather, since they take place in conjunction with the police, give presence to the state. Such efforts, she concludes, of citizens asserting their rights through social organizations, create openings and make demands for new ways of life in the process.

This chapter, then, looks at insecurity across multiple scales: insecurity at the level of the community (including threats from outside the community and from within), but also insecurity with regard to organizational failures (corrupt and hierarchical leaders).[3] Insecurity did not begin with neoliberal reforms but rather dates back to the colonial period—with the breaking up of indigenous lands, forced migration, shifts to new modes of production, and the vicious cycle of debt and dependency that resulted from colonization.[4] Yet neoliberal reforms, which introduced private capital as a solution to problems of poverty, also created greater inequalities and increased competition between and among neighbors for scarce resources.[5] This increased competition can cause people to distrust one another, fearing that their neighbors might be stealing or hoarding critical resources, and can turn into an exchange of harsh accusations. These daily tensions have forced MST to rethink their structure and to rebuild their organization to be more democratic and participatory, capable of creating order and holding leaders and rank-and-file members accountable through collective governance.

This change can be thought of as a form of grassroots citizenship: not as liberal individualism given to members as a right by the state, but rather a new model of local citizenship based upon ancient Andean principles of autonomy, self-governance, and participatory democracy. Sian Lazar (2008) might refer to this as the "collective self," or the idea that citizenship is not simply the liberal individualism imposed by Western societies on indigenous societies that were inherently or historically collectivist, where citizenship is creative and dynamic. Unlike Lazar, who is interested in how political subjectivities are produced between state and nonstate actors, I am interested in how grassroots actors pull pieces from their pre-Columbian past, which might be highly deterministic and essentialized, and use them as a vehicle to rethink democratic structures independent of the state. Security, then, for highlanders living in the lowlands, should be thought of in terms of land tenure, protection of the land and the community from violent threats (both outside and within), and governance. The Andean ideal of the ayllu—imagined as communally held land and collective forms of governance and control—becomes the framework for governing MST settlements. Modern ayllus are characterized by nucleated settlements, communal landholdings, rotational political and administrative offices, land redistribution, and rural tax collection.

MST takes parts of the ayllu model and adapts them to structure their political organization at the community, regional, and national levels. The state fractionalized land and territory through a model of citizenship that assigned property rights to individuals, but MST begins with the idea that land is more than a piece of individual property—it is a collective right. The occupation of land, or what they call a "reconquest" of sorts, is about reclaiming and reterritorializing indigenous control and autonomy over land and critical resources. Marcia Stephenson (2000), describing THOA's political, cultural, and ideological uses of the ayllu, articulates it as an Andean body politic in which the four parts of the Tawantinsuyu, the Inca empire, which was the largest empire in pre-Columbian America, were believed to represent a body: "For native peoples . . . its remembrance as it was, points to the reinscription of differences such that the ayllu becomes a political, symbolic, and geographical space for the enactment of resistant and subaltern identities" (14). These distinct parts of the Andean body politic—territorial reclamation, political structures, and geographic space—must come together to create a coherent whole. The dynamic relationship between territorial autonomy and the ability to provide a political infrastructure that sustains humanity is designated by indigenous conceptualizations of *sumak kawsay*,[6] or *buen vivir*—"good living." This "return to the past" logic provides a sense of territorial and communal security through a form of "collective" control and independent governance.

Managing territory or land as a collective then structures the entire political organization. The organization of the movement can be thought of as a set of nested dolls—family, nucleus (*núcleo*), settlement, regional bloc, departmental structure, and national leadership team. For example, the settlement of Pueblos Unidos consists of three hundred families divided into thirty núcleos of ten families each, with two coordinators, a man and a woman, to encourage gender equality. Several democratically elected representatives of the núcleo participate in commissions on production, education, health, communication, security, and political education. These commissions undertake projects such as alternative forms of production, agroecology, and community justice. The overarching purpose of this new ayllu structure is to reshape corporatist and highly vertical union-style structures into a horizontal, participatory, and democratic organization. These flexible commissions are responsible for the safety and security of the community, but scale up to ensure the functioning of the broader political organization. If something goes wrong, if someone attacks their settlement or threatens the collective structure of the organization, the committee convenes with rank-and-file members to discuss, debate, and come to some kind of consensus on an appropriate response.[7]

A GLOBALIZED DISCOURSE WITH LOCAL CULTURAL AUTHENTICITY AND APPEAL

At the level of the settlement and political organization, MST has adopted globalized indigenous discourses of usos y costumbres in order to enforce and promote this collective democratic structure. The question of why indigenous laws and customs now frame new MST settlements and organizational culture in rural Santa Cruz proves essential to this analysis. Why would movements like MST in lowland Bolivia rely upon the ancient Andean model of ayllu governance to inform their organization at the local, regional, and national levels?[8] How and in what ways does this represent a new kind of indigenous "bottom-up" citizenship, which came to define broader protest coalitions and the refashioning of the state? In part, the answers to these questions lie in the economic, political, and physical sense of insecurity wrought by thirty-plus years of neoliberal reforms. The homogenizing effects of the expansion of private capital, the withdrawal and retreat of the state, and new forms of dispossession have led to a creative and innovative indigenous politicking. Andean history and ideals of governance then serve as palimpsests whose multiple presences appear as a kind of layering over the past (Rappaport 1994, 2005) and create new meanings in obtaining and reclaiming rights, territory, and resources, in a moment in which detachment and displacement have become the norm.

While the ayllu might take on a particularly Andean form of organizing land relations, people, and collective administration of resources, the idea of usos y costumbres, self-determination and autonomy, did not occur in isolation. Shannon Speed (2007a), through her work with the Zapatistas in Chiapas, Mexico, describes such ideas as emerging out of "dialogic engagements,"[9] or between global governing organizations and local actors. Demands for indigenous rights and self-determination began to take center stage in the Zapatistas' public discourse and broader national demands for resource redistribution in the aftermath of the failed neoliberal policies of free trade between Mexico and the United States. They formed autonomous regions, began to implement their own local governments, and directed energies toward the task of developing independent systems of education, health care, and agriculture. Local forms of community governance (*juntas de buen gobierno*)[10] resemble MST's núcleos and decentralized committees dealing with the same issues. In the absence of the state, or with an ineffective one, these local actors have taken matters into their own hands; they have had to redefine liberal and neoliberal conceptualizations of rights and services often provisioned by the state.

While much of this might be happening on an international stage, it is important to recognize that the Zapatistas, like MST, had to adapt a global indigenous framework and put it into motion at the grassroots level. In her work with the Cumbales, Joanne Rappaport (1994) also argues that in order for these groups to recover territory, they had to assert a distinctly indigenous identity. They engage in what she calls "cultural invention" or "reinvention." The ways in which this took shape differed from community to community and from region to region. Instead of thinking about this as a smooth process of adopting a globalized discourse of rights to communal governance, Anna Tsing's (2005) concept of friction highlights the daily struggles and contradictions that characterize such work. Challenging the dominant view that globalization creates a clash of cultures, Tsing adopts friction as a metaphor for the tense and conflictive social relations and processes of interaction that make up the contemporary world. "A wheel turns because of its encounter with the surface of the road; spinning in the air it goes nowhere. Rubbing two sticks together produces heat and light; one stick alone is just a stick. As a metaphorical image, friction reminds us that heterogeneous and unequal encounters can lead to [new] arrangements of culture and power" (5).

Tsing reminds us that we cannot conceptualize movement, whether it be historical, political, or ideological, without friction, for while "friction slows things down, [it also] keeps global powers in motion" (6). MST's new model of collective ayllu citizenship, which relies upon prehistory, geographical or territorial reclamation, indigenous rights, and new

communal structures of governance, is ridden with tensions and frictions. Yet instead of conceptualizing tensions as slowing down political
movement, I illustrate how these frictions can lead to new insights and
innovations or reinforce a model of alternative governance.

INDIGENOUS LAW AND COMMUNAL DECISION-MAKING
AS SEDIMENTS OF PAST AND PRESENT

In terms of MST occupations and settlements, ayllu democracy informs
all areas of communal life and governance. The commissions organize to
make decisions regarding production, education, health care, and more.
In order to promote the idea of collective forms of governance, MST settlements must adhere to a set of rules or ideological principles. In part, these
rules have to do with building a functioning agrarian commune, but MST
organizers have also described this as restructuring social relations from
within at the very time when fears, distrust, and suspicion of the inten-
tions of both neighbors and community members are highest. Those who
break the rules or norms of the community face punishment, which can
be particularly harsh. For instance, a person accused of hoarding might
be subjected to a public beating, communal rejection and dismissal, or
denial of food to teach this person a lesson and serve as a warning to other
members contemplating similar acts. The security commission would
come together to decide the punishment as a "collective" force.

The ayllu model of governance can be seen as the historical sediments
and outcomes of the past that determine current distributions or redistributions of power and control (Postero 2007b). This model of democracy, with its embedded indigenous laws and customs, is a kind of *huella*
(a footprint or trace of the past), a reinvention of the pre-Colombian
form of governance that was transformed by the Spanish conquest. The
imposition of rule by the arrival of Europeans, who established their own
systems of law with respect to the creation of the state, had a dramatic
impact on indigenous systems, resulting in their complete destruction
in some cases (Van Cott 2003). After independence, with few exceptions,
states influenced by liberalism and positivism outlawed indigenous
legal systems and enacted policies to destroy legal distinctions among
ethnic groups. Some rural and isolated areas were able to maintain a
semblance of an indigenous justice system, but those closer to the centers of state power were incorporated into Western law and culture:
their justice systems were coordinated with those of the state, leading to

hybrid structures of governance. Customary law was comprised of those "uncodified concepts, beliefs and norms which, within a given community, define prejudicial actions or crimes; the selection of authorities and processes by which these should be resolved" (Sieder 1998: 98).

In mid-twentieth century, some states recognized aspects of indigenous self-regulation—usos y costumbres—for certain purposes, provided that such systems did not conflict with state law. Rodolfo Stavenhagen (1988) notes that in Peru, for example, the state allowed some community administration of land conflicts during the agrarian reform of the 1960s. And he found some mention of usos y costumbres in Latin American legislation two decades later. But the development of indigenous legal systems entered a new era in the 1990s when Latin American constitutions began to formally recognize their public authority and legal jurisdiction. After decades of activism and political organizing, states recognized indigenous peoples' collective rights, which were part and parcel of a broader discourse for self-determination. As Rachel Sieder (1998) notes, "customary law can be understood as a counter-hegemonic strategy used by indigenous communities to protect limited and conditional autonomy from the central state" (105). Furthermore, the ongoing influence of international organizations that turned toward the idea of culture for democracy building in the region legitimized such claims. International forums like the ILO 169 recognized indigenous laws and customs, provided that they did not infringe upon or undermine fundamental rights as defined by national or international law. In Bolivia, this "cultural" recognition ironically occurred during the nation's most contested neoliberal administration, that of Gonzalo Sánchez de Lozada. The 1994 constitution described the state as pluriethnic and multicultural, and Article 171 formally recognized the social, economic, and cultural rights of indigenous peoples, including the legal recognition of the "traditional authorities of indigenous and campesino communities" (Albro 2010a: 75). The progressive-sounding language of multiculturalism and cultural recognition within the constitution, however, did little to address structural inequalities and hard questions of material redistribution (Hale 2002).

"USOS Y COSTUMBRES" DEFINE COLLECTIVE GOVERNANCE IN PUEBLOS UNIDOS

In terms of community justice in MST settlements, ayllu stories— imagined as ancestral, community-based punishments for offenders—

circulated as justification for harsh punishment that taught someone a lesson. Silvestre Saisari remembered and told community residents about his grandmother's stories of life in an ayllu, and how everyone would gather *debajo de su pollera* (under her skirt) to listen to her. She would describe how people who did not obey the rules would experience *"castigos"*—punishments that were carefully thought out to be instructive. According to Saisari, it was important to make someone think, to reflect upon his behavior, and eventually to change it. For instance, he joked about how once a man had raped a woman in his rural community in Potosí. Instead of sending him to jail, people locked him up in a barn, completely naked, with his arms and legs tied to a post and with a pig who licked every part of his body. Saisari explained that this form of community justice would teach the man never to rape again.[11]

Similar forms of punishment were implemented in other MST settlements: a resident who violated community norms would be beaten or subjected to harsh manual labor, which reinforced a particular point about collective living. In the Pueblos Unidos settlement, community residents used collective memories of how their ancestors punished people inside the ayllu to create legitimacy for this system of governance to police minor internal problems such as petty theft, marital infidelity, and any form of physical assault or abuse. As one resident stated:

> There were petty thefts during the early days of the settlement. People would lose cooking oil here and other kinds of things like potatoes. In order to solve this problem, we created a justice system. The whole *directorio* [governing body] would come together and think collectively about a particular form of punishment for the criminal. "Let's do it like our ancestors in ayllus." The punishment for a first offender would simply be a warning not to do it again. The second-time offender would get physical punishment, or what they referred to as *castigos del chicote* [whipping], and the third-time offender would be kicked out of the settlement.

Stavenhagen (1988) relates an example from Oaxaca, Mexico, in which a man killed another in a drunken brawl and was ordered to marry the victim's widow and take care of her and the children. Although the Mexican state tried to intervene, the community and the individuals involved rejected this interference, and the sentence was honored (100). Sometimes, these punishments were performed with a kind of moral code, as illustrated by the Mexican example. Often, however, they included violent forms of punishment, such as the use of belts and whips in beating the guilty until they came clean in front of the entire community.

These kinds of punishments can be particularly harsh and reproduce the very hierarchies and power structures that progressive movements are working to eliminate. Rudi Colloredo-Mansfeld (2002), in his work with Otavaleños in Ecuador, notes that the economic forces propelling community justice in South America have been fueled by the severity of neoliberal structural adjustments. Crime, he argues, has increased, and national and provincial governments have lost the muscle and legitimacy to track down perpetrators, guarantee fair trials, and safeguard civil order. States have broken their pacts with their citizens, and community members feel more insecure. Extralegal justice therefore mushrooms, from vigilantism backed by conservative elites to beatings of street kids who pick pockets, to communal justice. This kind of freelance politics, he concludes, "produces divisiveness and moral estrangements manifest invidious segmentation" (653). Indigenous autonomy, while undoubtedly culturally and politically important, should not distract analysts from new forms of exclusion.

We might conceptualize indigenous resistance as partly emerging out of age-old regimes of labor control and suppression and colonial or neocolonial forms of violence. These sediments of colonial violence continue to shape dangerous terrains within city centers and peripheral rural communities. And yet this violence cannot simply be understood as one-dimensional—Europeans (or mestizos) pacifying resistant and militant Indians—but rather as the product of rotating regimes of violence and terror that influence the kinds of punishments MST members and indigenous organizations might impose upon community residents. In one example of how these indigenous rules and laws define individualized forms of punishment discussed below, we see a highly paternalistic and feminizing form of violence imposed upon a *cholita* (an indigenous person who lives in the city) that eerily resembles some of the *autonomista* (supporting autonomy) violence that mestizo youth committed against Indians in Sucre in 2008, when protesters marched in support of the Constituent Assembly. While some might argue that this kind of "vigilante violence" is about citizenship rights (Goldstein 2004), the ways in which marginalized actors thrust themselves into the public light, I see something much more at stake here when progressive social movements adopt and impose the same kinds of violent structures upon rank-and-file members and embed such practices within a cultural or ethnic identity discourse of usos y costumbres.

At a national-level MST meeting in the fall of 2007, a young MST woman sat next to former movement president Moisés Torres. While Torres was popular during the Yuquises occupation and supported the landless in the east during intense land battles, he lost a lot of respect within the movement for behind-the-scenes negotiating and self-interested political moves, and he was overthrown in the summer of 2006 at a national MST meeting. Lidio Julián (a regional leader from the Gran Chaco region), Silvestre Saisari (the departmental leader from Santa Cruz), and Wilford Colque (a regional leader from Ichilo) "refounded the MST" and refused to recognize Torres as the head of their political organization. As Colque stated, "We suspected that he remained loyal to the federation of campesinos and the unions and falsified documents for personal and political favors . . . so we began to question and challenge his actions. We gathered the rank and file in the eastern regions to *desconocerlo* [disown; i.e., not recognize him as president] and began thinking about a *refundación* or rebirthing of MST" (Wilford Colque, personal communication, October 2007).

Through a national ayllu structure of governance, regional and departmental representatives gathered to debate the problem, and eventually they reached a consensus regarding Torres's formal resignation from the organization as president. During these meetings, Lidio Julián became the president of the national-level organization in his stead. While Sian Lazar (2008) might argue that these accusations of corruption, or what she calls "*desconfianza*" (distrust), lead to a democratic and collective process in which the rank and file hold the power to ultimately make decisions, I have observed instances such as this one in which such processes appear to be highly undemocratic, often driven by power-hungry regional and departmental leaders. Decisions to *tumbarlo* (make a leader fall) can also divide the broader collective agenda, as these leaders often form their own groups with rank-and-file members and call themselves MST.

However, several months after this meeting, when MST gathered in La Paz to rethink their demands and platforms, a young woman sat next to Torres, since he was now a part of the rank and file. Eulogio Cortés described it as follows: "There was this cholita from Potosí who accidently sat next to Moisés Torres. People from Andres Ibáñez got really pissed because the eastern region had disowned Moisés Torres. They basically called a small meeting afterwards because they wanted to introduce *justicia comunitaria* in meeting spaces; they wanted to strip her and *guas-cearla* [whip her] publicly to teach her a lesson" (Eulogio Cortés, personal communication, October 2007).

Cortés said that the representatives from the movement listened to their argument, their frustration, and their desire to implement justicia comunitaria and finally concluded that "we shouldn't treat her like a whore, like a prostitute. She is a woman . . . and we need to treat women with respect," he recalls. "They basically wanted to strip her naked and beat her in front of the entire MST community for being a traitor, for defying our trust." After they proposed this form of humiliation, the woman from Potosí resigned from the movement and refused to talk publicly about this incident.

The use of an indigenous woman's body as sign and signifier of organizational disorder and chaos reproduces the very same state-based hierarchies of power and control through hyper-masculinized performances or rituals of violence. In his ethnographic analysis on the death penalty in the United States, Dwight Conquergood (2002a) describes such forms of violence as "awesome rituals of human sacrifice through which the state dramatizes its absolute power and monopoly over violence" (342). In this particular case, poor farmers who, through a particular kind of mimesis, reenact the same kind of rituals of authority and control pose a rather complicated dilemma. How do we begin to analyze these progressive social movements that reinvent similar state-based rituals of violence through extralegal punishment and reform? Poor indigenous farmers who have been beaten or violated by landowners are living symbols of the territorial and resource-based struggles, of the ways in which the law did not protect a particular group of citizens. But this paradigm complicates our framework of oppressor and oppressed, victimizer and victim.

This kind of gendered violence to enforce communal democracy at an organizational level very much resembles the spectacles described by Pamela Calla (2010) and Ricardo Montoya (2010) against indigenous peoples as a group of Indians marched in 2008 to support the Constituent Assembly in Sucre, Bolivia. A mob of armed civilians from Sucre, partially made up of university students, surrounded several dozen indigenous Morales supporters who had come from other regions to attend the ceremony inaugurating the new constitution. The mestizo youth forced the Indians to strip off their few belongings, then kneel, shirtless, and apologize for coming to Sucre. As Montoya describes it, the mestizo youth yelled, "Get on your knees [you Indian piece of shit] and respect the capital city!" "Respect Sucre!" and "Llamas [a derogatory term for Andean Indians], ask for forgiveness!" (6). Calla asks, "How can we understand this critical paradox of legitimizing rights to indigenous peoples through a new constitution, while simultaneously supporting old colonial forms of feminizing violence?" (2).

It seems as though the same paradox runs through this grassroots collective citizenship: ayllu forms of governance provide a more democratic and legitimate structure for indigenous farming communities to assume some form of autonomy from the state, but they can also reproduce similar hierarchies of power, violence, and gendered inequality. While the state no longer marks and claims the indigenous body, violence now takes the shape and form of extralegal youth groups taking matters into their own hands or leftist social movements wanting to strip a cholita and beat her publicly for disloyalty. These regimes of violence are not static. Instead, they travel from global actors and governing agents to local and regional elites, then to indigenous peoples. All the while, these models meld to create hybrid and distinct forms of rule. In this case, the creative mixing of indigenous rules of law and customs with Western models of individualized behavioral management resulted in incredibly infantilizing and patriarchal forms of violence.

Other kinds of tensions and frictions emerge as this ayllu model of governance moves from defining local communal structures to regional forms of governance. As this flexible model travels from community governance to organizing and structuring the democratic spaces of MST meetings, new kinds of tensions emerge regarding individual rights versus collective structures of governance, gendered forms of inequality, and power-hungry leaders who can often control and define the broader politics. The threats of beating the cholita help us understand how "encounters across difference" might lead to new dynamic and fluid cultural models of grassroots citizenship as rank-and-file members hold their leaders accountable and expose some of their stories of inequality and injustice.

The ayllu model of governance must be mobilized and reassembled at the regional level to make decisions about land politics, production, and more. An incident from Ichilo clearly illustrates the mobility of ayllu democracy, but also shows how frictions between individual landholding versus collective tenure can either threaten to dissolve the organization or revitalize the collective structure through the reinforcement of particular values. Daily insecurities and fears of losing land tenure, especially when settlers have no formal title to the land, enter into these regional debates and discussions.

One day in April 2006, I accompanied a group of MST organizers to a meeting in Ayacucho to discuss a proposal to convert the movement into a peasant union (see Figure 2). After many years of waiting for an escape from poverty, a group of squatters had decided that this would be a quick and easy solution to their problem of landlessness and lack of legal titles because it would guarantee ownership and enable members to sell their plots to the highest bidder. This, in part, was about the need for access to capital and instant gains. MST members, however, saw this as just a temporary solution to the ongoing structural problems of debt and dependency.

The meeting began at noon, when Wilford Colque led the group in an MST cheer: "*¡MST, esta lucha es para vencer!*" (MST, this fight is worth the struggle!). When the crowd cheered back, he added, "*¿Cuándo?*" (When?), and they shouted, "*¡Ahora!*" (Now!). Then everyone took a seat, energized by this impassioned call and response.

While the cheers and sentiments expressed a passionate commitment to this collective change project, members from one group, Núcleo Primero de Agosto, a community of Tierra Prometida, offered an alternative vision of change: a highly individualistic and capitalist-driven response to the problem of land inequality. Many community members had already traveled to Santa Cruz and filed their land petitions as individual rather than communal requests. This breaking of the collective contract had powerful symbolic and legal implications: it undermined the ability of the movement to collectively negotiate for communal land ownership and placed such power in the hands of a few individuals who simply wanted to buy and sell property. Consequently, the CEJIS lawyers had to pull the entire file from INRA until the problem was resolved. At the meeting that day, Pablo Mamani, a regional leader, attempted to reinforce the collective nature of the movement:

> When we speak of communal land, we are talking about the actual petition for a plot or parcel of land. An example is that if we petition for fifty hectares [per family], it means that we will need twenty-five hundred hectares for an entire community. This means that they will give the land title to fifty compañeros. For the twenty-five hundred hectares, you will receive only one title to the land, so that you will not be able to traffic land. This will protect the nature of the

FIGURE 2. MST–Tierra Prometida community meeting to discuss agroecology held in the nearby town of Ayacucho. Photograph by Eulogio Cortés.

organization as well. If not—if we give title to each individual compañero—you will get bored and will want to go to the city, and you will put your land up for rent or sell your plot to someone else, and then the organization will disappear. In this regard, we fifty compañeros must organize ourselves in a collective way, and the decision must come organically out of discussion, debate.

During the meeting, members engaged in an intense debate about the benefits of collective ownership of land versus the union-style structure, which afforded individuals titles to plots. Some worried about the slender thread upon which their survival depended. It was this sense of vulnerability that caused a number of peasants to support settlement conversion and fed their desire to sell their parcels to survive. Mamani spoke yet again in order to reinforce this collective model of ownership and governance and show why it is important in terms of communal stability and long-term economic security: "It is for this reason that we speak of a new land reform, land redistribution, so that we can all escape from this terrible poverty that envelops us. And not individually, because individually, the compañero, in order to plant two or three hectares, must get a loan from the bank, and the bank maybe will lend him money at 19 percent interest, and in a year he will be accruing more and more interest and he will become landless and finally maybe once again be working as a slave, working for the big latifundistas in this region. Is this what you want, compañeros?"

After several hours of debate, Silvia Vásquez[12], the CEJIS representative, intervened to distinguish between "possession" and "property." In a condescending way, she tried to explain the difference by using the example of a shirt, which is someone's possession but may be lent to another person, as contrasted with something that can be bought and sold. As her explanation lengthened, Mamani's face turned bright red and he stood up and said, in great exasperation, "Thank you, Silvia, that's enough!" He then pulled her aside during the intermission and told her, "It's not your place to intervene in organic MST matters. This is something the *gente de base*—the community—needs to resolve on its own. You are a member of CEJIS, not a member of the movement." In response, she turned to him and said, "Who are you? You aren't even a dirigente. Who are you to tell me what to say and what to do?" While CEJIS is a rather progressive NGO, this incident illustrates the increasing participation of human rights workers, NGO officials, and technocrats in MST affairs.

After isolating Vásquez, Mamani assumed the floor and declared his intention to open a "democratic" decision-making process, which was part of reassembling an ayllu structure at the regional level. One leader suggested, "We must talk, argue, ask questions, and eventually reach an agreement." Issues such as collective ownership of land must be debated for hours; individual members must work through their concerns and ultimately come to consensus. In this particular case, each núcleo broke up into small groups to debate the benefits of collective ownership. Two leaders, Pablo Mamani and Eulogio Cortés, circled the room, rotating into and out of the various groups. They referenced the ayllu of their ancestors and used Pueblos Unidos' alternative experiments of collective production and community governance as a model for reclaiming land and governance. They spoke to members about the ways in which individual land title and parcelization of communal plots have historically divided indigenous communities and eventually displaced them; they assured members that the MST model would bring an end to the vicious agribusiness expansion that preys upon poor families and their productive resources. A land reform settlement would guarantee permanence and provide long-term food and sustenance to its residents, while a union would lead only to poverty and inequality.

After several hours, the members of Primero de Agosto decided to remain a part of MST. They weighed the advantages and disadvantages of the collectivist model, and in the end, they judged it more beneficial to take part in a movement that could potentially offer substantial structural change than to choose immediate and probably self-defeating solutions to the problem of poverty.

Not everyone was satisfied with the decision. This posed a potential problem because in the past, dissenting members often chose to undermine the larger collective political and economic project of MST. At times, these individuals came together into separate wings of the MST regional base in order to meet their particular and often individual needs. There have been several MST subsections of the regional organization functioning with different principles and ideologies, which heightens confusion, animosity, and tension within the movement.

THE RIGHT OF ALL TO SPEAK VERSUS THE POLITICAL DISENFRANCHISEMENT OF WOMEN

Another critical tension that defines regional MST meeting spaces is the right of all to speak versus the political disenfranchisement of women. Earlier we saw the most visible illustration of the violence of gendered inequality within the movement; here, we see a silencing of voices—a less obvious example. Regional leaders like Mamani describe their organization as embracing a form of horizontal politics. He argues, "We stand against the European structure of union politics, where those who are in positions of authority define all forms of organizing. We are talking about another form of organizing, a horizontal structure[13] that allows the base to define the politics, and representatives have the same kind of capacity, the same right and the same responsibility to conduct business within the organization in a fair and equal way. This is why we talk about horizontal structure" (Pablo Mamani, personal communication, June 2006).

Despite such promise, however, the structure is not always egalitarian, and at times its vertical hierarchy resembles that of a union. Albro (2005) suggests that local associations employ a direct democracy that is transparent, horizontal, bottom-up, and nonhierarchical. Such a horizontal and nonhierarchical form of democracy promotes an idea of gender equality, which resembles Andean complementarity, or the idea that a man and woman form a conjugal pair. This might be the public discourse of democracy—words like *horizontality* and *equality* frame MST conversations—but this does not include the right of all to speak. The action of raising one's hand in a meeting, or *pedir la palabra*, is a highly masculinized performance in which compañeros assume the right to speak in political spaces; women often remain silent on many issues, afraid that their lack of political training makes their thoughts and reactions invalid. As one woman articulated, "These men are really *machista* and the women are afraid to speak up. Their ideas remain in their heads because they don't want to pedir la palabra. It's not that they are ashamed; it is that they are afraid; they have never participated in meetings, and they lack the kind of empowerment training."

While there is much talk of horizontal structures, MST meetings remain highly segmented along gendered lines.[14] The movement often fails to connect issues affecting women, such as job insecurity, health care, and child care, to a larger struggle for land. For example, while participating at the meeting in Ayacucho, a woman stood up with her infant attached to her breast and shouted, "Can we resolve this problem regarding the sindicato already? I [and other women here] cannot continue to take part in a twelve-hour meeting. We have hungry children at home; we have to cook for our families and tend to other responsibilities. You might have all the time in the world . . . but we don't!" (Rank-and-file MST representative, April 2006)

This tension between a discourse of horizontality and the political disenfranchisement of women lies at the heart of new territorially based movements in Bolivia. While MST leaders might proclaim that ayllu democracy encapsulates an Andean gender system based on a principle of gender complementarity, this romantic ideal of egalitarian structures comes to a halt on political meeting floors as women fight for a voice and push leaders to recognize gendered inequalities. At first glance, it seems that men define MST politics, but it is often women's physical labor that forms the backbone of the organization. Not only does information travel through intricate kin networks, but women mobilize friends and family to participate in protests and roadblocks. They also prepare food and do other "invisible" labor that makes the movement possible. The thread of gendered inequality, arising directly from union organizing, once again attaches to these new circles of MST politicking and fails to give women a central place in meeting spaces or to recognize their work as critical to movement building. Daily conversations and debates, however, push *machista* leaders to recognize gender's critical role in constructing a real indigenous-based territorial movement for landed equality and food sovereignty. While tensions can threaten to break down a collective structure and halt progressive movement, it can also lead to important discussions and new practices of incorporating indigenous women into the organization. For example, after these kinds of conversations, groups of women have formed commissions to begin to debate, discuss, and address the problems of gendered inequality and propose solutions to lack of female participation. Some of these include grassroots education focused on gendered inequality, workshops on political participation, and demands for more female leadership roles within the organization.

COLLECTIVE DECISION-MAKING VERSUS POWER-HUNGRY LEADERS

Besides gender inequality, corruption and abuses of power are some of the other daily struggles within regional politics. As seen in the earlier examples, Mamani tended to dominate much of the discussion regarding MST politics and organizing in this regional meeting. He might be a member of the "baoo," but as a seasoned organizer, he often assumed more power and expertise than others. In this context, it is not only gender differences but also the experience of the organizer that creates distinct hierarchies and power dynamics. Mamani speaks of the base as defining MST politics, but in reality his experience and expertise as a leader had a disproportionate influence on how people behaved and voted during the course of the meeting. This is a problem within the movement that extends beyond this particular incident. Those with experience and knowledge define the politics and, at times, manipulate the rank and file. Too often they fail to teach or bring people to understand through an in-depth educational process but rather take the efficient shortcut of speaking for them.

Lazar (2008) argues that this tendency should be thought of as individualism nested within the group structure. In an influential work, Xavier Albó (1977) identifies "the Aymara paradox" as the existence of a strong communitarian ethic within Aymara peasant communities alongside a tendency toward individualism and factionalism. He attempts to resolve the tension by proposing the concept of individualism within the group, whereby the group manages to synchronize the interests of different individuals through reciprocal help or common enterprise, with particular interests becoming unified through a common institutional matrix.

Lazar illustrates a similar process, not as a structural principle regulated through ritual practices of the ayllu, but as a political process fraught with tensions, failures, and difficulties. In the case of political organizations in the urban Aymara context of El Alto, the struggle between collectivism and individualism is absolutely central, as it is in MST political spaces.

MST leadership is often the terrain for struggles between the collective as an ideological force and on-the-ground practices of self-interested individuals (Lazar 2008). Despite often florid leadership descriptions of selfless service to the movement, the daily battles of on-the-ground MST leaders working within a limited budget, in an increasingly hostile, dangerous environment, and carrying heavy workloads for little compensation engender strong feelings of desconfianza, or group suspicion of the regional leaders and national coordinators. This mistrust is deeply embedded in the material terrain of fear and insecurity (instead of the structural or physical violence coming from agribusiness elites or young mestizo youth). It can be understood as an accumulation of daily fears exacerbated by a lack of state protection and few service providers, where people are in direct competition with one another for limited and sometimes scarce resources. Insecurity, then, is not just about outsiders invading or dismantling MST settlements but also defines social life within communities as suspicions or accusations mount, gain strength through rumor and gossip, and often target particular leaders as the culprit of this form of betrayal. As Lazar argues, "Corruption talk constructs and polices the frontiers between public and private if corruption is viewed primarily as people stealing resources for their private interests. In this case, making this distinction discursively connects the public to the group and the private to the individual, and has the effect of emphasizing a collective sense of self as more moral" (199).

In one instance, a regional leader was caught hoarding all official and public documentation of a land occupation in the Obispo Santiesteban region. People from across distinct MST núcleos had asked several times to see satellite photos of the property, INRA reports, and other documentation, but the leader refused to circulate the relevant paperwork. Members assembled to talk about this form of corruption, which they called "informational greed." They felt that he was "stealing, hoarding" the documents for his own purposes, possibly negotiating with land bureaucrats and government officials. An accusation of corruption is frequently the basis for removing a leader from a position of power, but more importantly, such an act reinforces the strength of the rank and file as the base of the movement. For example, when one faction within the movement organizes opposition to a leader, an effective tactic has been to accuse the leader of a specific form of corruption. Through democratic participation, the bases present their evidence of corruption to the entire group, and more often than not, the leader will fall, whether or not the accusations are in fact accurate and supported by a reasonable body of evidence. These actions, however unfair at times, promote both a strong respect for the power and authority of the base and a consequent sense of leadership accountability. A regional leader once said to me, "I am really afraid of the bases. I know that when we hold the next regional meeting, they are going to point toward all the things I have done wrong. Since the bases define the movement, I can possibly be knocked out of office" (MST leader, personal communication, August 2006).

The degree to which the threat of corruption promotes honesty in leaders' dealings with both movement members and powerful interests in the larger world is unclear. It is apparent, however, that MST leaders often think about the impact of the democratic process on their power as they negotiate their way through a circumscribed world of land policies, bureaucrats, and business elites. It is important to reiterate that rank-and-file members do on occasion falsely accuse leaders of corruption and informational greed, solely because of personal tensions or competition. As the accusations mount, it becomes more difficult to develop or maintain a stable cohort of movement leaders.

Lazar (2008) argues that it is paradoxical that such powerful collectivities have arisen at a time when the dominant economic model stresses competition and individual interest. "They should be seen as both a reaction to the neoliberal assault on more traditional class-based politics and a product of the concomitant reorganization of the economy," she writes. "Instead of a disappearing of class-based forms of collectivity, the poor and disenfranchised have reshaped themselves, drawing strength from past traditions and present circumstances" (208).

This return to the past or use of the ayllu to structure democratic governance at the local and regional levels proves invaluable in understanding one layer of grassroots indigenous citizenship. Collective forms of citizenship are not shaped in abstraction but rather in concert with people's economic and material lives. After all, this citizenship model emerges directly out of fears and threats of violence and the lack of any state intervention to provide support or services for rural farmers. The complicated terrain of violence—both external and internal—impels MST members to come up with an alternative form of governance and rule, relying on history as a guide for protecting territorial bounds, marking and claiming rights to territory, and constructing norms for settlements and political structures. Indigenous ideals (usos y costumbres), whether incredibly violent or not, protect MST settlements from these threats and rebuild trust among members through a horizontal and participatory system that holds leaders accountable for their actions.

There is no purity to such a political model. These reconfigured cultural models of governance are ridden with daily contradictions and tensions—the most extreme form being the violent spectacles of punishment imposed upon rank-and-file members who violate the norms of the organization, reproducing gendered and racist colonial regimes of power. The less extreme debates or tensions have to do with battles over individual versus collective ownership, union-style politicking versus ayllu democracy, and corrupt and power-hungry leaders versus popular and participatory power.

The idea of friction then proves key to conceptualizing political movement and mobility. This ideological framing of friction forces us to rethink movements as only forward moving, for friction can create cyclical and even backward movement. Yet friction can also lead to progressive, creative, and hybridized political structures and paradigms that mix the past with the present, indigenous traditions with Western forms of governance, and violent with nonviolent mechanisms of control. But all of this must come together into some kind of political structure that sustains landed relations, community, and alternative models of food production.

The next chapter turns to production processes and redistribution of surplus value. While the imagined ayllu must create some kind of structure for governing community and organizational life, it must also provide a framework for reinventing and rethinking agricultural production. The rescaling of agriculture to the local level through globalized and transnational ideas of food sovereignty and environmental stewardship can be thought of as "agrarian citizenship"—just as citizenship had to be unhooked from a highly individualized structure of land ownership and private property rights, ideas about citizenship also must be decoupled from an agroindustrial model of development. Grassroots movements are reinventing and rethinking citizenship as the ability of people to produce their own food on their own terms. If contemporary systems of food production, through the globalization of agriculture, have dangerously erased long histories of peasant food production, obliterated the importance of native seeds and culture, and might eventually destroy all possibility for producing for individual and national consumption, then movements are now using this concept of reclamation at a productive level to save food and food production as vital to indigenous autonomy and sovereignty. The idea of friction will continue to define new understandings of citizenship as MST communities rely upon mixed strategies of agroecology and large-scale farming, such as organic farming versus pesticide use, in order to simply survive and enter into the national and global marketplace. While MST, on one level, moves platforms like agrarian reform and food sovereignty to the seat of power and has effectively pressured the Morales administration to officially include these demands in the new constitution, on another level, the state continues to support agribusinesses and export-oriented crops like soy, simultaneously undermining such initiatives.

AGRARIAN CITIZENSHIP

Alternative Models of Production and Food Sovereignty

The MST organizers had secured a run-down brick building, possibly a school gymnasium or auditorium deep in the backwoods of San Pedro, for the event. Hundreds of campesinos were already gathered to hear about the alternative agroecological model MST–Obispo Santiesteban would promote in their new settlement, Pueblos Unidos.[1] Hot and sweaty bodies crowded onto several rows of broken wooden benches facing a small stage, where half a dozen MST leaders sat, looking down at the rank-and-file members. Many of the leaders had a ball of coca perfectly balanced inside one cheek, occasionally moving it from side to side in a rhythmic motion. Several organizers offered us a small plastic bag of coca as we set our things down on the cement floor (see Figure 3).

Two main issues were on the agenda: What would the campesinos' soon-to-be-titled community look like, and how would an agroecological area be constructed? As the meeting began, one organizer *pidió la palabra* (raised his hand), asking to speak to all those assembled:

> For five years, we have been fighting for Yuquises, since we first occu-
> pied the land in September of 2005. We have sacrificed long and
> hard—there were days without work, there were days during the
> *toma de tierra* [land occupation] when our children fell ill and we had
> no doctors or medical assistance. And now, we are about to receive
> title to this land from the government. This MST settlement has to
> change history. We have to begin thinking about the ways in which
> our economic model will stand against neoliberalism. . . . We have
> to think about the ideology of MST . . . it's not just about getting our
> little piece of land and working independently. This is about a collec-
> tive project with benefits for all. We have to think about how we will
> create a new system of production.

FIGURE 3. MST swearing-in ceremony in Tierra Firme, about ten miles from Santa Cruz. Photograph by the author.

The speaker, José Salvatierra, suggested that the settlers invent a wholly new economic model in order to meet their structural needs. As the meeting progressed that evening, many MST members discussed their distinct understandings of community. Ponciano Sulca, for instance, stated, "There is no fear, the fear is gone. The Pueblos Unidos that we are going to create is going to be a new form of life; it will be our communal land and territory. No one will be able to take this away from us." Luis Velásquez, a contract agricultural laborer who had studied agronomic engineering in Tarija, gave up his career to become a part of the movement. He suggested that the productive model *had* to be consistent with MST proposals for a new agrarian reform: "The Landless Peasant Movement stands against a neoliberal model in which agriculture is seen as a profit-making venture and productive resources are concentrated in the hands of cattle ranchers and large-scale soy producers. Our vision has to be farmer-driven, based on small-scale production, while at the same time being economically viable and ecologically sustainable." Velásquez paid attention to broader considerations, such as families' long-term food security, when making production decisions. Settlers expected such an approach to result in more on-farm production of the food that families required for self-sufficiency. For cash, they would need to rely on local markets, selling as much as possible to consumers in regional towns.

Silvestre Saisari used the ayllu as a point of reference for how MST might implement the proposed threads from the discussion to build a new agricultural model that could anticipate an alternative economic structure to large-scale production. "For this reason," he explained, "we need to talk about collective land distribution, one that is equal and fair, in order to get out of this terrible poverty. We are not looking to distribute land on an individual basis. . . . We must come up with another system; we must own the land and work collectively. This community can be like those of our ancestors. We could have the first ayllu in Santa Cruz. Our ayllu would include collective ownership of land, reciprocal work groups, redistribution of wealth and resources, and small-scale production."

As the community meeting unfolded, a series of unanswered questions emerged. In general, it was unclear how the many points raised by MST organizers and the rank and file could contribute to the development of an alternative socioeconomic and productive model that guaranteed food security. Especially important to this discussion was how the notion of the ancient Andean community could be transported from a structuring governance to an agricultural practice that would ensure both the survival of a campesino model of agriculture and long-term sustainability of these settlements.

THE AYLLU AS AN ALTERNATIVE MODEL OF AGROECOLOGY

As we saw in the last chapter, the discourse of the ayllu provided a democratic structure of governance within MST settlements and for the broader organization. The overarching theme of insecurity, wrought by neoliberal policies or the retreat of the state, manifested itself as fears of violence against the community, internal conflicts, and suspicions and fears of one another. Returning to the past, or finding a framework that relied upon indigenous beliefs and customs of holding people accountable for their actions and encouraging participatory democracy, offered a vision of hope for safety and prosperity. Here, the ayllu becomes flexible and elastic, as it is used for organizing people into productive units within the settlements and for promoting a model of small-scale agriculture and environmental protection. If the global agricultural model, as mentioned in the community meeting, places profit over people and commodifies humans as mere laborers and the environment as a playground for private capital, then this alternative model is about placing people back in the center and creating important connections between the socioeconomic and ecological spheres.

This discourse of an idealized Andean socialist community or utopia—premised on narratives of how their ancestors lived socially, economically, and environmentally—created an imagined cartography for respatializing agricultural production. MST's idea of food sovereignty and agroecology is deeply embedded in collaborative or collective forms of production. In order to build small-scale agricultural communes, members rely upon the rural Andean concept of *ayni*, which refers to reciprocity, whereby workers take care of one another, with the understanding that the favor will be returned at some point. The *minka*, or economic exchange among persons of differing socioeconomic or ritual statuses, in which a laborer provides work service in return for a meal or daily wage, proves essential to building infrastructure such as schools and health clinics in the community. Not only does the minka connect people to one another through a collective project, but it also ensures the long-term survival of such communities. While many scholars have noted that such models always relied upon a mixture of reciprocal relations and market-based exchanges for survival, MST leaders have revived and politicized essentialized notions of highland rural culture by establishing ayni and minka as forms of resistance to Western-derived, large-scale agroindustrial production.[2] In their reappropriation of this cultural model as antithetical to capitalistic endeavors, they enforce the social, collective, and reciprocal forms of production, in which all members of the community benefit from family farming.

These cultural frames then provide the possibility for sovereignty and independence. After years of relying on the state to redistribute resources, social movements in Bolivia have come up with their own language, structure, and system to reorganize control over land and territory. The politicization of indigenous values and symbols to reconfigure the economy and agricultural model poses an alternative to agribusiness expansion in the region. These movements are in a paradigm shift, from modes of contention associated with older forms of clientelist politics, dependency upon agribusinesses for their survival, and destructive forms of working the land, to new modes of living and producing that might lead to "the institutionalization and legitimization of new bearers and forms of territorial authority" (Gustafson 2011: 237).

This new socioeconomic and agricultural model also represents transformation of an individual citizenship model that links private landholding patterns and individual capitalistic gain. In the capitalist or liberal model of citizenship, individual gain represents entrée into the marketplace and particular social, political, and economic rights through advancement. MST's form of agrarian citizenship, on the other hand, is about encouraging "collective" rights for the community, food security for a large group of people, and sustainable lifestyles that will ensure the protection of ecosystems for future generations. As a key informant in Hannah Wittman's (2009) analysis of the Brazilian landless suggests, "Citizenship from an individual point of view is related to fundamental rights and guarantees of liberty, of the right to a name and title . . . [and other individual rights enumerated in the constitution]. But from the point of view of social advancement . . . for the earth and for the small ones of the earth, it is a collective project" (129).

Yet, this model of ayllu as a reimagined agroecological utopia that reconnects people to their food, agricultural production, and the environment is also riddled with contradictions and tensions. Agrarian citizenship, in the view of Hannah Wittman (2010), can be thought of as a model founded on the grassroots practice of reconnecting workers to food production and to the environment through systems of mutual obligations. While she might see this as a radical rejection of modern agriculture—or articulate it as the idea that rural producers have rights to the land and the environment but also responsibilities, connected to these rights, for maintaining the diversity of socioecological production and reproduction—I will illustrate the ways in which we can think about agrarian citizenship as conflictive, mixed, and more of a hybrid model than a pure one. Thus far, I have demonstrated that while the state has often defined citizenship for indigenous peoples, movements in Bolivia, like MST, are reconstructing ideas about "collective rights" through new forms of governance (indigenous usos y costumbres) and food production (built upon a model of reciprocal exchange coming from Andean tales of the ayllus). These ideas about rights and citizenship then emerge out of grassroots agendas and practices, which does not, however, mean that these practices remain pure, isolated, or detached from broader flows of capital and regimes of governance and knowledge.

FROM THE GLOBALIZED DISCOURSE OF
FOOD SOVEREIGNTY TO THE LOCAL AYLLU

As MST leaders travel to international spaces of organizing, their ideas and practices about alternative cultural and productive models become mobile. If peasants are at the center of this debate over reclaiming agriculture, then this section traces people's movement from local to international and back to the local. These transnational spaces of movement building, just as migrants' journeys across national borders—from western highland communities to the agroindustrial lowlands—have provided opportunities for the transport, re-creation, reassembly, and reinvention of cultural and political forms.

In June 2007, I traveled with a group of MST leaders from Santa Cruz to an international conference organized by MST-Brazil and the Vía Campesina on agrarian reform, food sovereignty, and social justice. The overarching intention of the conference was to study, exchange ideas, and understand the state of agriculture and land reform worldwide and construct specific collective proposals and platforms for the future.

The Vía Campesina has led the struggle globally to create alternatives to the neoliberal model of agriculture, proposing a concept of food sovereignty in the 1990s, which they defined as rights of nations and peoples to control their own food systems, including their own markets, productive modes, food cultures, and environment. Food, they argued, is first and foremost a source of nutrition and secondarily an item of trade (Desmarais 2002, 2007). These kinds of transnational spaces of organizing have been in the forefront of shaping this platform. The organization first discussed food sovereignty at its Second International Conference, held on April 18–21, 1996, in Tlaxcala, Mexico. Peasants and farm leaders who gathered there no longer saw potential in the concept of "food security"[3]—a broad-based concept that stated that all people will have food security when physical, social, and economic access to sufficient, safe, and nutritious foods meets their dietary needs—because they felt that the definition emphasized food production without paying close attention to how, where, and by whom food was produced (Wittman, Desmarais, and Wiebe 2010). It was within this context that the Vía Campesina worked with other organizations and civil society actors to further clarify and elaborate their food sovereignty framework. Both the World Social Forum and the Food Sovereignty Conference held in Cuba in 2001 created spaces for the elaboration of such a proposal or platform.

The statement, along with the Vía Campesina's 1996 World Food Summit document, is the most often cited international declaration of food sovereignty and was developed and signed by many of the same organizations that form part of the international planning committee on food sovereignty. The Vía Campesina fundamentally challenged who should speak on behalf of whom regarding food and agriculture; food sovereignty placed peasants and small-scale farmers clearly in the center of this debate. For this reason—the new networks of transnational exchange and support—a small group of MST-Bolivia organizers traveled to Brazil to share their experiences, participate in workshops, and learn from other Latin American peasant organizations (Desmarais 2002).

We met at the Viru Viru International Airport in Santa Cruz at 6:00 A.M. to travel to São Paulo. All of my fellow compañeros arrived with their identification, visa, and paperwork tied neatly around their necks. This paperwork, which the indigenous organizers held close to their chests, served as a symbol of new flexible forms of citizenship, where international actors and NGOs with an interest in indigenous rights, global warming, and environmentalism have provided critical funding to enable leaders to present their localized agricultural struggles and represent their peoples. International spaces offer forums for the creation and reinvention of an international notion of indigeneity—spaces where indigenous leaders might commodify the idea of the poor, colonized, exploited, and native populations that must be protected and discuss the rights that must be enshrined in universal human rights legislation. Indigenous leaders often use these spaces for the creation and circulation of symbolic discourses of Indians as connected to their natural surroundings,[4] which can prove particularly dangerous in failing to capture the complexity of their struggles to hold on to land and make a living amidst the expansion of soy for export-oriented production.[5] I have often witnessed MST leaders performing certain kinds of eco-friendly, indigenous citizenship models, where they feel the need to present a one-dimensional story to foreigners, NGO workers, and state and regional workers. However, in the private spaces of organizing and living, a more complex picture emerges.

Many scholars have written about these dangers of new "flexible indigenous citizens" as they take the global stage (Conklin and Graham 1995; Conklin 2001; Shah 2010). Alpah Shah argues that well-meaning indigenous rights activists can, in fact, further exploit the people they intend to defend: "The dark side of indigeneity suggests that local use of global discourses of indigeneity can reinforce a class system that further marginalizes the poorest people. This class dimension is likely to get erased in the culture-based identity politics it produces" (12). I am, however, interested in the flow from the transnational to local levels: How do transnational discourses travel to local communities, and how do they influence localized issues of food sovereignty and environmental stewardship? Additionally, how do indigenous organizers give food sovereignty a localized appeal? In the process, MST organizers alter meanings of such broad-based platforms, such that it has deep resonance for poor people who have lost their land, homes, and livelihood. This is not to say that some of these public discourses of indigeneity do not marginalize or create greater forms of inequality, as we saw in the last chapter. Rather I emphasize the fact that an indigenous language of rights has great creative appeal for Bolivia's landless peasants as they seek to rebuild and reclaim community, livelihood, and the mode or means of production. Rather than being passive recipients of transnational discourses, local people are actively exploiting the opportunities available to them in this moment when indigeneity has gained such global traction.

As movement organizers travel across national bounds, they experience new environmental surroundings, see problems differently, and analyze them from new heights. This plane ride from Viru Viru, then, represented not only a new form of mobility for most indigenous organizers, but also stood for the fluidity and transportability of fresh ideas, proposals, platforms—all made possible through international forms of travel and new globalized networks of peasant organizations.[6]

MOBILITY BY AIR AND SEEING THE PROBLEM FROM NEW HEIGHTS

Traveling by air was a new experience for most of the leaders in the group. They usually traveled together in agricultural trucks, on microbuses, and sometimes by foot—where the sights of the city and the countryside were quite visible and the smells stark. In the air, we were removed from the countryside, from the sounds of roosters, the sights of the unfolding landscape, and the smells of dirt, sweat, and humidity that define rural life in Santa Cruz. The plane was an artificial space: the air felt stale and compressed, and the windows were sealed shut and streaked with scratches and smudges, making it difficult to see outside. Still, we each grabbed a comfortable, reclining seat with a small white pillow and red blanket for added luxury. Saisari and I sat next to each other, with a Paulista (person from São Paulo) on our left-hand side, a businessman returning from a short trip to Santa Cruz.

Through awkward body language—which featured shrugged shoulders, glazed-over eyes, and reddish faces—it was apparent that some MST members felt uncomfortable with this mode of transportation, which placed agricultural workers side by side with elite businessmen, who take their mobility for granted.[7] People from distinct cultural, economic, and social backgrounds had to sit alongside one another, which is quite rare. It is not often that MST members sit next to and are forced to interact with the business elite. One MST representative turned to the businessmen in the first-class section who were trying to size him up with a deep stare. His eyebrows scrunched in anger and his face reddened with embarrassment. He turned and asked me as we proceeded through the aisle how much it cost to travel in the front of the plane, and why people pay to sit in that section. These complicated feelings of envy and anger defined our conversations about the business passengers on this direct flight from Santa Cruz to São Paulo.

This plane, unlike the trucks or the micros, also provided a satellite view of the altered productive landscapes and environmental surrounds of Santa Cruz, the Amazon, and the border of Brazil. Saisari pointed out particular plots of land that looked like green and brown patches to me but told him where and how soy was being produced. He was able to identify zones of deforestation and other regions of heavy pesticide use and soil erosion with confidence. Using images from the sky, he sketched a story of uneven geographical development. Saisari, from thousands of feet above the ground, was able to narrate a pattern of land use and destruction—just as these globalized spaces of conversation provided opportunities for landless peasants to learn about and see a much broader macro-economic picture: the agribusiness model of production and the connections between their lives and that of other small-scale farmers across the Americas.

As he explained the altered ecosystem, the flight attendant offered him a disposable cup of coffee and a plastic microwavable plate filled with perfectly shaped eggs and soggy toast. The organizers did not really like the food that they were served, calling it *comida pasada* (stale food). Saisari looked at it twice, as if trying to convince himself that he should eat before we landed in Brazil. When MST members traveled via other modes of transportation, they engaged in the process of collective food preparation on the side of the road, as we will see in the next chapter. We always carried organic foods from the settlements on our long journeys and quickly set up impromptu "kitchens" to feed large groups. This airplane meal, however, came right out of a box, representing the alienation of our global food system:[8] a prepackaged, microwavable meal that removed the consumer from the production process and took the pleasure and the joy out of eating. The social aspects of food preparation and sharing were disembedded from this meal.

These new heights, then, also illustrated the end result of large-scale agriculture, which is a parallel story of food—food that becomes commodified, packaged, and sold in corporate supermarkets. A new kind of food regime, which services airlines, business events, and meetings, symbolizes the loss of connection to land, production, and the processes of cooking and eating. This kind of mobility illuminated for MST members our dependence upon prepackaged and highly processed foods.

After several nights of travel, from international air travel to a bus that transported us from São Paulo to Brasília, we arrived at the fifth annual international conference. The energy and enthusiasm was high as chants and cheers filled the air. All conference participants wore red MST shirts with the slogan "Agrarian Reform for Social Justice and Popular Sovereignty." A well-known leader from MST Brazil took center stage with some opening remarks about the destructive practices of large-scale agriculture and the Vía's alternative proposal for food sovereignty:

> The problems of hunger and poverty in the countryside and the lack of markets for farmers' own agricultural products have been significant and multiplied during the last thirty years. . . . In effect, this union [of peasants and rural workers] has contributed to constructing a wider concept as far as food sovereignty is concerned. In the past, there existed a generic conception of food sovereignty—for example, peoples' right to produce their own foods. Now, we add duty to this concept, because all people that want to be free and independent are obligated to produce their own foods. Therefore, it is more than a right; it is a determination, a political condition. For that reason, we have come to apply this concept to all the territorial spaces: countries, regions, cities, and rural communities.
>
> We also managed to come to an understanding on the idea that food sovereignty is only possible if it takes place at the same time as political sovereignty of peoples. In order to be able to apply policies that allow autonomy in food production, it is necessary to have

political conditions that exercise autonomy in territories and toward the state.

Finally, we moved ahead with the idea of prioritizing agricultural techniques that respect the environment and are agroecological. In other words, [we must continue to find] ways to increase productivity and the autonomy of eco-agriculture administered in a sustainable manner, preserve nature for future generations, and produce healthy foods. (MST representative, public speech, June 2007)

This articulation at the international level of food sovereignty as a platform for reclaiming rights to land and autonomy represented the culmination of the daily labor of grassroots movements across the globe to protect national food systems and re-regulate the agricultural market, which had been deregulated under neoliberalism. McMichael (2008) described neoliberal policymakers as part of a rich man's club in which agricultural rules benefited Western nations and created great crises around food security in the global South. The lack of any form of protection of national food production created a flood of cheap imports flowing from North to South that undercut local farmers and gave transnational corporations free rein on speculation,[9] betting, or gambling on the futures markets of food commodities such as grain prices. This was, in part, what caused the "tortilla crisis" in Mexico in 2007, when people could not afford a staple part of their diet.[10]

Many poor countries in the South no longer have sufficient food reserves. They depend on imports for survival, but the prices of those imports skyrocket, then drop, and then skyrocket again (Rosset 2009). At the turn of the twenty-first century, 815 million people (777 million in the global South) remain food-insecure, unable to meet their daily requirements. Meanwhile, six corporations handle 85 percent of the world grain trade, and integrated, centralized control of the food chain, from gene to supermarket, intensifies. In the name of global development, this Northern model is exported as the solution to food insecurity, displacing farmers in both the South and North. As Nettie Wiebe, a Canadian farmer and recent member of the international coordinating committee of the Vía Campesina, remarked, "The difficulty for us, as farming people, is that we are rooted in the places where we live and grow our food. The other side, the corporate world, is globally mobile" (quoted in McMichael 2007: 266).

This international conference, then, was about building bridges across organizations, indigenous communities, and national identities in order to forge a platform for agrarian reform and food sovereignty. MST-Bolivia participated in workshops, listened to talks through small radios, which translated from Portuguese to Spanish, and interjected comments in subsequent discussions.

Following long days of workshops, our group received food badges for lunch and dinner that enabled us to taste different foods from the various regions of Brazil—organic food coming directly from settlements, made in collective pots, and served to thousands of international guests. This unstructured time during meals provided opportunities for organizers to share their struggles. As people waited for food, they talked about their journey to Brasília, discussed their organization or movement in their home country, and commented on MST-Brazil as a kind of model for organizing. Some of the delegates from Mexico shared their struggles over corn. In Mexico, 2.5 million households engage in rain-fed maize production, with a productivity of two or three tons per hectare, compared with seven to eight tons per hectare in the American Midwest. With the rise of corn imports over 200 percent under NAFTA, more than two-thirds of small-scale farmers have not survived the competition. One representative said, "We cannot try to win in a battle against the United States. It's not worth the trouble to plant. We don't have the subsidies or the machinery. And the direct result is hunger. We cannot feed our families" (Mexican agrarian organizer, personal communication, June 2007).

These kinds of informal conversations were critical to building transnational networks: organizers learned about the experiences of farmers in other parts of Latin America and compared strategies for combating hunger and food insecurity. Besides the sharing of stories, organizers also exchanged e-mail addresses, phone numbers, and contact information, creating a much broader movement. Many remained in e-mail contact well after the conference; some of the participants subsequently visited Bolivian settlements and led workshops on agroecology.

AGROECOLOGY IN THE MST SETTLEMENT OF ITAPEVA

But perhaps the most important educational part of the journey, rich with possibilities for taking such ideas and implementing similar projects in Bolivia, was our trip to an MST settlement called Itapeva to learn about

MST-Brazil's model of agroecology and environmental stewardship. The team of MST-Bolivia leaders had made some connections with a resident of Itapeva, who offered to take all of us to her settlement, which was not more than two hours from São Paulo. As we traveled, the landscape radically changed from one of congestion, deep black smog, and hustle and bustle to large green pastures and fields. There was a huge sign awaiting us reading, "MST 25 years of Struggle and Conquest." Itapeva appeared very different from most MST settlements in Bolivia. The houses were not temporary, but rather permanent, made of bricks and cement. There were small hammocks and swings outside some of the homes; occasionally we bumped into people reading books on their patios. Individual families had placed flowers and small vegetable gardens alongside their homes, beautifying this rural landscape. All the houses were about the same size.

We first arrived at Agrivilla 1, also known as barrio 13 May 1984, which was the date of the first occupation. We walked through the settlement, meeting families and hearing about the initial occupation, the joy of receiving title, and the early, challenging days of building community. The settlers spoke about their struggles convincing people to believe in a collective model of working and owning the land. Many had come from places where they were accustomed to working the land independently. There were also daily battles in convincing settlers to farm sustainably, as many simply wanted to rely upon genetically modified seeds and pesticides. This tension reflected recent academic work on MST, as Branford and Rocha (2002) note that many MST settlers have realized the importance of shifting from monoculture to an environmentally sustainable mechanism; as one settler said, "We're trying to do it in an ecologically friendly way without the use of chemicals, giving fish healthy foods that we produce ourselves from organic cassava, maize, and potatoes" (175). But this has never been an easy or smooth process. As Wolford (2011) notes, many settlers simply want to conquer the land for individual purposes, grow sugarcane, and make a quick profit off of this form of monoculture cropping. As one of her informants from northeast Brazil explains, "The plantation structure has maintained itself, and this means that the people here still think like this—this is the richest in the country, but unfortunately, the tradition is just to plant sugarcane" (132).

Besides learning about agroecology, MST-Bolivia organizers also heard about the benefits of agricultural cooperatives. We visited their dairy collective,[11] part of a broader marketing and supply cooperative (COAPRI) where one can join in the process and experience of making cheese. We traveled from one side of the building, where they produced the cheese, to the other, which housed the offices for supply and marketing. Besides public schools, which were trying to implement healthier alternatives for schoolchildren, some MST cooperatives have provided food through federal government programs such as the Food Acquisition Program (EAP), implemented by the National Supply Company (CONAB), which provides food purchases for registered entities, usually assistance facilities such as hospitals and APAES (Brazilian Association of Parents and Friends of the Disabled). The funds from these kinds of sales were funneled back into the settlement to provide necessary services like education and health care. Besides a dairy collective, this settlement was also planting herb gardens, using such medicinal plants as alternatives to Western medical practices, packaging and bottling extracts for curing illnesses and preventing diseases. Residents kept a small shop where visitors could buy some of these all-natural remedies.

More recently, Itapeva has been experimenting with alternative energy sources. Residents are building wind turbines and installing them across the long stretches of agricultural land. They described it as the only way to obtain real sovereignty. As one MST representative said, "Multinational corporations keep us dependent upon their energy for survival. This type of initiative will allow small agricultural communities to have sovereignty over their energy. We will generate energy for the people . . . not for big multinationals, whose big factories only destroy the environment" (MST Itapeva, personal communication, June 2007). Besides hearing about and seeing these projects for alternative energy, MST representatives from Itapeva took us through their agroecological schools and their collective radio station, which work together to promote an alternative vision of the economy, land reform, and sustainability.

This information then traveled from Brazil to Bolivia as organizers headed back to their settlements and attempted to implement similar kinds of projects. Silvestre Saisari and a few others returned to Pueblos Unidos, where they continued to try to convince people of the benefits of collective labor and agroecology. Yet this was an ongoing struggle, particularly as people remain convinced that individual plots of production are more effective than collective or communal projects. The Bolivian landless had to give broad-based ideas, such as food sovereignty and agroecology, a localized appeal by using their own historical and cultural frames of reference. Once again, through the imagined ayllu, they discuss the ways in which their ancestors lived, relied upon each other, and worked the land, as we saw at the beginning of this chapter. If ayllu democracy served as a cultural or political frame for organizing settlements in a more collective and participatory manner, MST organizers also realized that the economic and productive success of these settlements depended upon efficient management of labor and distribution of resources. Collective labor had to be the base for economic productivity, particularly at such a small scale, and for the creation of social wealth, which proved essential for the survival of these communities.

AYLLU AS AGRICULTURAL PRACTICE
WITHIN MST SETTLEMENTS

The MST model for community production is in part drawn from romantic ideas or memories of ayllus as independent and sovereign spaces, where people lived well off of small-scale agriculture. Many spoke about the importance of these ancestor stories in the early days of occupations, especially as community members struggled to organize themselves into communal work and production groups. As Braulio Cusipuma said:

> I remember in the first days of the occupation—everyone was really beaten down and tired. An encampment is not such an easy thing. There is no food, clean drinking water, or organizational structure. We have to create all of this from scratch. I remember a seasoned leader stood in front of all of us and said, "Compañeros, no one ever said this would be easy. We have braved difficult moments together. And now it is time to build a settlement on this land. And we must use our ancestors as a force. They lived in ayllus that functioned independently; they sustained a system of small-scale agriculture by organizing people into collective work groups, reciprocal forms of exchange, and an egalitarian structure of democratic decision-making. And this worked." (MST–Pueblos Unidos representative, public speech, April 2006)

When MST actually received title to the land, the ayllu served as a means of organizing distinct groups into productive units. The 190 families in Pueblos Unidos collectively own the 16.6896 hectares of agrarian land, which has been divided into individual and collective plots. Much of the land is not suitable for cultivation, but on the remaining hectares, the village cultivates soy and beans for the national market on a large scale.[12] Many of the residents have individual plots of land where they grow all sorts of produce for their own family consumption, some organic and some relying upon fertilizers and chemicals. There are also several community or collective farming experimental projects—for example, residents hope that the production of organic peanuts can lead to more sustainable development in the future.

In order to ensure some form of community protection, MST used the ayllu as a socioeconomic model to guarantee the survival of the collective. Saisari describes it as follows:

> Through collective forms of owning the land, we seek to prevent the trafficking of land and critical resources. This idea of collective ownership then informs how we build a sense of collectivity within the settlements. We use this ayllu model in order to strengthen the family economy and food sovereignty through the creation of community production units and by varying food sources, providing added value to organic production. We have strengthened community development and equitable sharing of natural resources, and protection of economic, social, and cultural rights will be guaranteed. (Silvestre Saisari, personal communication, May 2006)

MST members also mobilized the concept of ayni so that those who were elderly or disabled or unable to tend to the needs of their individual plot would be taken care of by the community. In discussing the appropriation of such rural cultural models to newly urbanized and marginalized spaces of Bolivia, Goldstein (2004) suggests that while ayni did not hold the same value in urban areas, community residents adapted rural cultural models during times of festivals and fiestas, as these reciprocal gift contributions helped with the financial burden of having to provide money, beer, and food. And Revilla (2011) argues that, in the absence of a strong centralized state to provide critical infrastructure to urban areas, systems like ayni and minka served to organize community residents into work parties that built pipelines for water distribution, health care centers, and schools. In a neoliberal era, where such marginalized and urban zones became "illegal communities," these cultural models served a practical purpose in mobilizing and collectivizing a workforce.[13] In the case of rural areas, such structures of reciprocal labor exchange also provided a sense of long-term security, as many community members were too old or frail to take care of their plots of land. Further, the collective work ethic of minka served as an organizational strategy for the building of community resources like health centers and schools.

As mentioned previously, ideas about how to "use culture" to define or redefine production did not emerge in a vacuum. Rather, international development agencies and local NGOs have been influential in providing this kind of information to MST and other social organizations. For example, Oxfam International has used archaeological evidence to reveal that three thousand years ago, pre-Columbian communities made vast modifications to their landscape. During this time, an agricultural system was developed that coped with environmental challenges, improved soil fertility, and made the land very productive. Recently, Oxfam and the Kenneth Lee Foundation have been working with communities in the lowlands to make use of this historical memory as a kind of guide to assist them in their efforts to build sophisticated agricultural technology, plant indigenous crops and species, and produce fertile soil. In addition to Oxfam, organizations like CEJIS also encouraged social movements like MST to recover and integrate indigenous habits, norms, and values into their practices of working the land. CEJIS, however, focused much more on the role of these "alternative structures" within the broader political process. The language of indigeneity then shifted from localized ecological projects to increasing political recognition and power at the national level. Movements in Bolivia take NGO ideas and meld them with their own creative strategies to come up with solutions that will work for their communities.

ENSURING FOOD SECURITY THROUGH ALTERNATIVE PRODUCTION

About ten months after Pueblos Unidos received official title, I finally made the long journey on the back of a semitrailer to see for myself how its experiments with food sovereignty and agroecology mapped out into this ayllu practice. The settlement was one large agricultural field, which appeared endless. There were about fifty to sixty thatched roof huts made of motacu, still temporary settlements, even though the settlers had now obtained official and permanent status. Residents immediately took us on a walking tour of their *chacos*, or small fields. They were proud of what they were producing and how they were producing it.

They led us down a winding and twisted agricultural road filled with overgrown shrubs and weeds. We were attacked by an army of ruthless mosquitoes and gnats, which gathered in the hundreds to form a kind of black dust blocking all visibility. While we carried several bottles of DEET spray, the MST organizers seemed unaffected by the *picasones* (little mosquito bites), as they called them, merely brushing the insects aside as they talked to us about how they were growing their vegetables and what they were growing. One organizer stated, "This Pueblos Unidos will be filled with production; no one will go hungry. Everyone will be able to live off the land. Then we will create roads, so that we can get our products out to market" (MST–Pueblos Unidos representative, personal communication, July 2007).

Another organizer spoke about the way they were experimenting with organic production and how using mixed forms of agriculture to prevent heavy pesticide use and trying to recover the soil after production were kinds of recovery of the past.[14] He also talked about using organic matter to improve the soil structure, which increases its water-storage capacity, enhances fertility, and promotes tilth, a characteristic of soil structure. The better the tilth, the more easily the soil can be cultivated, and the easier it is for seedlings to emerge. Furthermore, the settlers have relied upon green manure as a natural pesticide. Green manure helps to control weeds, insects, pests, and soil erosion, while also providing forage for livestock and cover for wildlife. Controlling insects, diseases, and weeds without chemicals is a goal of their system of sustainable agriculture. It was important for many of the residents to illustrate to us their creative use of globalized concepts like food sovereignty: to sit in the middle of their products, to show us their production, to pick a tomato or head of lettuce, and tell us its story of production.[15]

Continuing along this twisted path of agricultural landscapes, one resident wanted us to taste his juicy watermelon that had just turned ripe and was ready to be eaten. He cracked several open and encouraged us to eat our slices, even though the bugs swarmed around the melon and its delicious, sticky juice, which dripped from our lips.

As they sat in their chacos, many settlers recalled their struggle over this land, how they had been displaced and forced to live under bridges or in the parks without food. One woman said, "This here represents not only our home and community, but our independence. It's so beautiful that we can grow our own food and eat it. It means we're not having to rely upon others for our food. We can live the way we want to live."

FIGURE 4. Collective production of hot chile peppers in Gran Chaco.
Photograph by Kara Panowitz.

This talk of food sovereignty and autonomy, showing us the chacos and encouraging shared eating, could be thought of as grassroots performances of alternative models of production. This performed citizenship will become clearer through the twenty-eight-day march to La Paz, as MST moves, dances, and chants its way to the seat of power. However, in these private spaces of their production, MST members displayed, through a shared act of eating together and enjoying the fruits of their labor, the actual benefits of organic farming. The rituals of food sharing within the settlement opened up a space for dialogue and exchange, political conversations about food reclamation and the opportunity for foreigners to participate in their production, to understand and taste their food, made with their hands and their labor. In part, this was also an illustration of food that was produced, not with individualized slave labor in the fields, but as part of a collective and collaborative process (see Figure 4). Yet part of the new model of production was not solely about how food was produced and by whom, but also the social and ecological responsibility that farmers must assume in order to sustainably manage and protect their environmental surrounds.

Again, ayllu stories formed a cultural and historic basis for connecting themes on the sacredness of the environment, the crops that are grown for subsistence farming, and the use of natural fertilizers to contemporary struggles. As one MST organizer relayed to me in 2006, "In the Andes, our ancestors, who lived on ayllus, used something called 'raised fields,'[16] which provided drainage and improved soil conditions and temperatures for crops. It was an ecologically sound alternative to agricultural development based on expensive imported technology. We must be creative now in order to think about adapting such kinds of sustainable agriculture in MST areas" (MST-Ichilo representative, personal communication, August 2007).

Initially, environmental consciousness was not explicitly a part of MST's organizational or productive model. However, environmental and economic contradictions within the dominant agricultural paradigm compelled MST communities like Pueblos Unidos and Tierra Prometida to reimagine small-scale production and create long-term projects focused on issues of resource conservation and sustainability. In the field of political ecology, the idea of an "environmental imaginary" has emerged to describe the ways in which social groups reconceptualize the environment. The environmental imaginary has physical roots in the complex natural ecology of a location, but is molded by social perceptions of nature and its possibilities for human use and habitation. Watts and Peet (1996) explain that while environmental imaginaries stem from material and social practices in natural settings, they also guide further practice. Referring to landscape production, Denis E. Cosgrove (1998) argues that landscapes are ways of seeing, and MST's ways of seeing are directly influenced by the destruction of their natural environment and their emergent politics. Questions regarding how to recuperate dead soil, limit the use of chemicals, and reforest particular areas of the region have defined many political and farming conversations.

Tierra Prometida has been experimenting with both agroecology and reforestation projects, supported by Veterinarians Without Borders (VWB), an NGO based in Spain that focuses on rural development, primarily centering on issues of agroecology. Globalized discourses, such as food sovereignty and environmental stewardship, often gain local traction through NGO workers, technocrats, and the international flow of dollars and knowledge. Much of the work of NGOs in Latin America has turned toward governmentality, or the "conduct of conduct," and how power circulates through the inculcation of discourses and routines aimed at promoting individualizing and autonomous self-regulation (see Ferguson 1990; Paley 2001; Sawyer 2004, 2007; Ong 2006; Li 2007; Sawyer and Gómez 2008). Bret Gustafson (2009b) offers a more balanced interpretation of the ways NGOs could also offer a language for politicizing alternative epistemological frameworks. NGOs like CEJIS and VWB are not merely imposing a unidirectional model of governmentality upon MST; rather these are dialogical encounters, articulated connections across difference, whereby MST might receive financial support and learn from VWB *técnicos* (experts), who provide workshops, assistance, and training, while at the same time they experiment with their own models of agriculture, use and mobilize stories and narratives of their ancient Andean past, and create new models.

Veterinarians Without Borders defines its work with MST as follows: "We center our work in the defense and promotion of a strategy of campesino production that is collective with a strong agroecological base through participatory methods of learning and teaching."[17] A representative from this organization described the strategy it pursues as "using indigenous knowledge of plants to diversify production and protect forests and lands"[18] (Interview, June 10, 2010). Through the use and implementation of indigenous ways of working the land, VWB representatives have supported and built a model of agriculture in Tierra Prometida exclusively to defend territorial autonomy and the family-based, small-scale agricultural production that is central to this kind of self-determination. In one project, for example, settlers received direct financing from VWB to create organic rice fields; VWB provided the settlers with the seeds and materials they needed, but MST was responsible for the model of production followed. At the same time, MST organizers are beginning to think about and build connections with regional governmental officials for the creation of local markets in which to sell organic rice and other products. They hope that Evo Morales, through his new proposals for supporting small-scale farmers, will provide the supports necessary for getting these products to domestic markets.

MST-Ichilo has also focused much of its attention on the reforestation of deforested landscapes, which is part of its new socioeconomic and environmental imaginary. While deforestation and the illegal extraction of timber might have been the initial rationale for occupying this forest preserve, now, with the help of vwb, MST is using all kinds of native tree species, such as *mara* and *tajibo*, to diversify forests and replant landscapes that have been devastated by extractive industries. The sustainable plan for development is that, within approximately ten years, they would be able to use and sell the wood from these trees within regional and national markets. MST's alternative model of working the land and reforesting landscapes may produce moral and material alternatives to the crisis of agrarian capitalism. At the same time, however, its desire to make a profit off of such endeavors is never far from these projects.

TENSIONS AND FRICTIONS DEFINE A MIXED MODEL OF AGRARIAN CITIZENSHIP

While I have not directly witnessed this, there are rumors that Pueblos Unidos is no longer promoting solely a model of indigenous agroecology, but rather, has mixed agricultural practices of organic and monocultural production of soy in order to get out of debt quickly and bring much-needed funding to the settlement. However, there are social and ecological consequences to promoting a large-scale model of agriculture. As Miguel Urioste described it, "[the] mono export model—promoted by the World Bank for the past 15 years—is a lamentable demonstration of how those that decide public policies in the Third World do not take into account the enormous environmental costs or the lamentable economic and political effects produced by this model" (quoted in Burbach 2008: 3). This model of soy production has also relied upon the use of a single herbicide called Roundup. In view of the fact that the movement promotes the concept of environmental stewardship, this monocultural production of soy proves quite contradictory. When asked about the use of GMOs to promote soy production, an MST representative explained, "They aren't using any transgenic material, but they are using some fertilizers. . . . This is not organic production, but rather an easy way to gain entrée into the international market" (MST representative, personal communication, May 2011).

This kind of buying into the dominant logic of capital development and progress is described by Suzana Sawyer (2004) in her work on transnational oil and the role it played in Ecuador in shaping individual expectations, transforming allegiances, and defining what was an appropriate neoliberal subject. In the case of big oil in Ecuador, transnational corporations might lure people into supporting this model of development through gifts, trinkets, and international travel. As an Ecuadorian indigenous organizer said when speaking to a group of community residents, "Don't you see, you don't see clearly? They are blinding you and manipulating you with trinkets" (61). In Bolivia, it might be less blatantly obvious: it is not as much about the trinkets from agroindustrial elites, but rather, the predominant belief in the magic of the marketplace and the prevalence of powerful ideologies regarding regional citizenship as linked to international development, large-scale soy production, and quick cash. As described in Chapter 2, the regional agrarian elites promote a discourse and a practice of the limitless possibilities of large-scale agriculture for regional and local development. Ideas about modernity, development, and advancement are wrapped up and tied into this model; to regional elites, groups like MST that rely upon indigenous forms of agroecology are backward, primitive, and antimodern.

Agroecology might represent a threat to this agrarian capitalist class, as it presents alternative forms of development and long-term sustainability. Yet, many MST members are beginning to lose patience with the amount of time and resources that they are required to invest in such tedious farming activities. The lure of large-scale soy is that it can provide quick solutions to their problems and bring to fruition their dreams of grandeur and development.[19] But just as oil extraction offers the specter of development for indigenous communities, the same proves true for soy production in MST settlements. Community activists in Ecuador state, "Neither these gifts nor oil activity has brought development . . . rather, they have brought only misery, social and ecological decay, and *indígenas'* further marginalization from the national society. . . . We have a conscience on our side; ARCO [transnational oil] has the dollar. This is a struggle of *la conciencia contra el dolar* [consciousness against the dollar]" (Sawyer 2004: 80). For MST, the dollar sometimes wins out over the ideological and political consciousness.

AN INDIGENOUS-BASED MODEL OF
CAPITALIST DEVELOPMENT

In both Pueblos Unidos and Tierra Prometida, MST representatives romanticize about agroecological tourism, something they call "ecotourism," in which gringos and other foreigners would fly in from all over the world, live in cabañas, and experience this kind of indigenous-based environmentalism of the poor (Martínez-Alier 2002). When they imagine this, they often talk about building an airport for quick and easy transportation access to their communities, deforesting in order to build cabins or living spaces for the gringos, and altering the material surrounds in order to accommodate the needs of these foreigners. This model of development does not seem to coincide with the agroecological or sustainability frame. This tension between environmental conservation and economic development through tourism powerfully illustrates Linda Farthing's (2009) contradictory development model. While Farthing discusses the dilemmas that exist at the national level (the protection of the environment and discourses of indigenous rights mixed with policies of extractive industries), the same applies to this mixed model of conservationism and large-scale development plans at the community level. Farthing argues, "This predominance of economic over environmental concerns makes both healing Bolivia's environmental wounds and preventing future destruction an exceptionally difficult proposition. No past government has ever resolved this dilemma" (29). How do we make sense of this model of citizenship, which is fluid and attempts to incorporate alternative visions and cosmovisions of "living and protecting the environment" within a broader capitalist model of development?

Recognizing this tension proves fundamental to understanding the new dilemmas of indigenous grassroots citizenship and development, the ways in which localized struggles and conflicts begin to define broader regional and national discussions. Robert Andolina, Nina Laurie, and Sarah Radcliffe (2009) might describe this as "indigenous development" or "development with identity"(3), articulating the powerful ways in which ethnic identity has become a part of development thinking over the past decades.[20] Echoing Anna Tsing's (2005) work on friction, through a broad-based and multiscalar picture of transnationalism, they trace the ways in which members of indigenous organizations grapple with unanticipated consequences of their movement's political gains. While their focus is transnational, similar processes of negotiation seem to be at work at the very local level. Culturally appropriate development agendas as a form of what these researchers call "social neoliberalism" (9) prove particularly important as we strive to understand the uses of identity and indigeneity for strengthening institutions and building individuals' capacities to pull themselves out of poverty. While the model of analysis posed by Andolina, Laurie, and Radcliffe explains a rather unidirectional flow of knowledge and development, I will attempt to illustrate the complexity and hybridity of such mixings and envelopments.

This creative mixing of indigenous practice and large-scale development provides insight into new models of citizenship taking shape and form in Bolivia. Sian Lazar points out that citizenship has always been viewed as a bundle of practices between the state and the people, rather than simply a legal status (Lazar 2008). She struggles to understand incomplete citizenship, whereby those excluded come to influence the terms of their inclusion. Beyond the challenge to institutionalized citizenship that is posed by those who are marginalized, there might be yet another challenge to shaping citizenship posed by groups who wish to take over the state, and in turn are redefining the very terms of political participation and government. MST offers a distinct model of agrarian citizenship whereby members will scale these demands regarding food sovereignty and environmental stewardship up to the national government. Yet just as the grassroots movement is filled with contradictions and tensions regarding mixed strategies of development, so too is national legislation.

While many scholars have overlooked the critical tensions between the individual and collective, as well as between indigenous values and capitalistic logic, we need to spend more time inside these spaces. Within these tensions we can begin to find new, hybridized models of citizenship in which participants are both individuals and part of a collective, pushed and pulled by conflicting discourses: one privileging egalitarianism, rooted in tradition and the past, and the other privileging economic success, rooted in notions of liberalized markets and individualism. Conflictive grassroots or agrarian citizenship is not a clear, unidirectional model of citizenship, but rather is full of daily frictions and struggles to survive. Catherine Walsh's (2010) analysis is perhaps the most accurate description of these new and complex entanglements. She asks the following critical questions when referring to an indigenous-based development model of buen vivir in the case of Ecuador: "The crucial question is whether *buen vivir* is becoming another discursive tool and co-opted term, functional to the state and its structures and with little significance for real intercultural, interepistemic, and plurinational transformations? Does this model suggest a disentanglement of the colonial matrix of power? Or does all this rather suggest a new more complicated envelopment and entanglement?" (20).

Long legacies of colonialism, neocolonialism, regionalism, harsh violence, and displacement continue to define the ways in which indigenous communities and social movements strive toward an alternative model. As Walsh so eloquently articulates, this plural model is possibly the very envelopment and entanglement of old and new, of colonial and neocolonial legacies. Indigenous social movements do not simply jump to a pure collective model, and this collective model is not always so egalitarian or fair. At the transnational level, it might seem perfectly feasible to publicly promote alternative models of food sovereignty and agroecology as broad-based resistance to this globalized agro-export model, but the daily struggles due to increasing poverty, lack of resources, and lack of infrastructural support from the state prevent MST members from bringing such utopian visions of independence and autonomy to fruition. Instead, members adopt, as best they can, pieces of the alternative models that maintain great rhetorical appeal and are promoted as key to sustainability and egalitarianism. The result is a hybridization of these models, a necessary mixing of that which is described in the MST documents and speeches and that which is lived on the ground, in a moment of expansive capitalism, extractive industries, and environmental degradation.

Instead of viewing global-to-local flows as unidirectional, where neoliberal forms of governmentality have been imposed upon indigenous communities, I argue that this hybrid model represents the end result of these dialogical and conflictive engagements across difference. While some scholars might look toward these alternative projects as "indigenous utopias," to merely romanticize food sovereignty or agroecology in an era of expansive capitalism proves problematic. At the same time, to simply reject these creative approaches as "developmentalism" with social and/or cultural frames also seems equally problematic. These tensions between global actors, regional elites, and local community members might and do lead to creative plural imaginaries, new hybrid possibilities, and critical alliances between distinct organizations at a local level. This model of citizenship, and our analyses, must move toward understanding the multiple forms and layers of experiences and rationalities—the influence of the past upon the present, and the legacies of colonialism, neocolonialism, and violence upon these structures. However, we cannot lose sight of Arturo Escobar's (2010) insights regarding the possibility of a group of people who can dream of a better world and through both their imagination and practice can contribute to building these alternative structures.

The next chapter moves from communal spaces of governance and alternative forms and models of production to MST indigenous cultural practices in motion. It takes up what might be possible through these new kinds of plural imaginaries and moves from a hybrid and plural model of citizenship to one that is embodied, performed, and shaped in motion. My discussion of the Fifth March for Land and Territory emphasizes the idea that these platforms do not remain grounded in local communities. As people walk, talk, and discuss ideas for food sovereignty, they also move demands from the local to the regional and national levels. Ideas about rights and citizenship are being formed and shaped as people engage in these new and spectacular forms of protest, which bring broad-based and global attention to their struggles, invert age-old historic spaces of inequality, and demand reform at the local, national, and even international levels.

PART III

SYMBOLIC CITIZENSHIP AND NEW FORMS OF STATEHOOD

CHAPTER FIVE

MOBILE "INDIGENOUS" CITIZENSHIP

Marching for a New Agrarian Reform Law

We finally made it to the outskirts of the city of Cochabamba in the late afternoon hours, after fourteen days of marching from the lowland region of Santa Cruz to the upper valleys. The long line of protestors stopped for a short rest in the evening and began the journey again in the early morning hours from Sacaba into the Plaza 14 de Septiembre at the center of Cochabamba. While it was a short walk, it felt like an eternity; the hot sun beat down on our exposed necks, dried sweat and dirt stuck to our skin even in the wee morning hours, and the shoes we had worn for several days tightened with every step, rubbing against old blisters and sores. Despite the difficult conditions, everyone maintained perfect precision in the *columnas* (columns or lines),[1] which were two or three people across (all members of the same MST núcleo) and many deep, each rank-and-file member walking half a foot behind the person ahead. The protestors, while dragging their bodies along the paved terrain, kept a rhythmic motion, following the feet and the beat of the people in front of them.

Physical exhaustion and mental fatigue wore heavily on their dirt-streaked faces, yet their spirit and energy were high. Several MST representatives, with tired and cracking yet powerful voices, screamed in unison, "*¡MST, esta lucha es para vencer!*"

The crowd repeated, "*¡MST, esta lucha es para vencer!*"

And the leaders again: "*¡MST, esta lucha es para vencer!*"

The crowd followed in a melodic, "*¡MST, esta lucha es para vencer!*"

"*¿Cuándo?*" asked the leader.

"*¡Ahora!*" shouted the crowd.

"*¿Cuándo?*"

"*¡Ahora!*"

Several hundred protestors, following the rhythmic chant of the leader, banged on their makeshift drums and made lots of noise. Others chose to march with flutes and wind instruments, gasping for breath as

FIGURE 5. MST marching in *columnas* during the Fifth National March for Land and Territory, Cochabamba, November 2006. Photograph by Nancy Romer.

they continued to play songs from the Andes and the Amazon. The musical mixing represented the fifth attempt to bring these distinct indigenous communities together in protest for rights to land, territory, and agrarian reform. MST flags bearing the slogan "*Ocupar, Resistir, Producir*" (Occupy, Resist, Produce) waved high above the heads of the demonstrators, alongside *wiphala* flags, representing the distinct native communities of the Andes, now an emblem of the new plurinational state. These tribes had unified their distinct claims for land under a broader framework of rights to territory.

As the long lines of protestors approached the center of Cochabamba, city residents gathered on the street corners, clapping and cheering on the demonstrators. Some had brought small carts filled with plastic bags of water. They tied the bags and tossed them carefully to the demonstrators, trying not to break the columnas' orchestrated steps forward (see Figures 5 and 6). Others tossed treats and delicacies through the air to fill the protestors' empty stomachs. These flying objects created a circuslike appearance as people juggled and caught all kinds of commodities, quickly drinking and eating before arriving at their destination.

FIGURE 6. Protestors arriving in the Plaza 14 de Septiembre of Cochabamba, November 2006. Photograph by Nancy Romer.

Then, suddenly, the long lines of protestors crossed the last block of streets leading into the old city of Cochabamba and the productive spaces of economic modernization. Their destination was surrounded by the trappings of the West: fancy coffee shops, new and renovated government and municipal buildings, tourist offices, and hotels. The protestors stopped for a second to reconvene, and then they bulldozed into the plaza with collective might. Their bodies, once tired and weak, assumed new strength as they held their chests high and seized this space, infusing the main square with dynamic highland Andean cultural forms and practices. Some protestors danced in small circles, while others placed their wiphala flag in the center of the plaza. Others collapsed on the cement with their belongings, rubbing their sweat, dirt, and blood into the old colonial spaces of power and privilege. In the words of one MST leader, "The true MST performer is the one who brings from his breast the smell and color of his land, the mark of blood of the deaths that he has witnessed, so that the certainty of his struggle lives on."

Walking for days on this protest march with MST—from Santa Cruz to Cochabamba to La Paz—to support the New Agrarian Reform Law represented yet another form of mobility. It did not resemble the discomfort of traveling on the back of an agricultural truck or watching the landscape unfold from Santa Cruz to the northern peripheral regions in a congested microbus; rather this was about the use of the body—specifically, indigenous bodies moving visibly through national space. It was a kind of movement that required sacrifice and determination, pushing the body through a severe regime of pain in order to gain legislative rights to land, resources, and alternative ways of living. This march could be thought of as an embodied practice or performance, whereby protestors must train and use their bodies to achieve their ends (see Figure 7).[2]

Thus far, we have seen how grassroots agrarian citizenship is shaped inside local settlements and communities through ayllu practices of democracy and alternative ways of working the land. These kinds of protest marches are an embodiment of those same ideological platforms, shaped through the work of movement members. The marchers' bodies become vehicles, physically moving the ideological platforms through space and across scales as protestors place demands upon the state and push their bodies to the limit. These hyperpublic moments of pain and discomfort are not unlike what performance studies scholar Elaine Peña (2011) describes in her analysis of Mexican women's religious pilgrimages, where bruised and blistered feet, injured knees, cramped legs, headaches, and rug burns are expected and sometimes create a spiritual framework that gives rise to "communal corporal suffering" (102). In this case, they are the physical and emotive aspects of the new, mobile form of indigenous citizenship.[3]

This protest march can be conceptualized within the framework of spectacular displays of citizenship or citizenship rights. Daniel Goldstein (2004), while not focusing on protest marches in Bolivia per se, argues that spectacles call attention to and make dramatic the struggles of marginalized or invisible peoples: "Spectacles serve as a device to restructure patterns of inclusion. . . . By calling on their rights as citizens of the nation, those rendered silent and invisible to the ears and eyes of the state can find a stage from which to demand their inclusion through displays of national belonging" (19). While Goldstein looks at folklore and lynchings as two dramatic spectacles in which marginalized groups insert themselves into the nation-state, I am interested in exploring how performances of indigenous bodies and improvisational cultural practices infuse spaces with meaning, while at the same time reinforcing a

FIGURE 7. Graffiti on a wall in Cochabamba, "Marches and Roadblocks Are Forms of Nonviolent Struggle," November 2006. Photograph by Nancy Romer.

commitment to particular claims that indigenous peoples and the landless make upon the state. The physical pain and challenges of disciplining and moving bodies through space and the reassembly of their organizational structure along the march can be thought of as ayllu democracy in motion; discourses of food sovereignty and practices of cooking and eating were also put into motion in order to move demands from localized spaces to centers of power. All the while, the physical structure of the march and the organization of the marchers' bodies in space forced distinct groups to share histories and stories, and to engage one another body to body, a practice that is often rather challenging in the settlements. Yet, there is something about the constant motion and the process of enduring pain on a twenty-eight-day march that makes a collective politics possible—even if only for a fleeting moment. Festive culture, such as singing and dancing in the backwoods, reinforces this deeply embodied MST identity. But the demands of territorial reclamation and alternative forms of production—shaped at the grass roots, concretized in regional meeting spaces, and made mobile through protest marches—must be legitimized through constitutional and legislative reforms.

The Fifth National March for Land and Territory emerged out of four previous national-level indigenous campesino mobilizations for land, previously discussed. By May 2005, nearly ten years after the passing of the INRA Law, only 15 million hectares out of some 107 million had been effectively clarified in favor of campesino claims. The Fifth March, which took place in June 2006, called attention to the need to modify the failed law and pass a new Community Redirection Law, which included four pillars: land (the expropriation by the state and redistribution to peasants of all land that does not complete a social or economic function); mechanization (the distribution of tractors to the landless); credit (the creation of the Banco de Desarrollo Productivo, or Agricultural and Rural Bank [BDP], to lower interest rates for small-scale producers from 20 percent to 6 percent); and the development of eco-markets for ensuring long-term sustainability (Urioste 2007). This should be called an "agrarian revolution," in the words of Evo Morales,

> because we differentiate it from the so-called agrarian reforms of '52, of '53.[4] In those times, our grandfathers, our ancestors rose up, rifle at the shoulder, to recover the lands held by the *patrones* [agrarian elite]. And the MNR [Revolutionary Nationalist Movement]? The only thing they did was to try to legalize an armed uprising with the distribution of land. One of the errors of the reform was the individual parcelization, the lack of respect for the communitarian lands of origin. Another error was the creation, in the altiplano [highlands] and the valleys, of the *minifundio*, or the *surcofundio*, as some of our brothers say; and in the east, latifundio, where by the end there was no agrarian reform at all.[5] To differentiate ourselves, we speak of agrarian revolution . . . , [which] aims to provide land to those people without lands, or with insufficient lands, through state assistance. (Evo Morales, personal communication, August 2007)

Morales, while he had a plan for the new agrarian reform—or revolution, as he called it—had to legitimize and justify it with a performative and spectacular demonstration of his commitment to the *pueblos indígenas*. What better place than Santa Cruz, where agrarian elites had begun to resist such proposals? He gathered indigenous communities, social movements, and NGO representatives and provided transportation from rural areas to the city of Santa Cruz so that they could participate in this event.

A PUBLIC AND PERFORMATIVE DECLARATION
OF AGRARIAN REVOLUTION

Santa Cruz was a carefully chosen site in which to dramatize an alternative politics and indigenous citizenship through collective land rights and publicly confront the agrarian elites of the city. While elites might be performing a particular form of agrarian citizenship, as linked to transnational capital flows in city centers, public plazas, and through EXPO-CRUZ festivals, Morales wanted to create an alternative performance that responded to a history of colonization and then capitalist exploitation and that demanded the recuperation of latifundio land and called attention to the importance of redistribution. On that day in June, thousands of indigenous campesinos, peasants, and agricultural laborers congregated around a small stage close to the Chiriguano[6] monument. Some of the protestors wrapped themselves in wiphala flags, others carried the blue and white MAS banner, and still others had created signs made of cheap cardboard, sticks, and stones that read *"Tierra es Vida"* (Land is Life) or *"No a la Mercantilización de la Tierra"* (Stop Privatizing Land). Ponciano Sulca waved his MAS flag with one hand while his other arm hung by his side. He declared, "It is our right to own land. We live on the land; our parents lived on the land. This is our life—to work, to produce from the land for our families and for the city. We have to work to survive."

As people congregated around the stage, the clouds rolled in, hanging heavily as the sky turned a dark bluish-gray. Occasionally, military planes flew overhead to keep an eye on the protesters, their engines emitting an eerie whine as they passed. I stood with Deysi, an MST organizer dressed de pollera; Margarita Sulca, Ponciano's daughter; and another compañera from MAS. Hugo Salvatierra, the minister of agriculture, spoke for a few minutes about the historic significance of this day: "For more than 500 years, *you* have been oppressed, your land taken away, your communities and livelihood destroyed. But now, it is time for *you* to turn the tables." The protesters shouted their agreement in Aymara mixed with Spanish: *"¡Jallalla, hermano!"* (Yes, brother!). He, in turn, yelled in Spanish about the importance of the agrarian revolution for decolonizing Bolivia, and the crowd cheered in Quechua, "¡Jallalla!"

Then the protesters split into two large groups and started chanting, "EVO, EVO, EVO! The pueblo is with you!" Evo Morales, dressed for the occasion in an Andean shawl and colorful button-down shirt, welcomed everyone, saying, "I would like to thank all the organizations, social movements, and farmworker unions. We should also welcome the enemies of Santa Cruz. They are not happy because we are waking up this country with a new form of governance. This form of governing, our form of governing, is making history."[7]

Morales presented land titles[8] to sixty indigenous communities from different parts of Bolivia, giving official documents representing more than 7.5 million acres to small-scale farming communities in the departments of Beni, Cochabamba, La Paz, Oruro, Pando, Santa Cruz, and Tarija. He also promised the demonstrators that Bolivia's 2.5 million rural poor would receive titles to 20 million additional hectares of land over the next five years, a guarantee that meant 13 percent of the land would be given to about 28 percent of the population. The Morales administration controlled one-third of the land targeted for redistribution, while they promised to reclaim two-thirds from individuals and companies holding large tracts in the Oriente with no legal title. Morales declared that those who owned property legally and used land productively would not be affected, but those who had received property or obtained titles illegally through political ties to military dictators would forfeit their land.[9]

The skies opened and a torrent of rain was loosened upon all those present. However, the protestors remained at the Chiriguano statue, fixed in space and mesmerized by Morales's public performance of compassion and solidarity. As one MST organizer declared at the rally, "Evo is with us. He is with the poor indigenous majority. Such an event in the most conservative city of Bolivia, Santa Cruz, illustrated not only to us but to the entire nation his intention to implement laws that would benefit us, the working class and the poor of this country."

Then, as if they were his final words, Morales shouted in the midst of the torrent, "The great landowners of the Oriente are crying. They are hysterically crying because they know that their glory days are over. . . . We will seize their unproductive land and give it to poor campesinos!"

Several months after this public and performative declaration of an agrarian revolution, the draft of the New Agrarian Reform Law was stalled on the Senate floor. The members of the right-wing Podemos Party, which still held a controlling vote in the Senate, refused to support the new legislation. In response, landless peasants and lowland indigenous communities came together from around the country to discuss options for political pressure. According to MST organizer Silvestre Saisari, "The political climate in September was tense. . . . In mid-September, we presented the draft to the executive branch. In October, Morales sent the new legislation to the Congress, where it passed through the Chamber of Deputies. But then it was held up in the Senate, where the right-wing opposition party, Podemos, had the majority vote by one. They tried to create some concessions before passing the law. Their proposal was that the law should not include the reversion and expropriation of latifundio land. They wanted to simply redistribute state lands to peasants. Instead of creating solutions to the problem, they were creating more problems."

Further, the members of the CAO announced that they would create armed defense committees to protect their land against groups of peasants. Sporadic incidents of violence directed toward indigenous campesinos flared in the city of Santa Cruz during the summer months. By October 2006, the draft of the bill was still sitting on the floor of the Senate, but the members of Podemos refused to pass the new law. MST and other campesino organizations decided to take matters into their own hands in order to defend the position that land should belong to those who work it and to pressure the government to pass redistributive legislation. As one MST leader argued:

> We had to think about the political climate. Time was ticking away. It was already October 20 and the Senate wasn't going to meet again until the first week of December. That's why we had a national-level meeting with our legal advisers and our rank-and-file members. We asked people: What would we achieve through a mass mobilization? People agreed that we could use such a popular form of protest to gain support throughout the country and eventually pressure the Senate. We initiated the Fifth March as a lowland indigenous march for land and territory. However, throughout the journey, other groups from the valleys and the altiplano realized the importance of such a protest and they, too, joined us. It was the first time that east and west came together—campesinos from the Oriente and Occidente—poor indigenous people from this country joined forces to pressure the senators to pass the Ley de Recondución Comunitaria [Law of Communal Renewal].

The Fifth March then was about the importance of political pressure and visibility. Indigenous social movements (along with landless peasants) had to illustrate, through this sacrificial and performative demonstration of indigenous ways and customs, the importance of passing this legislation through the Senate. What becomes clear through MST's pivotal role in this process is how the very same structures at the grass-roots and regional levels must be reassembled and mobilized to keep people in order, to teach and enforce the importance of food sovereignty, and to use bodies as platforms for such demands.

THE ORGANIZATIONAL STRUCTURE OF THE MARCH

The ayllu model shapes democratic structure and physical organization within settlements and political spaces, but it was also assembled and re-assembled in motion when a number of MST communities came together to participate in the march. On the very first days of the march, MST organizers elected commissions, some of which included health, education, communication, safety, and agrarian reform. These MST commissioners then came together to comprise a larger decision-making body.

The elastic and mobile structure adopted by coordinators of the march proved considerably advantageous to the ideological and political development of the movement through geographical space. A horizontal structure of leadership enabled a cross-section of MST regional members to participate in commissions covering a variety of issues pertinent to the march. These commissions met every evening as a national-level body to discuss the progress of the New Agrarian Reform Law, the state of participants' health, and the safety of demonstrators. They worked collaboratively to create a supportive environment in which members exchanged ideas, debated, and eventually made decisions regarding the advancement of the march. As Arjun Appadurai (2002) argues in an article on neighborhood organizations and coalitions in Mumbai, social movements concerned with consciousness changing and self-mobilization can inculcate protocols that cultivate a nonhierarchical, antibureaucratic, and antitechnocratic executive structure. In other words, the organizational efforts involved a set of expressive decisions that aligned with the ideological framework of the movement.

MST's horizontal leadership also created an opportunity for the development of relationships across núcleos.[10] In the words of one MST leader:

> The commissions were a space in which to exchange experiences and ideas. I participated in the work group called Politics. We had meetings every evening, in which everyone sat on the floor of a large coliseum or gymnasium. There was no particular leader; we all led

discussions as a group *"pidiendo la palabra."* We had to know the proposal for the Agrarian Reform Law inside and out; we debated the proposal and discussed the implementation. Then we would meet with our regional groups or bases in order to transmit information from the national-level decision-making body to the bases. (MST representative, personal communication, July 2007)

Such a structure allowed for more equal participation and opportunity, fostered the building of political alliances, and promoted a quicker transmission of information from top to bottom. It is important to note, however, that such a horizontal structure of leadership is not without contradictions. Leadership, as we saw in Chapter 3, can be thought of as a terrain for struggles between collectivity as an ideal and the practice of self-interested actions by individuals (Lazar 2008). Some MST rank-and-file members asserted that their horizontal form of leadership was ineffective. Many community representatives who prided themselves on a sindicato background refused to accept a nonbureaucratic structure. They often assumed more powerful roles and made decisions for their particular community bases, as opposed to deferring to or consulting with the appropriate committee members.

One instance of this occurred when Juan Carlos Vedia, the regional leader of Obispo Santiesteban, decided to search independently for food and hoard it solely for his community, Pueblos Unidos, instead of abiding by the rules of the food commission. When MST members found out about his dissenting behavior, they strongly opposed it. The safety commission came together to decide on an effective punishment for Vedia, putting to use the usos y costumbres enforced in MST settlements and regional spaces of governance. Many suggested that Vedia be kicked out of the march altogether. Some described him as "not trustworthy," "a hoarder," and a "potential thief." They all decided that this was not someone that they wanted to walk, sing, and protest with for twenty-eight days. However, after much debate and discussion, the commission decided that they would give him another chance. They forced Vedia to apologize publicly to the movement about his actions and propose a plan where he—now part of the food commission—would come up with collective solutions for providing food to the entire movement. His hoarding of food breached the norm, fiery conversations followed, and eventually a solution was proposed: either abide by the rules or be eliminated from the march. Such an organizational style, by and large, creates a more democratic form of leadership, as community members are held accountable for their actions.

FOOD SOVEREIGNTY AND PRACTICES OF COOKING AND EATING IN MOTION

Just as ayllu democracy can be made mobile through protest marches, so too can food performances and practices, which do not remain grounded in time and space. They do not solely articulate the vision of the movement at the local level, but as people move, these discourses of "food sovereignty" turn into mobile acts. They can be assembled, reassembled, and reinvented in urban and rural areas, in the back of moving vehicles, along the sides of roads, and in the heart of national power. Cultural forms like the imagined ayllu or the tales of anticolonial ancestors take on new shapes as people extend their networks, mobilize their bases, and move across the country in a highly organized columna.

These food practices in motion teach people the ideology of the movement and forge or mark spaces en route with new meaning. An especially useful frame for exploring food practices is critical performative pedagogy, which is a teaching approach grounded in engaged and practice-based theory that challenges students to question domination. In other words, it is about helping students achieve critical consciousness. Augusto Boal (1979) took Freire's (1970) ideas regarding transformative learning and applied them to popular theater, where he described performance as a mirror in which one could change reality and transform a worldview. Similarly, the act of preparing mobile collective kitchens transmits ideas and sparks conversations about the need to reclaim food. These MST spaces allow members to share their day-to-day struggles and debate their ways of knowing. While tensions exist along the way, these embodied performances serve as a means to inculcate participants about the importance of healthy food and collective and alternative ways of "living well."

In MST settlements, members illustrated the importance of food sovereignty through elaborate show-and-tell stories of their chacos, but while they marched, members brought these ideas of food reclamation to new spaces, setting up collective kitchens along the road. While the idea of food sovereignty respatializes agriculture from the global to the local and re-creates social relations through new forms of working the land, the act of preparing an *olla común*, or communal pot, from which everyone is served, is a practice that also reinforces particular values;[11] it extends well beyond the individual bodily sensations of hunger to fulfill the needs of the larger group. Importantly, it is not the actual food that matters—the practice and structure of preparing a meal has embedded in it a hidden code regarding movement ideology: the importance of gender equality, collective forms of preparation and labor, and the redistribution of resources. In the words of one organizer, "Whatever we had, we figured out how to put something together to make a meal. It didn't matter if it was the best meal that we had; it just had to fill our stomachs so that we could keep walking. I lost ten kilos on the march. There were people who lost twelve kilos. We didn't eat well, but we ate enough to survive the conditions of the march" (MST representative, personal communication, November 2006).

During the march, the Food and Sustenance Commission mobilized its forces to travel through the designated rest zones in search of food at small stores and ask for donations of grains, fruits, and vegetables from churches and NGOs. They went out to the markets and to social and labor organizations, asking for support. According to one marcher, "In Cochabamba, informal market vendors, small shop owners, social service organizations, and public university students donated staples in solidarity; they gave large quantities to the national-level movement, and then we would divide that up to the regional bases for food preparation."

The plan for food preparation along the march was similar to the official vision of an MST settlement like Pueblos Unidos or Tierra Prometida: work should be divided equally, but remains gendered. While living in both MST settlements, I took part in collective kitchens, pooling resources and borrowing from several households in order to cook elaborate meals. A well-known MST quotation is *"Sin participación, igualdad de las mujeres, no hay socialismo"* (Without participation, equality of women, there is no socialism). Such a statement, while part of an eloquent discourse, did not hold true in practice. MST members joked incessantly about women preparing the pot for the entire community. As one MST organizer said to (and about) me, "Well, it is time for the *gringa* to use her usos y costumbres. Use your rights as a woman [*Usa tu derecho como mujer*] and cook a North American meal for the whole family."

This joke provides but one window into a gendered division of labor in which women often prepared the pot of food for the entire movement. Yet such forms of work were often described as "labors of love," not recognized by leaders and rank-and-file members as real political work, but rather extensions of women's household duties along the journey. The behind-the-scenes physical labor performed by women can be thought of as the backbone of movement politics, however. As women prepared the food, they conveyed ideas about resisting capitalist food systems and structures of inequality. As one female member stated, "It is as if we transmit our ideas about what a society should look like through food preparation. We each throw our ideas into the pot. If capitalism encourages people to buy from large supermarkets and chain stores, we used food from local markets and vendors. If capitalism separates food production from the labor process by encouraging people to buy frozen foods, we forced people to engage in a collective labor process."

Just like their predecessor, Domitilia Chungara, the leader of the housewives' committee Siglo XX,[12] these MST campesinas balanced everyday work in the domestic sphere with a deep commitment to movement politics. Despite MST's public discourses of gender equality, all signs point toward a landscape of inequality. As we have seen in earlier chapters, corporeal forms of punishment took on a gendered and highly masculinized violence, women's voices were silenced in regional spaces, and here we see the very gendered division of labor in preparing food. The preparation of large pots of food to feed protestors was some of the backbreaking movement work, yet it was not recognized as the heroic work of the organization. MST members like Ponciano Sulca often spoke about the real MST *guerrilleros* (guerrilla warriors) as the men who occupied the initial settlements, seized private property, and set up encampments. These hypermasculine war stories, often performed for large audiences, circulated as social and political capital within the movement. And yet the women, who often used their social networks to organize núcleos, worked double shifts in the house and in the political scene, and labored for hours over meals, never received the same kind of dramatic performances of heroic courage and strength.

Beyond some of the physical gendered labor, women also enforced and reinforced the ideological base of the movement, especially the importance of using organic food and supporting local markets, as they called into question the spatial logic of capitalism along the march. From the organization of work and labor policies on plantations, to the separation of labor from food production and consumption, to individual choices regarding food preparation, MST women questioned and challenged the existing model. As Margarita Sulca noted, "We did challenge the model by supporting local vendors; MST members went to the little corner stores and shops, to the peripheral *zonas* (zones), to ask for food donations. We refused to support the big-business model, steered clear of supermarkets and other large chain stores. And the food we prepared, although it wasn't by any means a balanced meal, it was mostly organic." Gradually, the organization shaped a new reality through food rituals.[13] By cooking and eating together, they engraved political meaning onto the built environment. It did not matter, however, where they landed to eat—it could be the backwoods of the Chapare, or conventional centers of rest and relaxation along the way, or the main plazas where they seized political power.

The act of preparing food in many ways resembled the practice of eating. As people assembled the olla común in motion, they transported practices and cultural models from the west to the east and from their MST community to the side of the road. Yet these cultural forms were never reassembled wholly intact or in any standard form. Sometimes they were formed and shaped purely as a political imaginary, and they were always filled with much contradiction. Along the march, the olla común had to be assembled in an instant, and practices of eating—such as who gets served, how, and in what order—also had to become part of this mobile and flexible structure, which reinforced ideas about power, gender, and status within the political organization. While Catherine Allen (1998) and Mary Weismantel (1988) argue that food can be used to create and reinforce hierarchy, MST members, despite obvious gendered divisions of labor, used food rituals to erase difference. For example, Allen asserts that the order in which individuals receive coca offerings has much to do with their social status—high-status individuals should receive *k'intus* (coca offerings) before those of lower status (105). Weismantel notes a similar phenomenon in the Ecuadorian Andes, as decisions regarding the order of food distribution indicate one's position within the household. She states that the women control not only the order of serving but a veritable arsenal of tools for expressing their opinions of those they serve (179). In practice, the dishes offered yet another scale on which social worth could be measured. But while women in Weismantel's households inverted power structures and hierarchies by selecting bowl sizes and portions of soup, MST women tried to mitigate age and gender differences by privileging the underprivileged at mealtimes, attempting to arrive at some kind of egalitarianism. They served the elderly and disabled first, women and children second, international volunteers shortly thereafter, and then the remainder of the rank and file.

This practice of collective cooking and eating along the road sparked all kinds of conversations. Similar to the performance of ancient Andean mythical tales that encouraged the landless to occupy unused lands, these kinds of rituals in motion also triggered memories about land occupations and distinct struggles in their communities: How do you organize peasants locally, how do you teach them to move beyond individual needs and desires to the collective, and how do you inculcate the value of collective work and labor? These questions filled mealtime with political discourse and purpose. MST members and leaders often commented on the individual survival strategies of their compañeros and their frustrations associated with organizing poor peasants into MST núcleos. Just as cooking a meal is a process, so too is the building of a counter-hegemonic movement. In this instance, the microscopic processes of food preparation, exchange, and consumption aided the movement's larger intention to teach people the benefit of collective title, agroecological work, and labor in motion.

EMBODIED PRACTICES OF AYLLU COLLECTIVITY: SONG, DANCE, AND PERFORMATIVE CULTURE

Food preparation and eating can be thought of as part of the MST *místicas* (mystique)[14] in which the movement uses symbolic forms and rituals to create and reinforce a collective identity. Like some of the other cultural narratives, these rituals along the side of the road strengthened resolve and provided vitality in the struggle for land and a better way of life. The overlapping of responsibilities and actions eventually culminated in the act of eating a meal together and singing songs about land reform and action.

Eating and mealtime provoked not only conversations, but also festive celebrations, dancing, and what I call "embodied ayllu collectivity." Often, there is a disjunction between the very public performances and discourses of collectivity and the practices of hyperindividualism, promotion, and extension of agrarian capitalism. In MST settlements, as members are shaping an alternative politics, daily performances of ayllu democracy are also riddled with tensions and frictions that define this form of grassroots or indigenous citizenship, as discussed in Chapter 4. But how can we think about the improvisational performances, songs, and dances as deepening and illustrating a commitment to the collective, through physical and impassioned sensations and movement, as they function within grassroots politics? Sian Lazar (2008) discusses this as a shared sense of identity through movement. I would like to extend her idea of shared identity through dance to understand how these practices construct a collective and mobile citizenship through feelings, sensations, and emotions. Lazar draws upon performance studies and dance scholarship to illustrate how people become rooted and connected to place through movement. Michelle Bigenho (2002) develops the idea of "experiential authenticity," or the fleeting feeling of sharing the experience of a performance with others and thus becoming rooted to people and places through bodily movement and the achievement of performative oneness with sonorous events (23). Like Bigenho, I am interested in the mobility of ideas and cultural frames in and through such performances. Building a shared identity then is not necessarily about belonging to the highlands or lowlands, or claiming a particular geographical grounding, or even about rights to a particular MST settlement—rather, it is about an ideological and flexible political framing of cultural and territorial reclamation that can travel, be uprooted, and be reassembled through such practices.

One night, with stomachs full and plates still dirty, MST members grabbed a few guitars and began to sing. The dusk turned into a deep, dark night, and a shower of stars rained upon us, creating a natural spotlight. An MST organizer began: "I ask those present if they have thought for just one second that the land belongs to us, not to those who already have so much. I ask those present if they have thought for a second that it is our hands that work the earth, it is our sacrifice and labor that gives life to the earth. We must tear down the fence and show that the land belongs to me, to Pedro, to Maria, to Juan and Jose."

The music performed during and after a meal was yet another vehicle through which MST emotively animated and inspired its bases while reinforcing a particular leftist ideology. Simon Molina, the son of a miner from Potosí, spoke to me about how music and song were important to the dynamics of the movement, as illustrated through both tomas de tierra (seizing land) and marches or protests: "During the land seizure in Santa Cruz," he explained, "we played music, danced, and drank into the wee hours of the night in Yuquises because we had to be alert and ready for battle—music was a way to keep people entertained, occupied, but also engaged and inspired."

It served the same purpose in the backwoods during the march for land. MST members engaged with the music by swaying back and forth. Some were even moved to sing, and since the lyrics were unknown to audience members, they improvised the verses. Often, the lines captured the feelings of individual members of the group at that particular moment. They sang about the long journey, the loss of two compañeros in an accident, and the aches and pains in their bodies. And then they danced.

The dancing in the backwoods during the march was similar to the kind of intense and rhythmic fiestas of movement in settlements, illustrating the power of the songs and melodies to move people. The musical sounds shifted from region to region, from Chaqueño rhythms to Andean *Huaynos*. The sounds and beats of the Chaco were high-pitched and rapid, expressing vitality and hope born of energy. While there were constant distinctions in the spaces of political organizing—veteran versus new MST recruit, women's roles versus men's, rank and file versus leaders—the dance floor created an egalitarian place where differences were momentarily erased. Highlanders and lowlanders experimented with different dance moves; people who barely knew one another became partners on the makeshift dance floor, with one partner placing his or her head close to the other partner's chest, feeling the fast-paced heartbeat of a stranger turned friend. As the sweat dripped, the partners followed each other's synchronized steps. Dwight Conquergood (2002b) describes soundscapes[15]—often referred to as differing acoustic environments that might define our understanding of space or place—as complex and dynamic, carrying with them the liveliness and immediacies of reverberations overlaid by worlds of interanimation and gesture that escape the silent page. Located in these soundscapes of meaning and movement are subaltern performances that scholars often overlook and underestimate: "Subjugated knowledges have been erased because they are illegible; they exist by and large as active bodies of meaning outside of books, eluding the forces of inscription that would make them legible and thereby legitimate" (146). Through such soundscapes and dancing during the march, people shared parts of themselves and their histories, and it seemed as though they were calling for the agrarian revolution through their feet, their arms, and their rapid movements. They marked this rural space as their own, a kind of politicized territory belonging to MST, which they would leave in a few hours to continue on their journey.

Through songs and bodies dancing and sweating together, MST members practiced, tasted, and touched for a fleeting moment this idea of collectivity: body to body illustrated a deepening of roots between people and an overcoming or melding of difference, while feet stomping on dirt created sociophysical connection to the land and environmental surrounds. But this connection was not grounded in one particular place, for it had to be something that could travel through the bodies of the protestors. It was not solely about conquering a piece of land, but rather about reclaiming territory across geographical divides and reinventing the nation-state as part of a broader move toward recognizing indigenous peoples as the first inhabitants of the land. As Lazar (2008) argues, "If dance is a citizenship practice, then, the citizenship here is not an abstract status or category of belonging, but concrete, physical and embodied, involving a sense of collectivity which includes a common relationship to a place but which cannot be taken for granted. That collectivity is neither homogeneous nor uncontested; indeed, the community is constituted precisely through hierarchy and distinction and is split into smaller collectivities . . . the fiesta is a moment of intense local belonging and an expression of Bolivian identity" (143).

These mobile fiesta spaces then are about a new kind of citizenship[16]— not linked directly to community, ethnic group, or a particular locality, but rather concerned with the construction of a flexible framing of mixing and melding traditions and of reclaiming small-scale agrarian culture and alternative mechanisms of production, which are now all redefining movements' relationship to the state.

The movement throughout the march in columnas was perfectly choreographed and precise. There was not much creativity or improvisation as people walked and talked. But these times of rest, the sing-alongs and dancing deep in the forest, were improvisational. These times were about being out of order, inventing in the moment, adding to and adjusting, and making culture flexible. This represents some of the new creativity of movement building that has yet to be sufficiently analyzed. Perhaps it is in these spaces that new imaginaries and ideas about how to reassemble the socioeconomic and human environment are not only hatched but experimented with, critiqued, and elaborated (Escobar 2010).

This form of embodied and mobile claims of citizenship rights does not fit within a conduct frame, or the frame of governmentality where NGOs have unidirectionally influenced the shaping of movement-based ideology. Nor does this kind of model fit within the neoliberalization of consciousness (di Leonardo 2008), whereby broader political and economic forces have created highly individualized and self-help kinds of strategies (Gledhill 2005). Rather, this model points toward the possibility for building and creating new cultural and ideological forms and placing them in motion, taking them directly to the seat of power and transforming indigenous-state relations. Some of these spaces along the march are far from the eyes of the public, far from media attention, and far from international and transnational spaces of organizing. Yet they are valuable spaces for thinking about the imagination of movements and the construction of alternative models of politicking across regional, ethnic, and racial lines, and the possibility for incorporation of all of this into a new national body.

While these backspaces of the march might illustrate the out-of-order or improvisational capability of movements, MST members had to continue on the highly organized and precisely choreographed journey toward La Paz. The last part of this analysis looks at this movement of indigenous demands through national space, or as Nancy Postero (2007b) would describe it, how this physical movement of a rights-based discourse has broadened the meaning of democracy for all members of society (223).

RETERRITORIALIZING POWER AND RIGHTS
THROUGH CLAIMING NATIONAL SPACE

The last stage of the Fifth March occurred on November 27, when approximately two thousand MST members and lowland indigenous protestors arrived in this highland city of El Alto. From an altitude of 13,400 feet, the Alteños look down onto the adjacent city of La Paz, which sits in a crater-like bowl high in the Andes. In this overcrowded and congested urban area, one could barely move through the streets leading to *La Ceja*, the "brow" of the city, or main market area. Vendors filled the sidewalks, selling products ranging from electronic items to everyday household goods. Rundown hotels and *alojamientos* (motels) shaped the grim cityscape. Homeless people sleeping on the curb were a permanent fixture. Buses queued in an assembly-line fashion, waiting for passengers to board. Black smog from stationary vehicles created dark circles in the thin air, making it difficult to breathe. Garbage piled up in the streets, and there was no running water or sewage system; people simply lifted their polleras to urinate on the side of the road. The graffiti on the walls, "*Basta el reformismo del MAS, Revolución Maoista Ahora*" (Enough of the reformism of MAS, Maoist Revolution Now), enclosed the claustrophobia of the streets, the intense poverty, and the lack of public services in satellite cities like El Alto.

As protestors finally crossed the city limits, they were greeted by their Aymara brothers and sisters, union leaders and organizers, and neighborhood organizations. It was at this point that the protest scene grew from two thousand to nearly thirty thousand: the miners dressed in their classic garb with hardhats and sticks of dynamite, mothers outfitted de pollera with children on their backs wrapped tightly into colorful Andean shawls, and the many landless—some barefoot, others with worn-out sandals—who had walked from Oruro and Potosí braved the cold air of El Alto. In the midst of wiphalas rippling in the wind and the sound of *pututus* (ceremonial horns), the two groups, lowland Indians and highlanders, sealed a solidarity pact with the ritual sacrifice of a llama.

Neighborhood organizations and local schools came together to provide protestors with a place to sleep and eat. Food donations from local markets, neighborhood organizations, and even individual families flooded the open space of the university. Participants set up an olla común in order to provide food to this large group. Yet something was quite different this day. Members of mine workers' unions, neighborhood organizations, and federations filtered into MST's bases to share in the festivities. The march coordinators did not assign a particular group or núcleo to anyone, yet everyone found a place to eat. They shared ideas regarding organizing struggles and strategies, problems emerging in distinct parts of the country, and the importance of forging a larger campesino-indigenous movement, especially during moments like the passing of new legislation. Afterwards, their stomachs full, the demonstrators rested for several hours.

El Alto has been described as ground zero for many protest movements, especially national-level demonstrations to reclaim and recuperate natural resources such as water, gas, and land. This final site on the march served as the launching pad for governmental negotiations. Its location near the international airport and directly above the seat of government gave residents the power to stall all forms of business, both national and international.

At 5:00 A.M. the following day, the marchers organized into their columnas in order to descend into La Paz's main plaza, the Plaza San Francisco. As they walked down the slope, they sang "*Que se acabe, que se acabe esta marchasa*" (Finish, finish this long march). They arrived at their final destination at rush hour that morning,[17] cheered on by the thousands who lined the city streets to welcome them.[18] The old drummer who had led the entire march dropped to his knees, kissed the ground, and collapsed, exhausted. At that moment, the crowd broke into the Bolivian national anthem, placing emphasis on the chorus: "From our country, in a high-pitched voice, in glorious splendor we proclaim: We will die before we live and work as slaves! We will die before we live and work as slaves!" The song set the stage for what was to come: civil disobedience in the very heart of the legislative and executive seat of power. And this occupation of the plaza and the subsequent singing of the national anthem illustrated the impermanence of space. Indigenous Bolivians, as the original inhabitants of this space, demanded that their homes and communities be returned in order to decolonize the nation-state.

Such a powerful performance of pan-indigenous solidarity and nationalistic sentiment led to a public declaration by President Evo Morales supporting passage of the New Agrarian Reform Law. He asserted before the massive crowd, "This lucha for land and territory is the same as those of the ancestors of Tupac Katari, and we are still in this fight. We need to make this proposal legal today in order to begin to recover land that belongs to our ancestors. We will take back latifundio land . . . I am part of this struggle, I am part of you all . . . and I state, actually I declare before all of you that we will put an end to the unproductive latifundio."

As Nancy Postero (2007a) recently argued, Evo Morales's public discourses, while often evoking utopian visions of Andean culture, always serve a particular function: they negotiate spaces for social and political reform. In this particular instance, by invoking the struggle of his Incan ancestors, Morales stood in solidarity with the indigenous campesino movement and encouraged the protestors to continue marching to the Senate. As with the místicas performed by MST in the plaza of Cochabamba or in the backwoods of the valleys, Morales, as president of the republic, used performance to mark national space with meaning and open up a new arena for radical political change and agrarian reform, a theme to which I will return in the next chapter.

From the Plaza San Francisco, the massive crowd broke down into columnas one last time in order to seize the Plaza Murillo, the center of cultural and political power. As soon as they arrived, a well-known indigenous leader, Natalio Izaguirre, proclaimed, "We are staying here in the Plaza Murillo. We aren't going anywhere until these changes are passed. We are exhausted, sure, but we are here to reclaim our rights from those land speculators who have taken our lands all over the country" (Natalio Izaguirre, personal communication, November 2006).

The massed marchers remained in the plaza long after sunset. Some chewed coca for energy, while others sang revolutionary songs and danced into the night. Through their Andean dances, stories, and tales in the Plaza Murillo, they used highland indigenous culture as a conduit for reordering and cleansing Bolivian society of the stain of colonialism, which they believed had been further tainted by the evils of capitalism and neoliberalism (Rivera Cusicanqui 1987; Postero 2007b). Through occupying the very heart of political and legislative power, they began to infuse, mark, and redefine national space with an alternative vision of an indigenous counterpublic sphere (Stephenson 2002). Protestors turned the plaza into a tent settlement, thus galvanizing national attention and laying down roots in the very center of power. The thirty thousand people refused to move until they received a written contract: they wanted a statement confirming a new kind of agrarian reform, not a minimalist or conformist effort like the Agrarian Reform Bill of 1953, but a radical change.

As they marked this space culturally, the protestors also transformed the legislative and executive bodies of government through a spectacular demonstration of popular participation and indigenous culture. The senators could not ignore the sheer number of people camping in the Plaza Murillo,[19] and so the new agrarian reform bill finally passed through the Senate that very night. This act transformed grassroots ideas into essential legislation, which would benefit the poor as opposed to agrarian elites, and which would begin to undo a history of unequal landholding patterns. MST and other social movements "do not only want to be recognized by the state; they want their president to enact what philosopher Nancy Fraser calls a [radical] politics of redistribution" (Postero 2007a: 22). Recognition had been meaningful in the past, but MST realized that national and international recognition was not enough: true dignity and prosperity must be tied to significant material and structural change.

The march illustrated the power that grassroots movements now have in moving demands across geographical space in order to transform critical legislation. By carrying platforms on their backs, debating and discussing the laws en route, and conducting civil disobedience in the heart of power, they made visible their claims and placed just enough pressure on senators to pass the new agrarian reform bill. Their bodies—aching and bruised, scratched, beaten, and injured—became the repositories of new citizenship claims.

Yet what is interesting to note here is that such spectacular performances and demonstrations of culture and "radical change" do not always lend themselves to the intended conclusions. While indigenous movements in Bolivia have focused on constitutional reform and legislative claims for citizenship rights, what has become clearer in recent years is the increasing vulnerability of national legislation—even nation-states—as compared to transnational power and influence. This proves to be a crucial paradox of our time, particularly in regard to resource politics. Indigenous peoples and landless peasants place much faith in altering their national constitution; the reconstruction of laws proves deeply symbolic and material, as these communities seek to undo long histories of subjugation and racism. However, the question of the power of the state or even the power of laws remains murky, as transnational oil companies in Ecuador bulldoze over any environmental protection policies, as mining corporations in Bolivia disregard the new Rights of Mother Earth—which drew deeply on indigenous concepts in writing natural and legal rights on biodiversity, water, and clean air into the constitution—and as extractive practices continue to rely upon large amounts of water and destruction of environmental surrounds, all in favor of profit. Suzana Sawyer (2004), in the wake of the 1992 indigenous mobilization for land reform, was somewhat hopeful, arguing that "indigenous agency continually disrupted elite Ecuadorian national narratives rooted in, and routed through, the conquest . . . the act of capturing political space and challenging constitutional powers on this infamous day was a barbed indictment of colonialisms, imperialisms, and racisms, past and present" (222). I am less hopeful that such agency has the ability to undo these legacies of colonialism, imperialism, and racism.

This analysis now turns toward the role of movements like MST in Morales's Bolivia. While this march might have been illustrative of the ways in which movements make mobile their cultural practices, learn in motion, and bring demands to the seat of power, movements like MST have also been important to the rethinking of a nation. Yet fierce pushback from right-wing elites in the eastern region, working in collaboration with multinationals, led to the passing of a severely compromised constitution. The original proposals for redistributing land and wealth, implementing food sovereignty, and providing support to small-scale farmers dramatically shifted as elites managed, through similar forms of protest, to pressure the government to push their statutes through as written law. The next chapter then begins with the passing of the new constitution, yet traces back to the rightist resistance, which began with the public declarations of the New Agrarian Reform Law. The symbolic passing of land legislation in Bolivia has not eliminated the age-old power relations and the latifundio in the east, nor has constitutional reform provided material and structural support for small-scale farmers to survive off of organic production. So while movements might be redefining citizenship rights in the twenty-first century as cultural and symbolic rights, what structural and political-economic change has simultaneously occurred to heal these deep scars of colonial and neocolonial inequality?

CHAPTER SIX

A SOCIAL MOVEMENT STATE

Indigeneity in Morales's Bolivia and
a Compromised Constitution

The Ceja in El Alto is a bustling urban sector characterized by the rapid movement of people from the high mountains to the basin of La Paz. Many of the pedestrians are searching for microbuses, which line up one behind another, heading down to La Paz, the basin of the mountain. Most of the women, who have migrated from rural Andean communities to this urban, peripheral city, wear layered pollera skirts and bowler hats. The men dress in a range of hand-me-down or secondhand clothing, including warm winter coats and boots. The Ceja is usually congested; people shove one another to make their way onto the buses, while young boys or *ayudantes* (drivers' assistants) yell out the routes, shouting over one another as they compete to be heard. The air is always heavy and marked by thick clouds of pollution originating from the old Toyota microbuses. Hundreds of small-scale vendors set up along the Ceja, some selling black-market DVDs, others household items and goods, and still others cosmetics and everyday soaps and shampoos. Some vendors have their own *puestos* (informal stalls), while others simply set up cloth blankets on the road to sell their items. At first glance, this is a chaotic urban environment of marketplace competition and sale, hustle and bustle, but it is also framed by the majestic and serene mountaintop glaciers of Illimani.

As one walks along the *avenida* leading to the Ceja, one sees small restaurants and shops with images of the Aymara revolutionary Tupac Katari, the anticolonial hero who led an army against the Spanish in the eighteenth century and held the city of La Paz while under siege for four months. In the end, he was tortured and his body ripped apart by horses. Inside the municipal offices, such as those of the Alcaldía, or the Planning Department, hang more contemporary posters of Evo Morales, dressed in a blue suit with Andean fabric running down his chest, clenching his left fist. Appearing directly behind Morales, almost like a shadow, is Tupac Katari. Bold white lettering above their heads reads, "*Katari, La Rebelión . . . Evo, La Revolución*"; and gold lettering on the bottom of the

FIGURE 8. Tupac Katari poster hangs behind President Morales as he presides over final passage of the new constitution. Photograph by Eulogio Cortés.

poster proclaims, "Evo Morales Ayma, President of All Bolivians" (see Figure 8).

These signs of Tupac Katari are everywhere, graffitied on the cement walls of buildings, hanging as calendar images inside the makeshift homes of Alteños (people who live in the city of El Alto), and even sitting on the dashboards of microbuses. On a grander scale, close to the Ceja, stands a seven-meter-high statue of Che Guevara made of recycled scrap metal, peering toward the Christ the Redeemer statue, where the heart of Tupac Katari is said to rest. As legend goes, Katari's right arm was taken to Ayo, his left arm to Achacahi, one leg to Chulmani, and the other to Caquiaviri, but his heart is said to remain, embedded in the statue of Christ overlooking the city of La Paz. In the famous Inkarrí myth when the parts of his body reunite, he will rise, take back his kingdom, and restore harmony in the relationship between the earth and her sons. This rebirth of sorts will fulfill the promise he made at his death: "I will return, and I will be in millions." This phrase has become a popular quotation, picked up by movement activists, NGO officers, and even Morales, who proclaimed that the time has come for *pachakuti*: "*pacha*" (time and space) and "*kuti*" (upheaval or revolution). The term *pachakutí* has popularly been used to refer to a kind of cataclysmic reversal.

HISTORIC RECLAMATION AND THE PASSING OF A NEW CONSTITUTION

On January 31, 2009, nearly three years after the Fifth National March for Land and Territory, hundreds of activists gathered in El Alto to mark the passing of the new Bolivian constitution on a site that held great cultural and symbolic value. Initial cries to rewrite the constitution came out of the populist resource movements of the late 1990s and early 2000s. Part of Morales's 2005 presidential campaign platform promised to create a constituent assembly, responsible for rewriting the document and incorporating indigenous nations and peoples into the nation's legal framework. Comprised of movement activists, urban popular organizational leaders, and middle-class progressives and nationalists, this diverse group began their work on August 6, 2006, in the colonial city of Sucre. In the end, the proposed constitution would require that two-thirds of the 255 deputies or 51 percent of the Bolivian electorate support the document in a popular referendum. Due to sustained right-wing opposition, it took more than two and a half years to build this support for the constitution,[1] and even then, the final document was severely compromised from the initial movement proposals of the late 1990s to 2000s. The new constitution was finally approved by 61.43 percent of voters in a national referendum on January 25, 2009. As popular journalist Benjamin Dangl (2009) notes, "Among many other changes, the document empowers Bolivia's indigenous and Afro-Bolivian communities, establishes broader access to basic services, education and healthcare, limits the size of large land purchases, expands the role of the state in the management of natural resources and the economy and prohibits the existence of US military bases on Bolivian soil."

Despite the compromised legislation—which eventually incorporated a form of departmental autonomy and made several concessions on land tenure—movement activists continued to support the MAS Party and its leader, Evo Morales. They listened on a rather warm January day as he declared, "This is the second independence, the true liberation of Bolivia!" The speech was an important strategic performance, linking legislative shifts to historic indigenous claims to land, territory, and resources. Morales chose El Alto as the site for the signing of the constitution because the city had served as the base for both Katari's 1781 siege of Spanish-controlled La Paz and the more contemporary resistance movements of the 2000s, and therefore it had great symbolic value. Morales spoke at length of Katari's legacy, describing the passage of the new constitution as the continuation of a struggle sparked, in part, by Katari in his fight for indigenous liberation. In conclusion, he declared, "After 500 years of rebellion against invasions, against permanent looting, after more than 180 years of resistance against the colonial state, after 20 years of permanent struggle against the neoliberal model, today, on the seventh of February of 2009, a new Bolivia is born." As he finished speaking, his voice echoed across the altiplano.

This opening speech in El Alto illustrates the power and mobility of social movement tactics—the strategic use of historical memory and performance of Andean indigenous symbols and figures as a language of change and political transformation. These cultural shows, evoking the spirit of Tupac Katari as a guiding force, emerge directly out of Bolivia's resource movements, particularly those deployed by the Cocaleros and MST. This is not surprising, since Morales emerged from one of the most important resource movements of the twentieth century, the coca-grower resistance. The Cocaleros used a reified understanding of indigenous peoples as first or aboriginal peoples who had an inalienable right to cultivate coca[2] because of their deep historic, cultural, and territorial ties to it (see Grisaffi 2009). This strategy, similar to the one used by MST, excavated the reified and unchanging idea of the ayllu as an essentialized and pure indigenous community, based upon the values of reciprocity and redistribution and untouched by broader forces, as a platform for reconquering land and territory. Ayllu democracy then serves as an organizational structure for horizontal and participatory forms of grassroots citizenship and as a model for alternative ways of living and working the land. As we have seen, however, while the discourses and performances of pure indigeneity might advance broad-based movement goals, MST members' daily practices of democracy and agroecology are hybridized and are not fully realized in relationship to this vision.

In this chapter, I look at the use and mutability of indigeneity as a language for political transformation and legitimacy. This language has infused movement tactics and performances, which over time have scaled up to inform the construction of a new and inclusive state. The mobility of grassroots proposals and the performances of Andean indigeneity as a tool for reform contributed significantly to the solidification and extension of support for the MAS project. Morales's savvy use of cultural frames of reference evolved new forms of identification with the state. His performance of anticolonial heroes like Katari forged a shared historical and territorial narrative and promoted the construction of a collective identity, a partnering of sorts between movements and the state.[3] These cultural, historical, and territorial performances powerfully linked distinct groups of people to the idea of participating in decolonizing the state, as they see their own history and cultural practices informing the reconstruction of legislation and national forms of governance.

The language of indigeneity and cultural performances then became part of Morales's two-pronged agenda to "refound" and "decolonize" the state and to illustrate how such marginalized practices could become a part of a public discourse to create a new kind of Bolivia. Gustafson (2009b) has noted that "MAS bridges indigenous histories and territorialities which exert a decentralizing pressure and a discourse of plurinationalism charged with a deeply felt sentiment of popular nationalism, tied both to visions of a strong, developmentalist state and to active control over economic production, especially over Bolivia's strategic natural resources" (2009b: 254–55). Indigenous philosophical tenets, cultural ideas, and social models of territorialized governance might lead to a more robust recognition of indigeneity and, in turn, of how these tenets might transform law, economics, and forms of governance (Escobar 2010; Gustafson 2011).

With the gradual passage of his legislative agenda, Morales cemented his commitment to movements with a grandiose ceremonial or performative event. Thomas Perreault (2011) notes that many years prior to Morales's nationalization of gas, in 1996, during the second round of neoliberal reforms, a Bolivian journalist, Mirko Orgaz García (2002), referred to the privatization of Bolivia's hydrocarbons as the "Tupacamaruzación of YPFB [Yacimientos Petrolíferos Fiscales Bolivianos, state-owned oil company, YPFB]," in reference to the Inca leader Tupac Amaru, who was hung, drawn, and quartered by the Spanish in 1572. The mythical and historic linking of an administrative dismemberment to the quartering of the body of Tupac Amaru by colonial forces asserts and solidifies "Bolivian national identity, rooted firmly in Andean indigenous culture—an identity which transcends space and time" (Perreault 2011: 10). But more than this, it also links contemporary struggles over land, territory, and sovereignty to age-old colonial battles, whereby the quartering of an indigenous body can also be interpreted as part of a historic dismemberment leading to the breakup and expropriation of critical national resources—in other words, linking ideas about land, territory, and nationality to deep indigenous history and roots. When Morales nationalized gas in 2006, he also evoked the martyrs of the Chaco War fought in the 1930s between Bolivia and Paraguay over the Gran Chaco region, which was thought to have oil resources. Morales "rearticulated this contested region within a nationalist history, naming the state nationalization plan the 'Heroes of Chaco Decree'" (Gustafson 2011: 226). Morales's performances, in the context of legislative change and movement transformation, make use of indigenous and cosmopolitan visions as the historic rationale and justification for broad reform.

This combination of political and economic changes mixed with cultural performance as justification for overturning legacies of oppression and subjugation proves important to understanding why many social movements like MST continue to support Morales, despite the compromised status of his proposed legislation. Many movement activists say, "We support Morales. We *are* a part of the state" (Adolpho Chavez, personal communication, July 2010). While people privately might critique the contradictions, tensions, and struggles of this nation-state, they also refuse to *tumbarlo* (overthrow it), as they have done in the past with other neoliberal regimes. On one cold day in July 2010, up on the altiplano of Bolivia, I sat with several guerrilleros from the Gas Wars who spoke to me about their concerns with the Morales government. Roberto Mamani took the floor to describe his concerns: "We brought this government to power. Our protests, our demonstrations, and the lives we lost in October [referring to the Gas Wars in October 2003] really paved the way for someone like Morales to gain power. However, the demands that we put on the agenda in October 2003 have not been met. What we have rather is a reformist government that uses highland indigenous culture and promotes a symbolic politics. Sometimes, we talk about how this is very similar to the 1952 Revolution and the MNR's cooptation of peasant movements and uprisings in order to implement a conservative and imperialist agenda. At the same time, we realize that this might be our best option right now. What alternatives do we have?"

This discussion highlighted complicated new relationships of identification with the state, for Morales as a political figure was birthed out of Bolivian social movements, but movement activists—particularly MST activists—do not romanticize Morales's "decolonizing initiatives." Rather they point toward the contradictory uses of indigeneity solely to promote a reformist agenda. Yet what is most striking about this conversation is the fact that these gas warriors also realize the dilemmas and limitations of any change arc by noting that Morales might be the only option in this political and economic moment. Despite their frustrations, many movement activists continue to support the MAS agenda. Morales has been able to rally hundreds of thousands of people to defend legislation, particularly when it has been besieged by right-wing vitriolic attack. The ongoing national-level and constitutional struggles in Bolivia have largely been the result of sustained resistance from the eastern oligarchy, working in alliance with transnational U.S. agribusinesses like Archer Daniels Midland (ADM), Cargill, and Monsanto. Rightists in the east have also mobilized indigenous symbols and discourses in order to legitimize and "make authentic" their claims to regional autonomy. Their use of similar cultural and political tactics has been quite effective in stalling the new constitution and advancing their alternative legislative agenda, which is primarily centered on land (in direct opposition to the New Agrarian Reform Law) and issues of autonomy (indigenous versus departmental).

Just as Morales has masterfully crafted an Andean anticolonial narrative for "decolonizing the state," linking social movement demands to an overarching state-based agenda, elites have manufactured a shared historic, regional, and cultural narrative that connects distinct groups across race, ethnic identity, and class to an idea of departmental autonomy or independent statehood or regionhood, which in turn gives elites full control of the resources in their territorial domain.[4] Chapter 2 traced the ways in which elites, under new threats of indigenous power, held on to historic rights and privileges through ever-greater control of city centers and rural provinces; but what has not been discussed is that these elites have also been working on ways to build a broad-based movement, forge a collective identity, and scale their demands up to the national level. While discourses and performances of globalized citizenship rights through agribusiness parades and festivals proved effective in mobilizing Cruceño elites, the Right had to flexibly reinvent its narratives and performances in order to effectively block Morales. Reengineering the historic cultural, racial, and territorial tensions between highland "Collas" and lowland "Cambas," elites crafted a masterful tale of an oppressed region that had been invaded by Andean forces that relied upon antiquated, communitarian forms of economic relations, usurping their resources and revenue to build a social democratic and redistributive state.

RIGHTIST PERFORMANCES AS HISTORIC
AND TERRITORIAL RECLAMATION

Almost immediately after the Fifth National March for Land and Territory and the official passage of the New Agrarian Reform Law in November 2006, conservative elites in the eastern region created alternate forms of spectacular cultural performance and resistance. Fear helped to ignite and fuel the project to build the right-wing movement. Lowland Cambas feared that, with majority control, MAS could enact a radical agenda of communitarian development benefiting Morales's highland constituents and harming the interests of lowland elites dependent on speculative landholding and export-oriented industries. Thus, the right wing quickly mobilized its forces and organized opposition to the new agrarian reforms. Just as Morales used Andean symbols of Tupac Katari's struggle to redefine the nation as plurinational, right-wing elites had to politicize certain lowland cultural signs and symbols in order to validate their campaign for decentralized rule and place significant pressure on the government to stall or reverse such reforms.

This new movement was undergirded by lowland indigenous myth and history that previously had been scorned by the right-wing oligarchy. This historic contradiction is both interesting and curious. More to the point, while there had been a racialized rejection of certain kinds of Andean indigenous peoples by regionalists, they simultaneously appropriated and subordinated another kind of Indian, the Guaraní, whom they refer to as "Our Indians" (Gustafson and Fabricant 2011). Conservative elites in the nineteenth and twentieth centuries may have rejected the Guaraní as savages and antimodern, but civic committee members and agribusiness elites[5] now politicize historic tales of the Guaraní as having historically stood against the invasions of Andeans. For several weeks after the passage of the New Agrarian Reform Law, elites in the city of Santa Cruz organized hunger strikes in the central plaza. These strikes were joined to marches and demonstrations replete with signs and symbols of the Guaraní as lowland warrior, prepared to stand against invasions of highlanders and defend regionalism, sovereignty, and rights to territorial autonomy. This right-wing movement and narrative were similar to the coca growers' and MST's politicization of culture as homogeneous, whereby they claimed historic rights to land and livelihood. Regional elites also had to resurrect a similar origin story, one in which

Cambas who were under threat by the continued expansion of the Inca empire had to bring the Guaraní soldier back to life to protect their borders. Still, the hypermasculinized and warriorlike stance of the Guaraní had to be made mobile and flexible enough to incorporate the later arrival of European elites, working-class mestizo Cambas, and even productive Collas. Like the Guaraní warrior, these otherwise distinct groups had to come together to defend their territorial rights and spaces from Andean expansionism and from the usurpation and transformation of an independent, well-developed, and capitalist region into a part of a communitarian, social-democratic state.

And so, in their parades and performances promoting regional autonomy, Cambas evoked this myth of the Guaraní warrior who tried to stop the overwhelming force of Inca—or Andean—expansion in the sixteenth century.[6] In their reinterpretation of this event, they constructed performances that represented the Guaraní militia as refusing to fall to the powerful forces of the Inca army. Signs of the Guaraní were culturally transmitted, appearing on T-shirts and even autonomy paraphernalia. Distinct groups that live in the lowlands were increasingly drawn to this narrative because they felt personally threatened by Andean migrants' taking their lands, occupying city centers, and "stealing" limited jobs in a contracting economic environment.

More surprisingly, some Andean highlanders who had come to Santa Cruz in search of the "land of opportunity" and had done well also defended right-wing claims. In many cases, these relatively privileged Collas went beyond the generalized rejection of the highland Indian, which was part and parcel of autonomy platforms, choosing instead to distinguish between the "deserving" and "undeserving" Collas. This discourse of the noble and deserving savage defending autonomy in order to promote a particular capitalistic model of upward mobility was most evident in the Civic Committee meetings. In a women's Civic Committee meeting in June 2010 where members from peripheral barrios (El Plan Tres Mil and Villa Primero de Mayo) were organizing an autonomy parade and festival, a young Colla migrant dressed de pollera stood up and declared,

> Evo Morales humiliates us. . . . My name is Paulina Santos Vargas, and I come from Potosí, and I have lived in the land of the Oriente for a while. . . . This land has woken us up. We are able to eat well, to live well, and we have cars. He who works is able to have cars and land here. He who does not work, the lazy, the *maleantes* [bad asses]

who don't work, they won't have anything. . . . It is for this reason that we have to defend [as Colla women] this place we call Santa Cruz. We must fight with Rubén Costa [governor of Santa Cruz] for autonomy. . . . The people voted for him, and we must continue to support him and the autonomy battles here.

The young Colla migrant described the Santa Cruz department as a land of opportunity, and therefore she used the overarching discourse of autonomy in order to promote this model of economic development. Rather than employ a universalizing, racialized, anti-Colla discourse, she distinguishes between the good—the Noble Savage, who is productive and entrepreneurial—and the bad—the Nasty Savage, a political and militant Colla invading the lowlands. These militant Collas are the lazy ones, the maleantes who do not take advantage of the limitless opportunities and resources in the region.

The Guaraní warrior in this context does not simply pit highlanders against lowlanders, but rather reframes the legend as the "productive Indian" who now must defend the region that has become his second home against unproductive invaders seeking to benefit from his hard work. This land of opportunity has opened its doors and borders to Collas, providing market-based solutions to problems of inequality and poverty, and it is not their responsibility to support invaders looking for a quick and easy fix off of their backs. These powerful "pull yourself up by your bootstraps" discourses, or transpositions of structural problems of poverty onto individuals, create a discursive and ideological justification for elite control of city spaces and systemic exclusion of "militant Collas," whom they view as "perceived threats."

These discourses of defense have taken on a sweeping racialized and class-based dynamic, as many mestizo working-class youth in Santa Cruz have stepped up attacks on anyone who dresses de pollera or looks like an Andean Indian. They describe their present undertaking of the mythic work of the Guaraní warrior as a call to control Andean migration to the lowlands and protect city spaces from anarchy. Camba youth joined defense committees in the late 1990s and early 2000s to protect agrarian lands from MST invaders and city spaces against Andean expansionism. One such defense committee, UJC, became the subject of much controversy due to its militant and militaristic activities in support of the Santa Cruz autonomy movement and in opposition to the Morales government (Fabricant 2009). When I asked these Camba youth about their role in promoting autonomy and defending lands and spaces, one young man responded that he had to evoke the warriorlike spirit of the Guaraní in order to "defend democracy," adding, "We *must* protect this city and our provincial areas from anarchy" (UJC member, personal communication, May 2006). Just as Tupac Katari is often easily mobilized as sign and symbol of "plurinationality" and historic forms of reclamation for MST, elite symbols of "Our Indians," especially the Guaraní warrior, are mobilized as a powerful counternarrative to stop Andean migrations, which represent a threat to free-market capitalism. Such strategic uses of indigeneity then become the justification for either transforming the status quo (in the case of MAS) or protecting it (in the case of right-wing regionalists).

This kind of politicization of indigeneity, whether the narrative of the Andean revolutionary or militant Indian standing up to colonial forces in El Alto or elite tales of the Guaraní Indian resisting Inca expansionism, signifies how history and cultural forms can be excavated, remade, and politically recycled by distinct movements. As noted earlier, Morales's use of Andean indigeneity has become part of his broader agenda or initiative to legitimize new forms of statehood. The evocation of revolutionary figure Tupac Katari, whose legacy represents the possibility of a rebirth of the indigenous masses to overthrow colonial powers, solidifies Morales's relationship to social movements and dramatizes the passing of the Constitution. Alternatively, the Guaraní warrior has been reconstructed by rightists to promote a platform of decentralized autonomy, protection of private property interests, advancement of market-based economics, and business models of resource extraction. These opposing factions' detached and disembedded uses of indigeneity have created an open canvas on which movement actors can paint their versions of native narrative in order to give their positions legitimacy. These uses of indigeneity can easily erase the real story of conquest and subjugation, slave labor conditions, and rotating regimes of power and violence, placing European Cambas and agrarian elites in a space of victimization and the highland Indian and MST occupiers in a place of power. The erasure of history and cultural, material, and territorial ties poses a significant threat in an era in which mobilization is tied to the power of a narrative and resources and environmental landscapes are being radically altered and politically contested.

Still, rightists of Santa Cruz had to build other symbolic structures onto the narrative of "Our Indian" if they were to scale up their struggle from the regional to the national level and pose a significant threat to new forms of statehood designed by indigenous peoples. Thus, the right wing came up with its own embodied and spectacular forms of "enacting democracy." One can draw several parallels between leftist social movement tactics, such as the March for Land and Territory, and elite performances of "direct democracy," which featured indigenous people presenting their demands and claims in the seat of power. In effect, the structures of direct citizenship developed by the Left were being appropriated by the Right. The intention was to orchestrate events that represented lowland groups taking matters into their own hands, making visible and bold their demands and mobilizing collective identities of shared regional, cultural, and ethnic affiliations publicly in order to pass critical legislation.

Importantly, agrarian elites had to rally enough people to draw attention to the fact that their battles were also a just and democratic cause. This political show demanded the mobilization of the same kinds of cultural symbols deployed by the Left. In this instance, the symbols were enacted by youths sporting T-shirts, some of which read "*Iyambae*"— roughly, "We are a pueblo without a ruler" in Guaraní—and others featuring the face of Evo Morales inside a large circle with black cross running through it and drops of blood dripping from the image, indicating that his regime was yet another kind of violent dictatorship (see Figure 9). Yet the organizers of the movement understood that their claims could only be legitimated through the materialization of a spectacular gathering of half a million people, which was popularly referred to as the *cabildo del millón* (or town meeting of a million people) at the Christ Statue in Santa Cruz,[7] to dramatically respatialize matters of governance from the president of the republic to regional political figures (see Figure 10). This was just one of many creative tactics of "embodied democracy"[8] intended to create enough pressure to tip the balance of power in favor of the right-wing Camba oligarchy movement. Governor Costa ended the cabildo for autonomy with a proclamation, and asked the participants, "If the Constituent Assembly approves a political constitution of the state that violates the *ley de convocatoria* [law of assembly] regarding the two-thirds majority vote and the referendum for autonomy, do you stand against such an illegal constitution? Do you give full and total power to the governor of Santa Cruz to implement a decentralized regime that allows for a social-democratic state of rights?" Each time, the crowd shouted a hearty "Yes!" in reply.

FIGURE 9. Anti–Evo Morales
T-shirt worn by a Camba
attending a cabildo.
Photograph by the author.

The leaders motivated the audience at the event through chants and the rhythmic language of call and response. This discursive sing-along climaxed with a frenzy of popular votes for a new autonomous Santa Cruz government, which ultimately resulted in the de facto transfer of power to the governor and Civic Committees, with a mandate to implement a new constitution for an autonomous nation severed from the western highlands. Although the autonomy statutes enacted through this cabildo and later public elections were ultimately held to be illegal by the Supreme Court of Bolivia, the force of the autonomy movement and its pressure tactics convinced the Morales government to negotiate. Most important, this event put Santa Cruz's autonomy movement on the national agenda.

Cabildos such as this are political rituals, not unlike the spectacular protest marches described in the previous chapter, that transform vague ideas into statements of dramatic clarity. Signs and symbols of historic and territorial connections to the region of Santa Cruz, embodied and plastered onto mestizo Camba bodies—such as the green and white Santa Cruz flag, which appeared as painted graffiti on bare chests and heads[9]— is not unlike the rich symbolism used by indigenous protestors on their

FIGURE 10. Camba youth holding flags of Santa Cruz at the Gran Cabildo.
Photograph by the author

twenty-eight-day sacrificial march—the wiphala flag, red MST flags, and symbols of agrarian reform. Singing songs glorifying the beauty and productivity of Santa Cruz, telling stories of the historic marginalization of the region, and displaying new embodied forms of democracy, participants in cabildos make abstract concepts visible and concrete. Over time, these symbols, as part of a larger movement, were translated into legislative proposals—a palpable manifestation of this political formation's vision of justice. To paraphrase Victor Turner (1969), justice lives only in performance, only so far as its rituals are ongoing concerns. Protestors in Santa Cruz, including a fair number of highland migrants, came away from these events feeling that justice had been served. The rituals effectively linked cultural differences, historic reclamation, and contemporary resource battles to structures of democracy and justice, independent of the nation-state.

These tactics were quite successful, as the Constituent Assembly was paralyzed for months. Finally, in February 2007, MAS and the right-wing political parties reached a settlement in which each article of the Constitution would be approved by two-thirds of the commission in charge of it, and then by the entire body, concluding with a public referendum for final recognition of the full text. With this compromise, the Assembly ended its seven-month break and began its work on the content of the constitution.

As Postero (2010) notes, the tensions that were present at the Assembly's beginning never lessened. Commissions assigned to tackle the challenging issues of land reform and autonomy (both departmental and indigenous) tried to work amid constant argument. After a failed recall referendum in August 2008,[10] these tensions escalated in early September into what Morales termed a "civic coup" (*golpe cívico*), which culminated in an attempted overthrow of his administration (see Gustafson 2008; Fabricant 2011). Autonomy activists seized state buildings, burned several down, and stole important documents from NGO offices.[11] Following the unsuccessful coup attempt, the U.S. ambassador to Bolivia, Philip Goldberg, flew to Santa Cruz to meet with Governor Costa, one of the leaders of the autonomy movement and Morales's antagonist. Due to these secret meetings and the United States' regionalist alliances, Morales expelled Goldberg on September 10, 2008, declaring him persona non grata for having conspired against democracy. Goldberg's expulsion sparked right-wing violence on September 11, the thirty-fifth anniversary of the overthrow of Salvador Allende, Chile's democratically elected president. Regionalist elites in the lowland department of Pando opened fire on Morales supporters, wounding hundreds and killing thirteen campesinos (see Gustafson 2010; Soruco 2011).

Unintentionally, this blatant and spectacular violence directed at indigenous communities and poor farmers created a groundswell of popular and global support for the new constitution, and international organizations sided with Morales. The shock of this event turned the tide of public opinion and led to negotiations between the state and the autonomy movement leaders. In a few weeks, they had crafted a negotiated constitutional settlement whereby all parties agreed to put the document to a public vote. MAS, however, had to make several substantial concessions, primarily due to oligarchic interests on land reform, grandfathering in existing large landholdings and limiting Morales's ability to hold office indefinitely.[12] In exchange, departments won limited autonomy[13] and the ability to administer their own revenues (Postero 2010). The referendum took place on January 25, 2009, and the constitution passed with 60 percent of the vote.

FRICTIONS WITHIN A SOCIAL MOVEMENT STATE
AND A COMPROMISED CONSTITUTION

Over time, the pushback and creative politicking by the right wing led to what many refer to as a compromised constitution. While social movements were instrumental in shaping the new legislation, and Morales often called upon activists as a force to defend the legislation, their initial proposals and ideas were significantly compromised because of powerful oligarchic resistance and reach. It was within this context that the national constitutional concessions were negotiated. Perhaps most dramatic were the concessions made on land tenure. MST's strategy, as discussed in prior chapters, had been to attack the center of oligarchic economic power in the east by seizing latifundio land. Movement members physically embodied their protest, squatting on unproductive land and in turn pressuring government officials to survey and redistribute property as part of a state-based policy. Due to this sustained political practice in the eastern region and MST's successes as a national-level movement, the New Agrarian Reform Law legitimated the seizing and redistribution of much of the unproductive land in the east. In turn, oligarchic elites saw this legislation as the most threatening to their economic power because it directly challenged their rights to private property and limited the possibility for expansion of monocultures and other export-oriented products.

The first and perhaps most devastating concession for movements like MST has been the administration's refusal to implement the state's right to militantly seize unproductive land from latifundios in the east. As Sinclair Thomson (2009) remarked in an interview:

> The final constitution was the outcome of struggles between popular social forces and the government and oligarchical interests in the lowlands . . . and this constitution is disappointing for indigenous peoples. The Constitution does not allow for the redistribution of existing agricultural estates. The vote on Sunday has set a new limit on the size of agricultural properties. Right-wing forces based in the lowlands were very concerned about any kind of agrarian reform happening as a result of the political process in Bolivia. And they were fighting tooth and nail to prevent the redistribution of existing lands in the country. And in the end, in the final

negotiations between the government and the Right . . . the government made a major concession.

The state's retreat was especially disturbing to movement leaders because of the concessions that were written into the legislation earlier. It is important to articulate the legislative strictures of constraint on such seizure. As Fernando Garcés (2011) notes, "the most serious issue of this shift in relation to land is that . . . individual holdings that are now restricted to five thousand hectares are not retroactive" (62). This essentially means that existing landholdings of about five thousand or more hectares are not subject to expropriation and redistribution, essentially sustaining the age-old and highly unequal landholding patterns in the east. The government conceded on this point in order to bring political opposition into some kind of consensus to approve the referendum on this draft of the constitution. According to Thomson, "The MAS virtually lost control and legitimacy in the lowland parts of the region [in 2006–7]. So I think it made this concession in order to try to reconstitute legitimacy and authority in the country as a whole and leave some concrete legacy in the form of the constitution."

Another source of movement disappointment was that Morales convinced MST to work alongside the government on indigenous and collective land titling instead of continuing to seize land through militant strategies in the Oriente. More militant leaders felt betrayed by the outcome of this bargain. Garcés (2011) might refer to this as the "domestication of the indigenous" (47). While he is essentially referring to the state-based co-optation of indigenous forms of autonomy, originally crafted by the Unity Pact, the same language of pacification or domestication of militant movements can be used when describing how landless movements have had to surrender to the compromised politics of the state. Since Morales assumed office, they have been encouraged to stop seizing or occupying latifundio lands in the east, but the constitution has not officially recognized the need to take back preexisting haciendas and lands. Despite the fact that the latifundio continues to exist, MST has abided by this, hoping to title lands to indigenous peoples as collective property rights. Morales pacified these more militant movement tactics in order to maintain a solid pact between movements and the state—currently, they advance his agenda instead of working against it.

In regard to land, Miguel Urioste (2010) has several recommendations for improving the legal framing of the agrarian reforms. First, the state needs to explicitly add articles strengthening public institutions like INRA, which have been historically weak, disorganized, and lacking in effective systems that help track land ownership. By and large, such institutions have worked to benefit and expand the interests of regional elites. Secondly, the flow of international and transnational dollars needs to be controlled and directed. Historically, international cooperation has dismantled and weakened the capacity of the state to intervene, so if Morales wants to build a strong and centralized state, these transnational corporations must also be controlled, regulated, and monitored. Third, for a real agrarian revolution, the center and source of economic power—large-scale landholding—needs to be attacked. Morales must begin to actively advance a political agenda that includes seizing the lands of oligarchical elites. Another weakness of the land reforms has been the lack of financing for productive infrastructure (e.g., housing, access to health care and education, roads, irrigation systems, electrification, and credit). This was evident in and through the daily struggles of Pueblos Unidos. Consequently, a fourth policy prong must emphasize state investment and rural development. Fifth, and perhaps, most important, this administration needs to combat land-grabbing, which continues to be a major problem in the Oriente. Despite proposals to support movements like MST, which in fact has resulted in support for seeds, infrastructure, and technology, there has been insufficient control and regulation of land hoarding. In part, this is a consequence of oligarchical power. In addition, it is a product of a dynamic global economic demand for alternative sources of energy leading to urgent and aggressive searches for food crops that can be turned into agrofuels or the production of cash crops in peripheral areas of South America. For example, the promotion of a biodiesel market has also been part of a dynamic political economic process and has been accompanied by further consolidation of unequal landownership, deforestation, expansion of monocultures, and new forms of accumulation by dispossession (D. Harvey 2003) or the forced expulsion of peasants from lands (Urioste 2010).

If Morales continues to inadvertently support land appropriation by the oligarchy for biodiesel industries and not simultaneously create strict regulations regarding land seizure or redistributions to dominant economic interests, his administration will continue to foster uneven geographical development, social and economic inequality, and intensifying political instability. As Urioste (2010) writes, "It is a perverse consequence of free trade agreements, of the immorality of investors and countries that move between two codes: the tiny foreign aid flows for development on one side (including the Millennium Development Goals of the UN) and the huge subsidies to the financial sectors which caused the global crisis. . . . Land grabbing is a disastrous modernization of colonial relations of dependence that will enhance food security for rich and emerging countries at the expense of worsening conditions of poverty and malnutrition in poor countries" (7).

FOOD SOVEREIGNTY AND STATE SUPPORT
FOR DOMESTIC FOOD MARKETS

Another problem beyond the constitutional concessions has been the overwhelming influence of transnational corporations on Morales's form of state-making. This dynamic has ultimately weakened the possibility of enforcing radical legislation or reforms. Jeff Webber (2011) describes this continued dependence on transnational corporations as part and parcel of Morales's "reconstituted neoliberalism" whereby he continues to rely upon the extraction and exportation of primary raw materials, such as mineral wealth and hydrocarbons (227). The process of extracting and industrializing raw materials occurs in direct partnership with transnational mining, petroleum, and agribusiness corporations. Within this compromised context, the state has negotiated a percentage of resource wealth for redistributive purposes. By working in alliance with multinational corporations, Morales is constrained in carrying through on his constitutional or legislative proposals regarding reinvestment in small-scale agriculture, developing domestic markets, or protecting the environment, because this model of extraction continues to rely upon the exploitation of workers, lands, and natural resources, all in the interests of private capital. More concretely, while many of MST's ideas regarding reclaiming control over seeds and food sovereignty made their way into the new constitution, the overwhelming presence of multinational corporations in the east means that support for a model of agriculture that relies upon genetically modified products and large-scale hypermechanization of farms will continue. To enforce legislation reclaiming food as the right of people—specifically, allowing local communities to decide and implement their own agricultural policies for sustainable production and distribution—will require a new level of statecraft and protectionism. Working hard on such proposals as food sovereignty and the right to food at a grassroots level and launching them into physical and legislative motion during the twenty-eight-day march from the lowlands to La Paz paid off for organizations like MST when these items were included in several articles of the constitution. Article 16, for instance, states that all people have the right to food and water, and the state has the obligation to guarantee food security through a healthy, adequate, and sufficient diet for the entire population. According to the FAO (Food and Agriculture Organization), this inclusion is a result of the efforts between the FAO and the Bolivian government. The April 2007 conference and training that resulted from this union, "Basis for Constitutionalizing the Right to Food," and the discussion between the FAO and the Constituent Assembly were paramount to the inclusion of food in the new constitution. The document also recognizes food sovereignty in Articles 310 and 404. Article 310 promotes economic democracy and the achievement of food sovereignty for the population by requiring state companies and state-owned enterprises to provide Bolivians with rights to natural resources and strategic control of production. It also requires them to "promote economic democracy and the achievement of food sovereignty of the people." Article 404 touches on the importance of sustainable rural development through its emphasis on food sovereignty and security. Moreover, part 3 of the constitution, under the heading "Integrated Sustainable Rural Development," deals with a fundamental part of the economic policies of the state, which is to give priority to those efforts that promote common economic undertakings and the assembly of rural people. Its emphases are on security and food sovereignty: increases in productivity and sustainable agricultural practices, livestock, manufacturing, agroindustry, and tourism; the ability to compete commercially; the articulation of internal structures of agricultural production and agribusiness; the achievement of better conditions of economic exchange of the rural productive sector in relation to the rest of the Bolivian economy; the significance of and respect for indigenous peasant communities; and the strengthening of the economy of small-scale farmers.

Once again, we see the radical ideas of movements reflected within this new constitution. The contradiction, however, is that the passages regarding food sovereignty will be radically compromised if Bolivia continues to remain deeply embedded in transnational flows of resources and dollars. In June 2011, the Morales government presented to the Bolivian Congress a legislative measure to reduce the use of genetically modified foods. Until now, genetically modified seeds were allowed only for some export-oriented soy crops. Simply constraining GMOs however, is not going to reduce the dependency upon chemical inputs and international or trans-national influence in agribusiness. There has been too much pressure from external global forces, combined with regional might, for Morales to resist, relatively detached as he is from the movements that gave his political career a powerful arc. Multinational agribusinesses stand against the proposed agrarian and food reforms, just as corporations like Cargill and ADM, which have control of the soybean and sunflower production in Santa Cruz, and John Deere, Monsanto, and Calgene promote genetically modified seeds. This has placed a significant amount of pressure on their business affiliates in Santa Cruz to maintain Bolivia as a friendly, open market for agroindustrial development. As one MST leader noted, "The government is fomenting the production of GMOs . . . but as campesinos this does not convince us as the best way to produce or work the land. We want to be able to certify our seeds, the native seeds that we are produc-ing. However, the government does not have the strength, the economic resources, or the power to limit the use of these GMOs" (MST-Ichilo repre-sentative, personal communication, July 2011).

Clearly, it has been very difficult for Morales to independently undo the legacies of monoculture export-oriented models, which are detrimental to sovereignty over food and natural resources. Bolivia is a country with much debt and little national revenue, and it does not have much choice when it comes to continuing neoliberal trade policies and supporting the export of cash crops in the lowlands. This lack of decision-making latitude in turn undermines Morales's projects of collective land reforms and agroecological approaches to farming. While food sovereignty might be written into the constitution, the legal framework of a nation-state alone does not provide sufficient resistance to the pull of powerful trans-national corporations and businesses in shaping industrial choices, developing and instituting international regulations, and forging power-ful political connections. Even with strong social movements, regulation and development outside the neoliberal framework are increasingly dif-ficult in this political and economic climate.

MST and the Vía Campesina have responded to this complicated issue of food sovereignty in the constitution by pressuring the state to strengthen its regulatory capability. As Vía Campesina representative Ramiro Tellez (2007) wrote:

It will not suffice that this principle be written simply into the new constitution, be named in new laws or given the status of a ministry or some other governmental program. The political will of the State will be necessary to deepen a genuine comprehensive agrarian reform, to rescue and respect our native seeds by not allowing the introduction of GMO seeds, that will support the productive culture of the small and medium producers. . . . There must be guarantees of markets for peasant and indigenous products but by means of a fair market for the people. Above all the human being should be at the center of development for which they should receive adequate social services such as health and education and a healthy and adequate diet.

As we have seen in this chapter, the same kinds of tensions that affect grassroots movements—legacies of race, racism, uneven geographical development, unfair trade, and market economies that support large-scale development—also define the contradictions of the Morales state, which struggles to implement progressive policies. Morales's efforts to reroute control and reinvest in small-scale producers clearly remain deeply entangled in historic and more contemporary practices of international and regional capital. While he might have assumed a certain amount of political power, economic control remains in the hands of the oligarchical elites in the lowlands who successfully placed enough pressure on his administration to gain significant concessions in the constitution and in their international economic interests. Admittedly, the legal advances of movements are often minimized by the multinational and transnational corporations that continue to define the economic and productive model of state-based redistribution, which is dependent upon primary resource extraction. And this narrative of movement building, statecraft, and capitalist response, as well as ongoing global development, bring us back full circle. More to the point, global capitalistic interests, combined with regional elite investments in the extraction of primary materials for an external market, continue to undermine indigenous territorial rights, alternative utopian projects, and the long-term prospects of environmental sustainability. As noted, this model inherently relies upon the destruction of environmental surrounds, the rerouting of natural flows, and the ultimate displacement of small-scale farming communities.

While indigeneity as a language and discourse of rights has provided opportunities for new kinds of alliances and solidified allegiances between grassroots movements and the state, it has not structurally altered people's material realities. Many rural indigenous communities,

MST settlements, and urban peripheral barrios are barely surviving without the appropriate forms of state protectionism and radical redistribution of wealth promised by the MAS regime. MST's initial hope that this government would seize and redistribute lands, provide critical material support for agroecological projects, and build domestic markets has not yet come to fruition. Thus, discourses of indigeneity continue to represent a powerful pull that mobilizes and, over time, creates an oppositional politics. However, this oppositional movement politics is falling short in both the development and implementation of its vision. When these indigenous-based performances are not linked to sustained national, regional, and local reinvestment and programming, they fail in their transformational potential at the level of practice. Indigeneity has, at times, simply been used as an empty signifier to promote a model of development that continues to place its core faith in the capitalist market as the principal engine of growth and industrialization. Clearly, this model has not reduced or altered historic forms of inequality and uneven geographical development. The Morales period is one of high rates of export-led growth, based in hydrocarbons and mining minerals, and low rates of spending. While government revenues spiked, social spending decreased, and rates of poverty and social inequality showed little alteration. Precarious, flexible, and unprotected labor conditions have remained in place, as there have been few jobs created outside of the informal economy (Webber 2011). Indigenous-based discourses and platforms, if not tethered to a concrete economic plan of national development and redistribution, job creation, and protectionism, remain only another distant, abstract language of political transformation.

So where does this leave us? Jeff Webber (2011) might suggest that instead of romantically aligning with Morales or the MAS party, as many left-wing academics have done, North American scholars and activists should form new alliances with the truly exploited and oppressed, "the real revolutionary and anti-imperialist forces," who while demanding decent wages and better working conditions may also be standing against the Morales administration. This suggestion, however, fails to recognize that the same contradictions riddling Morales's government are likely to appear in these so-called anti-imperialist forces. As we have seen through extensive analysis of MST and other organizations, although many projects of social movements have worked at a grassroots level, these movements have failed to develop solutions for restructuring the state or disentangling Bolivia from international and transnational webs of control and power.

Instead of concluding on this rather grim note, I return at the end to some of MST's initial proposals for working the land and reinventing socioeconomic relations. While indigeneity was a tool used to promote progressive agroecological projects, it also effectively linked culture, race, and ethnicity to an economic and agricultural agenda. Further, its creative and flexible strategies of moving demands across space have reshaped our understandings of how the grassroots can influence state-making. While the Right quite effectively appropriated similar strategies, slowed the pace of reform, and ultimately compromised Morales's political power, there might be forces that are beyond their control. I return to the radical possibilities of social movements working in collaboration with a state in a moment of new ecological crisis, which offers both a challenge and an opportunity for moving such collaborative work to the next stage of development.

Critically, MST and other indigenous social movements have become increasingly concerned with the topic of climate change. Their frame makes the explicit connection between greenhouse gases in the air locally and the fact that the global North's burning of fossil fuels is increasing global average temperatures, which has greatly affected poorer and more vulnerable countries in the global South like Bolivia. MST has been concerned with some of the effects of climate change, which have included increasing floods and droughts in the lowlands, affecting food production, food security, and sovereignty. Movement leaders have declared that the expansion of the large-scale and mechanized model of agriculture will only exacerbate such problems, and they have indicated that little time remains to undo or possibly reverse such dramatic alterations. Their platforms, strategies, and even organizational capacities will be tested as they confront greater challenges. Simultaneously, however, they realize that the language, symbolism, and contemporary power of indigeneity must be linked to concrete plans for sustainability, preservation, and models of adaptation. One question that is being asked by movement leaders is how and in what ways Andean, pre-Columbian forms of working the land and conserving water can provide solutions to these problems. Their preexisting, though tense, relationship with the state may also prove critical in the next stage of creating more robust and popular platforms for change. In effect, MST's prior experiences—building its power through the historic reclamation of indigenous identity, creating collaboration with government officials, and proposing alternative forms of resource extraction and new possibilities for economic development—may well be the foundational elements of the next stage of movement politics working to address and solve a burgeoning series of ecological crises. I end, then, with the idea that political-economic and ecological crises could possibly lead to new forms of creativity, innovation, and ways of governing.

CONCLUSION

Revisiting Indigeneity in Resource Politics
and the Battles That Lie Ahead

This book has examined how landless and dispossessed peoples have redefined our understanding of citizenship in the twenty-first century through their elastic redefinition of Andean indigenous cultural forms, which in turn have come to restructure socioeconomic relations and forms of governance. Significantly the language of indigeneity has also greatly informed the creation and building of a new plurinational state, where native peoples have been critical to remapping a national agenda.

Historically, indigenous peoples have been on the margins of the state. This point is most vividly illustrated by indigenous people's being denied the right to vote or participate in national politics until the mid-twentieth century. This new era of resource crisis,[1] however, has brought with it a turn toward indigeneity as an idiom of change, transformation, and an alternative political-economic model. In part, the transition and use of indigeneity as a movement force for change can be traced to the earlier era of denial of citizenship rights. Interestingly, that epoch was also marked by the transformation and consolidation of communal lands into private property—part of this era was defined by the state gaining more power and control over native peoples through the breakup of historic territorial ties. Shifting regimes of power throughout the nineteenth and twentieth centuries were accompanied by new forms of pacifying and suppressing indigenous peoples, whether through control of land, community spaces, places of learning, or even their bodies. These threads of oppression and subjugation were ultimately woven into the Bolivian state-making agenda, which sought to eliminate the rich history of indigeneity from centers of power and control. It was not until the late 1980s and early 1990s that what had been rendered invisible in an earlier era was reshaped and translated into a dominant political practice. Indigeneity offered a language for negotiating new relationships with the state. The harsh effects of neoliberal reforms, which consequently intensified forms of inequality, displacement, and poverty, forced otherwise distinct groups to cohere politically across regional and historic differences. This period of social and political consolidation of both political grievances and historic identification in large part served to make their claims generalizable. As neoliberal reformers marched forth, armed with the magic of market discourse as the solution to poverty and inequality, distinct indigenous groups came together, forging an alternative language of indigeneity as resistance to the free market capitalist model, which was perceived to be producing growing displacement, exploitation, and misery.

The shifting ground of both economic globalization and its political arm, neoliberalism, when combined with the multicultural turn in the 1990s, helped to pave the way for a new and explosive politics of land reclamation and reappropriation. Lands—in many cases, large extensions of land in the east—were turned into large-scale and export-oriented sites of production, which ultimately removed many small-scale and migrant farmers from the production process. Neoliberalism in urban areas was often characterized by a slashing of the state budget and antilabor legislation. This model of economic austerity and privatization resulted in a draconian slashing of a cross-section of services and a systematic denial of rights to workers and landless peoples. These trends, in combination with the rise of a powerful, regional oligarchy in the late twentieth century, further marginalized indigenous people in their relationship to the land and to their living and working arrangements within the city. Santa Cruz represents perhaps the most powerful example of the denial of citizenship rights that continues to define indigenous people's subordination and alienation.

MST, which emerged in response to these conditions along with other Bolivian social movements of the 1990s, embodies a new form of insurgent citizenship. It is through the politics of building a mass movement that dispossessed laborers have taken matters into their own hands—for example, by occupying latifundio lands, pushing the limits of legality and rights to private property. If the state was prepared to turn a blind eye to the massive accumulation of land by single families in the Oriente, then an independent resistance was required, with a militant movement politics that offered the opportunity to reoccupy land and reassert historic property rights. However, with the absence of an effective state or even a regional body of governance that might protect landless peasants, movements like MST had to invent their own way of controlling and protecting semi-autonomous occupations and eventual settlement sites. Reclaiming lands without effective means of control would only fail, particularly in this neoliberal era of governance with its ever-greater forms of "inse-curity," such as the hypermilitarization of particular coca-growing areas of the Chapare brought about by U.S. coca eradication policies, or the global-regional power of the agribusiness model in the east, whereby powerful elites can hire paramilitary groups to protect their lands from "invaders" like MST.

Within this context, the culture or language of indigenous ways and customs became necessary to implementing a political and agrarian practice of redistribution. In this way, culture became a form of commu-nal and agrarian protection—a shield, if you will—from destructive dis-course and ultimately a way to form a common identity in opposition to the global-regional forces placing new pressures on peasants' ability to survive and sustain themselves. As we have seen through the case of Pueb-los Unidos, these indigenous discourses emerge from both grassroots resistance and global dynamics, which transcend national borders—con-sider, for instance, international and national NGOs, indigenous social movements, and transnational peasant conglomerates. Over time, how-ever, this language of cultural identity must be anchored to a place and historic moment and thus transformed into a shared historic and col-lective experience. MST accomplished just that by transporting Andean cultural imaginaries of the ayllu to new spaces of lowland production. It was on this basis that distinct forms of collective and participatory democracy were constructed, social relations were reconfigured, and new rationales for discipline and punishment proffered. As was noted in Chapter 3, collective structures of governance modeled on historic and mythic understandings of the ayllu, unlike vertical union-based organi-zations, did not punish simply to punish, but rather, to teach community residents a lesson and incorporate them back into the community. The ayllu or imagined ayllu also respatialized agricultural production by cre-ating collective opportunities for farming, providing a model of ancestral techniques and organic methods to protect and preserve the land, thus better ensuring that peasants would be able to provide enough food to sustain themselves. This social reconfiguration politically and economi-cally delinked residents from their historic and ongoing dependence on agrarian elites and transnational corporations. And yet, although these ideas had a certain power, they were not grounded to community life. They made cultural practices mobile and generalizable—assembled and reassembled parts of their history in order to create a sustained politi-cal practice and reinvent community. Moreover, although the movement might seize land, long-term relationships to either the land or self-built governing structures were at best fragile because of the uncertain status of legal claims and the power of the forces that could be arrayed to reclaim the land for the oligarchy. To actualize this sociopolitical vision to claim rights to land and resources required a scaling up of these practices to national levels of governance.

In a situation such as this, indigenous bodies prove crucial to the development of new citizenship practices. As this book has indicated, this stage of citizenship enactment requires that indigenous and landless peasants carry demands through geographical space to place pressure on the government. Their bodies, which have been marked, worn, and torn frequently through a globalized agricultural system of virtual slave labor, have been essential to reclaiming and seizing rights at a local level through occupation. In sum, bodies become vessels for moving platforms through national geographical terrain as they endure difficult conditions—for example, on marches to La Paz to pressure the government to pass legislation—while simultaneously creating a sense of collectivity and commitment to alternative agrarian projects in and through motion, dance, improvised practice, and political and personal risk.

Through their mobility—their physical movement and their assembly and reassembly of cultural practices and flexible platforms—activists have helped to shape a more inclusive state and contributed to the rewriting of critical legislation. As indigeneity and the incorporation of movement demands into national decision-making by political elites has produced new forms of state-making—most importantly, leading to the inclusion of issues such as land reform, food sovereignty, and autonomy in the new constitution—there have also been several limitations to this culturalist discourse of change.

The new plurinational state of Evo Morales, while it aspired to radically transform economic and social relations, has not been able to transport indigeneity into decision-making circles. Consequently, Morales's capacity to mobilize historic memory and performance as part of a legislative power to advance a radical platform for change or an alternative to the capitalist model has been deficient. In part, this can be explained by the powerful countermovement work of oligarchical elites, who use strategies and tactics that mimic leftist social movements, forcing the MAS government to negotiate and compromise on many reform fronts, particularly in regard to land in the east. As land represents great economic and political power, it is not surprising that old oligarchical families continue to hold on to large extensions of land and resist transformative change. Their effective countermovement politics have served to sustain the age-old colonial tensions and fuel the agroindustrial model.

At the level of the state then, the Left's strategy of using indigeneity as a shared identity, historic memory, and springboard for a radical land reform agenda has been countered by the oligarchy, and at best, it has only resulted in incremental change. Multinational corporations and agrarian elites continue to hold on to economic power—while the possibilities that indigenous ways, customs, and traditions can lead to radical political and economic change have proven limited. Yet again, elites have managed to tip the balance of power in their favor by limiting the mobilization potential of indigenous practices through imaginative counterstrategies, economic might, and national-global influence. Their capacity to penetrate the state politically through their economic and social power has hurt the ability of grassroots movements like MST to scale their agrarian utopian project up to the national level. This power has compromised Morales's politics, as he directly and indirectly supported unequal land tenure systems, export-oriented crops, and departmental autonomy. This political context dictates that MST members and other small-scale farmers must adapt to the new state politics and tilt their production in this direction if they are to compete in the broader economic structure.

While I have turned briefly to what has been possible through the multiple uses of indigenous-based discourses, motion, and language at the grassroots level, and have summarized the limitations of such an approach at the national level, I now shift attention to political possibility in an era of radical ecological shift and crisis. This context demands that the state reconstitute itself with a powerful and transformative economic and political agenda. In the past, social movements have been highly adept at using their pasts to create a shared collective identity, which, for example, meant fusing the distinct political ideologies of the Marxist miners and agrarian corporatist unions and resisting the neoliberal agenda of the state. As Garcés (2011) notes, however, what is going on in Bolivia now is different than the recent historic experience of the miners' struggle against the state or the landless peasants' struggle to capture state power. Although indigenous social movements have recently recognized the importance of reinventing the space of the state, the state's arc of change has not been very steep because the Morales government has not been an effective partner. What has transpired is that MST's initial proposals have been significantly diluted, and over time, this has led to a kind of "domestication" or pacification of social movements. The question then becomes, can Bolivian social movements reinvent themselves once again in this new era of ecological crisis and possibly push the state further left? And if so, can Bolivia serve as a model for other parts of the world undergoing similar economic and ecological crises?

NEW ECOLOGICAL SHIFTS AND THE
PROBLEMS THAT LIE AHEAD

While shifts toward indigeneity have facilitated great symbolic and cultural strides for indigenous peoples, they have also failed in many respects to alter material and economic realities. But it is possible that ecological shifts will challenge movements and the state to move beyond indigeneity as a free-floating signifier and reframe how ancient Andean techniques of the past can be used to inform the environmental struggles of the present. One hotly debated topic of recent concern to movements like MST and the Bolivian state has been how to adapt to radical temperature shifts. These warming trends greatly affect environmental surrounds and make it more difficult to farm and sustain alternate agroecological models.

Bolivia, like other countries in the global South,[2] has contributed minimally to the problem of the planet warming. It has spilled very little gas emission into the atmosphere, but ironically—and consistent with the inequitable distribution of both wealth and waste between the first and third worlds—Bolivia has been and will continue to be one of the first nations forced to deal with the consequences. Bolivia's highlands are already experiencing water scarcity, which can be directly traced to global warming and melting glaciers.[3] In consequence there has been less available fresh water, hotter and stronger sunlight, an increase in pests and diseases, and the extinction of various kinds of crops. In the lowlands, climatologists are tracking heavier rains and floods, droughts that have caused forest fires, and more erratic seasons that they attribute to this emergent ecological dynamic.[4] A question that must be raised in this context is how the Bolivian state can help to shore up this increasingly fragile ecological terrain. How will the state, working in conjunction with movements, embed social, economic, and environmental programming into a coherent and comprehensive set of policies that creates maximal adaptation to changes that are both inevitable and potentially disastrous? Most important, these radical climate changes are exacerbating preexisting problems of racism and uneven access to basic resources like water and food and ultimately will lead to the destruction of lands and ecosystems. And yet the social movements struggling to redress these historic grievances recognize that as time runs short, they must work in collaboration with this state to develop and implement pragmatic solutions for water scarcity, declines in agricultural production, consequent food security crises, and more largely, the material survival of the poorest sectors of society.

For these reasons, Morales has begun to restructure the symbolism and content of his politics beyond "indigeneity." For example, he has taken the lead internationally and has folded movement leaders into conversations about climate debt,[5] proposing that highly industrialized nations in the global North be obligated to pay ecological reparations to third-world countries in the global South. This reparations movement has served as an umbrella for a diverse coalition of international and national organizations, NGOs, and social movements. Their primary intention is to hold the global North accountable for the damage it has done to the environment. As Angélica Navarro, Bolivia's climate change negotiator, stated, "Millions of people . . . are suffering from the effects of a problem to which they did not contribute. In addition to facing an increasingly hostile climate, countries like Bolivia cannot fuel economic growth with cheap and dirty energy, as rich countries did, since that would only add to the climate crisis—yet they cannot afford the heavy upfront costs of switching to renewable energies like wind and solar" (quoted in N. Klein 2009: 2–3).

In 2009, despite Morales's and the coalition's demands, the UN Climate Change Conference in Copenhagen, which offered hope for an international treaty on reparations and global warming, ended in failure. Developed nations failed to formally acknowledge their role in global warming, refused to commit to significant emission reduction, and ultimately did not recognize their monetary obligation to investment in the global South, which would have helped less affluent nations successfully adapt to climate change.

In response, Morales organized his own conference, called the World People's Conference on Climate Change and the Rights of Mother Earth, in Tiquipaya, Cochabamba, in April 2010, which brought social movement activists together from across the globe. Their agenda was to address and popularize the distinct third-world problems associated with climate change. The planning for the conference began a few months before the physical event, as seventeen working groups were authorized to explore a series of topics ranging from climate debt to food sovereignty, to the structural causes of climate crisis. Each of these working groups had an open e-mail list that facilitated the development of an initial document (Building Bridges Collective 2010: 31). Within this virtual context, working groups debated critical issues and proposals, which Morales in turn was expected to present to the UN climate change committee. As one representative from Brazil stated, "This summit is very important because it is one of the few times that people bring their struggles, their flags, and their opinions directly to decision makers. This is a unique moment" (Democracy Now 2010). Once again, much like the forging of the Constituent Assembly, Morales relied upon a broad base of movement and NGO support—this time, social movements from across the globe—to bring material solutions to the surface, legitimize demands to the international community, and rapidly address the policy implications of climate change. The World People's Conference on Climate Change illustrated the new possibilities for participatory democracy through virtual media and ultimately showed the role social movements have played and can play in creating broad-based change. Unfortunately, however, the same kinds of frictions that plagued Morales's regime in bridging the power of indigeneity and real economic transformation have also affected these global discussions.

Morales opened the People's Conference with an impassioned speech linking the capitalistic system to Andean cultural and social norms and values. He invoked historic understandings and meanings of the *Pachamama* (Mother Earth) stating, "We are here [in Cochabamba] because in Copenhagen, the so-called developed countries failed in their obligation to provide substantial commitments to reduce greenhouse gases. We have two paths: Either Pachamama or death. We have two paths: Either capitalism dies or Mother Earth dies. Either capitalism lives or Mother Earth lives. Of course, brothers and sisters, we are here for life, for humanity, and for the rights of Mother Earth. Long live the rights of Mother Earth! Death to capitalism!" (quoted in Democracy Now 2010).

Just as MST or movement activists might use the romantic idea of an ayllu as a counter to capitalism, Morales publicly enacted Pachamama and buen vivir as globalized indigenous discourses to protect Mother Earth from forces of extraction and environmental degradation. This discourse had great appeal for many of the conference participants. As one participant noted, "Copenhagen was basically for the authorities. It was for the leaders of the countries. This is a gathering of the people. And as people who suffer the consequences, we share our concerns and our expectations. This is a movement. It is a first step to mobilize the whole world, to search for another kind of civilization, another kind of relationship with nature." Another participant declared, "We are hoping for results, that those brothers who have contaminated our Mother Earth, or the Pachamama, as we call it . . . [will] acknowledge this situation. And we want them to adapt to the planet, that they stop the abuse, and that they stop polluting our environment" (quoted in Democracy Now, 2010).

While movement activists were hopeful, arguing that this kind of people's summit was the only way to include movements in processes of change, tensions emerged between Table 18, which was comprised of CONAMAQ[6] representatives, and Morales. These frictions powerfully illustrate the ongoing and potentially explosive conflicts between the use of symbolic politics to promote political platforms, on the one hand, and the need for concrete plans or proposals to halt the influence of transnational capital, on the other. Groups that wanted to expose the contradictions between the Bolivian government's external globalized discourses of indigeneity as inherently anticapitalist and Morales's ongoing support for domestic mega-projects and reliance on extractive industries had set up Table 18— officially dubbed "the table on collective rights and the rights of Mother Earth"—prior to the conference's opening, and it was highly conflictive. For instance, during the Climate Summit, local communities five hundred kilometers away in the highlands of Potosí took action against the San Cristobal Mining Company, owned by the Japanese Sumitomo Corporation, the world's third-largest producer of silver and sixth-largest of zinc. Grassroots activists and community members who were frustrated by the extraction and contamination of water resources and the inaction of the Morales government blockaded the company, occupied its offices, and began overturning trains full of mineral ore close to the Chilean border. As researchers from Building Bridges Collective (2010) indicate, this was a real clash between Morales's words and discourses and the continuation of long struggles against extractive industries (36). At approximately the same time, three hundred Weenhayek, Tapiete, and Guaranís from the Gran Chaco also conducted demonstrations against the Morales administration, which had authorized oil operations in their territories.

In this context, Table 18 was an example of a social movement that had historically supported Morales but more recently had pushed back against his administration in order to expose some of the contradictions between empty symbolic discourses and the continuation of a neoliberal agenda. This is not the first or only incident of progressive movements aggressively confronting the Morales administration.[7] Despite these ruptures, he has, in general, been successful in keeping such groups whole and reaching a consensus. In this instance, many of the grievances were voiced by Aymara and Quechua leaders who had been actively involved in Morales's administration and helped forge the constituent assembly. Rafael Quispe, the leader of CONAMAQ, said, "Table 18 is going ahead whether the government likes it or not, and it does not only deal with Bolivia's problems" (quoted in Weinberg 2010: 22). The table, according to Quispe, would be convened in the streets of Tiquipaya, outside the official conference, if it was not allowed into the conference. Referring to the Bolivian government, he said, "We are not opposed to the process of change, nor are we against the forum, but it is important to deal with problems in our own house" (23). Because Table 18 demanded both the expulsion of all extractive resource industries and government adoption of a new development model based on the ayllu and local self-sufficiency, or what indigenous political leadership called the "Andean cosmovision," it was barred from the meeting for having violated one of the basic principles of the conference, namely that *mesas* (discussion tables) should meet during particular hours and within the bounds of the official summit grounds of the Tiquipaya campus of the University del Valle. Angered by Morales, Quispe noted, "The government says capitalism or Pachamama . . . but this government is neoliberal and capitalist.[8] It's all a political show. Evo's election was a step. But the marches, strikes, blockades that brought him to power are continuing" (24).

THE PASSING OF THE LAW OF MOTHER EARTH

While some movements, like CONAMAQ, remained adamantly opposed to symbolic discourses without material gains, others have pointed to the legislative successes that emerged directly out of the World People's Climate Summit. For example, in April 2011, the Bolivian Congress passed the Bill of Rights for Mother Earth, which draws deeply on indigenous concepts viewing nature as a sacred home. The law reads as though it were drawn from an ancient Andean text: "Mother Earth is a living dynamic system made up of the undivided community of all living beings, who are all interconnected, interdependent and complementary, sharing a common destiny." The law recognizes the legal rights of nature, specifically the rights to life and regeneration, biodiversity, water, clean air, balance, and restoration. This Bolivian law mandates a fundamental ecological reorientation of the nation's economy and society, requiring all existing and future laws to adapt to it and accept the ecological limits set by nature. It calls for public policy to be guided by sumak kawsay, rather than the current focus on producing more goods and stimulating consumption. In practical terms, the law requires the government to transition from nonrenewable to renewable energy; to develop new economic indicators that will assess the ecological impact of all economic activity; to carry out ecological audits of all private and state companies; to regulate and reduce greenhouse gas emissions; to develop policies of food and renewable energy sovereignty; to research and invest resources in energy efficiency, ecological practices, and organic agriculture; and to require all companies and individuals to be accountable for environmental contamination, with a duty to restore damaged environments (Buxton 2011).

Raul Prada, a well-known Bolivian sociologist, notes that even with significant pressure from social movements, transitioning to an economy based on the concept of buen vivir will not be easy. There is no simple exit strategy from an extractive economy to a more radical "green" alternative. He states, "We clearly can't close mines straight away, but we can develop a model where this economy has less and less weight. It will need policies developed in participation with movements, particularly in areas such as food sovereignty. It will need redirection of investment and policies towards different ecological models of development. It will need the cooperation of the international community to develop regional economies that complement each other" (quoted in Buxton 2011).

Ultimately, creating this alternative "green" economy is a challenge far too big for Bolivia to tackle alone. As Prada recognizes, the ecological and social crisis is not just a problem for Bolivia or Ecuador; it is a problem that everyone, sooner or later, will have to confront. He suggests that we will need to pull together a broad array of researchers, indigenous peoples, and grassroots activists to develop concrete alternatives to the dominant systems of exploitation. This is not an easy task (Buxton 2011).

While this law seems critical in moving toward new forms of development, it is important to note that national laws have not held commensurate power in relation to transnational corporations and multinational conglomerates to prevent their either rewriting or disobeying laws that do not comport with their interests. Protection of Mother Earth might become merely another symbolic discourse as critical industries, such as mining and hydrocarbons, continue to search for opportunities to pursue their unsustainable development practices and ply their political power to overwhelm any form of resistance to their maximal profit-making agenda. But as Prada adds, "This is an ecological and social crisis not just affecting Bolivia, but affecting all of us" (quoted in Buxton 2011).

No matter the difficulty and challenge, this much is clear: whatever hope exists to alter the present course of events largely rests with social movements such as those in Bolivia, working in collaboration with a left-leaning state and proposing alternative structures and solutions to a mounting environmental crisis. What, then, could be possible regarding the implementation of a radical project of change in response to the ecological crisis? In my estimation, a number of the key elements of a movement structure, platform, and political practice already exist. MST, for example, offers an invaluable example of how a movement built upon a militant mining and agrarian legacy mobilized cultural forms to implement alternative agrarian structures, invest in collective structures of governance, and push for long-term sustainability projects to protect the environment. While at times its project has been deficient, particularly at the national level, MST has nonetheless produced concrete victories and offered a way of reimaging a leftist project for change. Of special importance at the moment is assessing the potential contribution of MST's grassroots structure for combating climate change. Equally important, though, is the question of what hope this structure offers for effective collaboration with the state in a moment of crisis. The questions of whether mobile, mutable cultural practices and political formations can be an effective strategy for combating transnational capital clearly remain unanswered.

ECONOMIC CRISIS MEETS ECOLOGICAL CRISIS

What I wish to posit is that as people across the world begin to see that the structure of economic relations is connected to the social, ecological, and environmental crisis, then they will also recognize how movements like MST may provide possible alternatives. My first presupposition is that the ecological crisis is emerging out of our economic system. The latest phase of capitalism, the neoliberal model, has turned land and productive resources into disposable commodities that are being rapaciously exploited and discarded. In the search for quick and easy solutions regarding resource extraction, regimes of accumulation have raped the land and destroyed the natural rhythms and fragile relationships of ecosystems. As

David Harvey (2006) notes, in the early stages of capitalism, people were turned into laborers, disconnecting them from home, land, and productive processes. In later stages, there has been an increased focus on the recircuiting of greater concentrations of over-accumulated wealth, and in turn, the intensified use of hazardous chemicals, the appropriation of land, the destruction of natural habitats, and the privatization of all things public. To a certain extent, the web of socioecological life has been ripped apart at its seams. In Harvey's effort to relink the economic, the ecological, and the social, he calls for new kinds of analysis that place the logic of property and capital deeply inside this so-called "web of life" (75). Referring to Marx's classic theoretical point regarding our dialectical relationship with nature, Harvey argues, "In transforming our environment we necessarily transform ourselves. . . . If the relation of man to nature is seen as dialectical, as a matter of internal relations, then the particularity-universality problem is directly confronted. On the ecological side, therefore, we have to understand how the accumulation of capital works through eco-systemic processes, reshaping them and disturbing them as it goes" (88). But as he argues, the social and cultural side cannot be evaded as somehow radically different from their ecological integument.

If we begin to reembed the historical, the economic, the social, and the environmental into this "web of life," then we will also begin to see some of the lacunae within the indigenous-based environmental movements bubbling up in the global South. Harvey notes that "the idea of crisis, imminent collapse, or even 'the end of nature' plays an overwhelmingly powerful role in shaping most varieties of environmental discourse. The appeal of this rhetoric to the left is partly based on displacing the crisis and collapse rhetoric about capitalism from class conflict to the environmental issue" (1998: 1). He offers a poignant critique of popular eco-socialists like John Bellamy Foster (see Bellamy Foster 2000; and Bellamy Foster, Clark, and York 2010), whose metaphor of "ecoscarcity" and the idea that "we are headed over the cliff into some kind of abyss (collapse) or that we are about to run into a solid and immovable brick wall (limits)" is offered without a political economic framework, and therefore proves rather simplistic (D. Harvey 1998: 2). Instead, Harvey provides a platform for thinking about environmental problems as intimately linked to Marx's idea of dialectical materialism: we must conceive of ourselves as embedded within an ongoing flow of living processes that are individually and collectively affecting us and that we in turn can influence through our actions. First and foremost, Harvey effectively links the environmental crisis to the world's most vulnerable populations: the poor, the marginalized, and the working classes. Secondly, he argues that environmental impacts have a social bias—class, racial, and gender discrimination is evident. Lastly, he notes that some risks and uncertainties can strike anywhere, even against the rich and the powerful.

If we use Harvey's three critical points as a springboard to political action and strategic thinking, we begin to see how MST might have been ahead of its time in enacting a politics of cultural reassembly and movement-building in the midst of the global economic and environmental crisis. All of Harvey's critical points are like disks in the backbone of this social movement. First, MST developed a way to link distinct groups (mestizos, indigenous farmers, and small-scale vendors) in a struggle to reclaim land and territory. Leaders realized at the earliest stages of their movement-building that the economic model of expansive capitalism and agribusiness was leading to both displacement on an unprecedented level and the consequent rapid expansion of the informalization of work in the cities. Their solution—to mobilize and use the cultural histories of the most vulnerable peoples as a generalizable and flexible force for politicizing and militarizing—was both imaginative and, in many instances, effective, especially at the local level. Yet they realized in the process that it was not enough to simply occupy or reclaim land locally without the push to simultaneously create collective systems of governance and ambitious alternative forms of production. Only in this way could local struggles be reembedded into the larger national attempt to incorporate a broader national project of historic and sociocultural reclamation. Still, MST realized that these kinds of reclamations at the local and national level required a new economic structure. Necessarily, working the land and protecting it had to be a fundamental part of this socioeconomic and ecological model for campesinos, and thus the movement was born. MST members have felt the environmental and ecological shifts more powerfully than any other group because they have been close to the land for their livelihood. Within this context of land dependence, they have had to construct long-term proposals for adjusting to climate change and ensuring food security, working alongside international conglomerates like the Vía Campesina, all the while attempting to maintain a stable relationship to the land. This productive land, however, disappeared as it was redistributed to agribusiness. The multiple challenges for MST were of course daunting.

Harvey's call to reinsert class into our discussions of the environment has become a part of MST's overarching frame, which named culture or indigeneity as a language or discourse of political action. Although MST does not articulate class in the way the radical mining unions of the twentieth century did, it uses culture and indigeneity to undo a system of slave labor and to reconstitute discourse about the nexus between class and culture. Its cultural frame eliminates the reality of dispossessed peasants who depend upon landlords for their survival and in its place creates an alternate model of self-sufficient food production for poor farmers. As Harvey (1998) states, "We need, in the first instance, to understand the specific class content and definition of environmental issues and seek alliances around their resolution. The politics of this kind of environmental improvement can then replicate that which limited the strength of the working day as the working class's power of attack grew with the numbers of its allies in those social layers not directly interested in the question" (3).

While MST at a local or grassroots level might use indigeneity as a political language to reembed the social, the cultural, the economic, and the material into an alternative model of agriculture, we are still left with a gaping hole between the social/cultural and economic/material at the national level. This is a profound contradiction that raises a number of questions: How can grassroots movements effectively scale their practices up to redefine an economic and political agenda at the level of the state?[9] In what ways can the power of these movements, working in collaboration with the government, halt the overwhelming flows of transnational capital and influence? Are there ways in which MST's cultural, political, and economic practices could potentially provide alternatives in a moment of crisis? These are pressing questions because as we ruminate on these issues, time is indeed running out for essential parts of the fragile ecological balance that has sustained the poor and working classes.

THE ROLE OF MOVEMENTS AND
THE STATE IN AN ERA OF CRISIS

Out of the crisis—particularly in reference to the resource crisis, the privatization of water, proposed privatization of natural gas, and food insecurity—the possibility for a distinctive form of organizing and reconstruction of the state has emerged. A number of political leaders and intellectuals understood the potential for transformative change from 1998 to

2005, particularly the possibility of grassroots movements to redefine and reroute transnational capital. The power of these populist movements, along with a particular kind of leadership, halted a proposed plan to privatize natural gas reserves and pushed for the Constituent Assembly. Bolivia is a key example of the transformative power and potential of populist movements to redefine a national agenda. Movement leaders used and mobilized indigeneity as part of a broader politics of transformation, reclamation, and redistribution of rights and resources, and Andean indigeneity became a powerful alternative to neoliberalism.

Many social scientists and observers referred to this period in Bolivian history as "the Revolutionary Epoch." Mexican historian Adolfo Gilly wrote, "A revolution is not something that happens in the State, in its institutions, and among politicians. It comes from below and from outside. It happens when centerstage is taken over—with the violence of their bodies and the rage of their souls—precisely by those who come from below and outside." Referring to the Gas Wars of 2003, he goes on to say that in "the present Bolivian case, what they were demanding was the resignation of President Sanchez de Lozada" (quoted in Webber 2011: 45).

This truly was a kind of people's revolution. Still, as Jeff Webber (2011) argues, it is important to separate the notion of "revolutionary epoch from social revolution" (46). He suggests that the concept of "revolutionary epoch" provides a way to understand that revolutionary transformation is possible but not predetermined. The concept of social revolution, on the other hand, is concerned with accounting for and measuring the depth and consequences of lasting structural change that has been won through the popular struggle of a revolutionary epoch. That was largely the case in Bolivia between 1998 and 2005.

However, in the aftermath of these populist uprisings, the Morales years (2005–present) have also exposed an array of struggles and problems, notably the entanglements of legacies of colonial and neocolonial influence, and the fact that foreign capital defines resource redistribution; Bolivia remains wedded to a model of extraction, exportation, and semi-nationalization or industrialization of resource wealth. Simultaneously and contradictorily, it has also become clear that this model of extractivism has run its course. Water runs scarce in the altiplano, for example, because northern parts of Santa Cruz have no natural buffer and are exposed to more severe weather patterns due to deforestation. And yet, private interests continue to accelerate their extractive agenda, ignoring these growing tremors of ecological rupture. The increasing gulf between critical resource flows and availability will bring more difficult choices and political struggles to rural and indigenous communities. Once again, these communities will have to invent adaptive mechanisms and devices. This time, however, if solutions are to work, they will have to be politically, socially, and economically commensurate with the crisis. That means that these communities must forge political alliances with the state, take their movements to the national level, and create large-scale alternative forms of economic production.

Is it possible for such a large-scale movement with an ambitious agenda to succeed, given the kind of transnational capital arrayed against it? If there is any hope of it, we must ask if there is some way to shift our discourse to help us understand how a strong and centralized state, within a popular and participatory democratic framework, can, in this era of ecological crisis, be created out of movement struggle.

Bolivia teeters on the brink of an economic and ecological crisis that continues to loom over the political landscape. As Neil Smith (2009) has said, "Out of crisis might come great possibility for Revolution. . . . As anger at the economic crisis builds, as old movements remake themselves, and as new movements emerge around (and often combining) issues as diverse as immigrant rights and police brutality, environmental destruction and labor organizing, decimated social services and indigenous rights, a political reconstruction of the left is urgent" (57). The challenge that lies ahead will, in large part, be framed by the following question: How can movements realign their interests, separate their immediate and short-term aspirations for capital accumulation from state politics, and reconstruct their radical project from within the space of the state? For as we know, in a comparative context, no real redistributive or protectionist legislation has ever been possible in the United States without the working-class power and the strength of progressive social movements and labor unions pressuring for workers' rights, labor control, and environmental protections. In the absence of such class struggle and pressure, states will remain relatively ineffective in resisting or offering alternative policies to transnational and extractive agendas. But Bolivia has these kinds of movements, and it has a relatively sympathetic state. The challenge is for movements to redefine transnational agendas and prevent the state from co-opting or dismissing their projects and proposals.

As people's lives are unraveling—whether due to brutal attacks on economically stable employment, struggles for the right to unionize, or widespread ecological crises,[10] which in turn tend to destabilize and uproot whole populations—there is an urgent need for the new social projects and political practices of the Left. Social movements in Bolivia perhaps represent the most advanced and politically savvy experiments in the uses of culture to advance alternative economic agendas. Intellectuals and activists alike must create the appropriate forums to move beyond a symbolic politics and to imagine and put into practice radically new structures of equality and redistribution that could work feasibly at the level of the state. As Smith (2009) has indicated, "one earns one's freedom and life when one takes them every day by storm" (64).

In the past, "taking them by storm" would have meant armed revolution and seizing state power, for this has been the history of radical change in Latin America. From the Mexican Revolution of 1910 to the Cuban Revolution in 1959, to Central American revolutions in the 1970s, the model of redefining a state has been the seizing of state power through revolutionary forces and the implementation of new regimes of governance. Bolivia's most recent epoch of movement change has been quite different. Although the era of multicultural reforms brought with it new symbolic and "passive" revolutions of incremental change, it did not lead to a restructuring of Bolivia's economy. Economic and ecological transformation will only happen when workers, aligned with peasants, indigenous peoples, and the global North and South, seize their rights by storm. But seizing rights also means moving beyond simply making constitutional change to a transformative political and economic rethinking of the role of the state as a strong and centralized body with the capacity to create a truly redistributive and protectionist agenda and the power to reroute transnational capital. As Harvey (2006) has argued, social movements, aligned with the state, must reembed in discourse and in political practice the social and the cultural with the material, the economic, and the environmental.

In the end, I do not mean to imply that indigeneity as a political vehicle is unproductive, for it has led to radical transformations in our understandings of legal frameworks and state structures. And yet the discourse of indigeneity alone will not solve the problems of uneven geographical development, increasing inequality and poverty, ecological problems of severe drought, flooding, and water shortage, and more. Bolivian social movements must come up with concrete proposals for how to build self-sustaining agricultural communities, new and alternative forms of energy relying upon power from sun and wind, and productive engines that do not continue to destroy the environment and have the potential to create jobs and stimulate the economy. Ultimately, Bolivia, in alliance with social movements from the global South and North, must rein in foreign capital, which preys on lands, landscapes, and state structures. That is the daunting challenge for Bolivian social movements. If they get it right and show the way for grassroots movements to work in collaboration with a state to reinvent a better economic and political model, they will provide a far-reaching directional beacon for other nation-states undergoing similar kinds of crises around the globe.

NOTES

INTRODUCTION

1. The MAS party originated as a political arm of the indigenous peasant movement in the department of Cochabamba in the mid-1990s. It was anti-imperialist and anti-neoliberal, and it was modeled on the assembly-style, rank-and-file democracy of the peasant unions in the region. Its primary social base was the Cocaleros.

2. Santa Cruz elites sometimes use the idea of the mestizo or mestizaje as an alternative to the indigenous turn. The notion of mixing, according to elites in Santa Cruz, privileges and gives priority to European and "Western" ideas regarding economics, forms of governance, and even urban advancement, ultimately mobilizing an implicitly racist and biological model of race (Gustafson and Fabricant 2011).

3. Many of the soy producers in Santa Cruz also rely on speculative unproductive landholding (*tierras de engorde*, "fattening lands") for capital accumulation. As Gustafson (2006) notes, "this agrarian pattern and its attendant dependence on transnational export sectors reinforce the opposition to both a redistributive land reform and the nationalist policies for establishing sovereignty over natural resource exploitation" (360).

4. The failure to do prior consultation violates international agreements ratified by Bolivia, such as the UN Declaration on the Rights of Indigenous Peoples and International Labour Organization 169. Also, more surprisingly, it violates the new Bolivian constitution approved in February 2009 (Kenner 2011a).

5. The new law fails to satisfy demands for consultation of indigenous peoples. Morales, unwilling to modify his position, stated on October 13, "They want the consultation to be binding. That's impossible; it's nonnegotiable. The constitution and international law mandate previous consultation, and we will always respect that, but letting a group of families tell us what to do would mean paralyzing all of our work on electrification, hydrocarbons, and industries" (Andean Information Network 2011). In the international arena, TIPNIS representatives have filed a formal claim with the United Nations, accusing the government of violating their rights by executing a contract for the construction of the highway before securing their consent. A UN representative in Bolivia requested a suspension of all construction activity underway on the section of the road outside TIPNIS until an agreement is reached.

CHAPTER ONE

1. *Sindicalista* tradition refers to the union-based structure of organizing in Bolivia. The 1952 revolution involved an alliance of sorts between the bourgeoisie and the agrarian peasantry. The initial phase can be described as an active subordination of Indian peasants to the state. The second phase can be described as the peasant-military pact, which allowed unions to bargain for land and productive resources

from within a repressive military state. (For more on this, see Klein 1969; Malloy 1970; Dunkerley 1984; Grindle and Domingo 2003; Gotkowitz 2008.)

2. Stearman (1985) and Gustafson (2006) illustrate more explicitly this geography of uneven development, as the plaza, or *casco viejo* (old city), associated with the traditional power elite, historically represented the colonial center. Beyond the old center, the city is surrounded by *anillos*, or rings formed by circular roads, which become progressively poorer and more dangerous as one moves toward the periphery.

3. The word *colla* (or *kolla*) comes from the Quechua word *kollasuyo*, the name of one part of the Inca empire. Within this zone, one ethnic group called Kollas was eventually assisted by the Incas in defeating its ethnic competitors. The word later expanded to describe people living in the Altiplano around Titicaca. The inhabitants of the Santa Cruz region are known as Cambas, a Guaraní term for "friend." It was first applied to the peasant class in ways synonymous with "peón" or "slave." However, as time went by, elites have reappropriated the term to incorporate all lowland peoples whom they categorize as culturally, regionally, and ethnically distinct from their highland Indian counterparts (see Pruden 2003). *Bolita* means a small ball, or marble. Argentineans use the term to describe Bolivian immigrants living in Argentina and working low-wage jobs. It has many connotations, among them the suggestion that all Bolivians are short, dark skinned, and inferior to Europeans.

4. Historical memory and performance prove critical to understanding how these tales are narrated and retold through the bodies and actions of contemporary activists. Many scholars have focused on the use of historical memory as central to oppositional identity formation and movement building in Bolivia (see Delgado 1994; Farthing and Kohl 2007; Postero 2007b; Arbona 2008). Primarily, however, they have centered their attention on the Andean region, since the mining unions, the backbone of the labor movement, have been considered the most revolutionary segment of the Bolivian working classes. June Nash's (1979) pioneering work on the miners in the mining camps of Siglo XX describes historical memory (specifically, rituals from the pre-Conquest era) as important in the shaping and strengthening of working-class consciousness. Magdalena Cajías de la Vega (2004) and Juan Arbona (2008) argue that these histories and memories of struggle in the mines proved necessary to "translating" miners' political and militant identities to new urban, peripheral spaces like El Alto, which became the primary sites of miner "relocation" after neoliberal reforms.

5. This term, originally derived from Marxist economic theory, refers to the linked processes of accumulation and annihilation of wealth under capitalism. From the 1950s onward, the term has been associated with the Austrian American economist Joseph Schumpeter who adapted and popularized it as a theory of economic innovation and progress.

6. *Mit'a* directly translates as "turn" or "season." The Spanish conquistadores utilized a system of turn-taking, such as the exchange of labor for the building of roads, in order to sustain the empire.

7. Beyond exploitative labor relations, Postero (2007b) notes that the Spaniards used other forms of humiliation in order to control and subjugate Indians. She quotes Gilly (2003), who suggests that this was materialized through practices of corporal punishment, paternalistic treatment toward subordinates, separation of work and

living spaces, and visual differences in clothing; these were everyday practices that reproduced inequality and inferiority, marking bodies as "other" and spaces as belonging to particular groups of people.

8. While THOA worked in the highlands on indigenous rights and reconstituting the ayllu, CEJIS (the NGO supporting MST), in the lowlands, began using indigenous identity and providing training through seminars, workshops, and scholarships to indigenous social movements to increase their political recognition. The organization focused on their leaders and on the rights and entitlements of indigenous peoples, including political recognition of their existence and culture, institutional recognition of indigenous peoples' traditional political systems, and recognition of indigenous peoples' dual identity (Bueno and Datta 2011).

9. International donors and funders have had a similar Andean bias in terms of funding projects that center on reclaiming historical pasts, ways of living, and farming.

10. *Cruceño* was a term used to describe a person from Santa Cruz, usually an elite. However, in order to unite distinct groups in a struggle against Morales and their highland indigenous counterparts, regionalists have appropriated the term *Camba*.

11. It is important to note that the rubber era and the rubber boom (1860–1914) were the beginning of the consolidation of wealth and power in the lowlands. Lesley Gill (1987) argues that the new laws that gave elites control over jungle lands represented the first governmental attempt to exploit natural resources and divide up native lands. While the rubber boom was short-lived, those Cruceños who formed import-export houses, which primarily exported rubber to Europe and imported high-priced manufactured goods, were able to diversify their activities and transition into agriculture (Gill 1987: 27–28). For instance, many of these original families began to exploit timber concessions across northern Santa Cruz.

12. The Oriente region occupies the whole of the northern and eastern part of the country, or more than 70 percent of the territory. As opposed to the Altiplano and the cordilleras, this is a torrid area, consisting of plains, and the Amazon forests to the north.

13. Between 1955 and 1960, the Bolivian state channeled resources through the Inter-American Agricultural Service. Most of the investments focused on large-scale production in Santa Cruz. By 1961, close to 50,000 hectares of rice and 80,000 hectares of sugarcane had been sown. The land allocation resulted in a skewed distribution. The first mechanism was oriented toward Andean migrants of rural origin, which created a large class of small-scale landholders and peasant producers who depended on outsourcing its labor in order to support household economies. The second mechanism was concentrated on larger landholdings in the hands of a smaller class of capitalists that focused on export-oriented agriculture. Soruco, Plata, and Medeiros (2008) argues that of land allocations greater than 10,000 hectares, between 1952–93, 81.26 percent went directly to private individuals and 10.1 percent went directly to small-scale producers. This created radical class differences and uneven distribution of access to land, means of production, and materials.

14. The difference between classic liberal political theory and contemporary neoliberalism, as John Gledhill (2005) notes, is "[contemporary neoliberalism's] elision

between a market economy and a market society, to the point where the latter seems to engulf life itself" (340).

15. Multinationals as the ambassadors of democracy have consolidated power in the hands of a few, gained complete control over resource wealth through new international rules benefiting Northern nation-states, and managed to extract and hollow out Southern peripheral provinces and rainforests. Neoliberal policies have put the squeeze on the environment in concrete ways. In the case of Brazil, like other nations in the global South, the government slashed millions of dollars from environmental spending in the wake of IMF-enforced cuts. The country's environmental enforcement arm had its budget reduced by 19 percent, which weakened its environmental regulating body.

16. The United States moved to regulate world agricultural commodity markets via programs of liberalization, culminating in the WTO-centered corporate food regime of the 1990s. The progression from multinational markets to transnational complexes grew out of geo-economic arrangements as global capitalism shifted gears in the late 1970s and 1980s. The stable organization of nationally regulated economies, with fixed exchange rates pegged to the dollar, gave way to an increasingly unstable organization of transnational economic relations governed by floating exchange rates, offshore money markets, and financial speculation. As national controls on capital movements eased, transnational corporate activity expanded, and development agencies like the World Bank identified exporting to the global market as the preferred strategy for states and firms (McMichael 2000). By the 1980s, the United States had moved to regulate world agricultural commodity markets via a program of liberalization in the Uruguay Round, culminating in the WTO-centered food regime. Politicians and bureaucrats then replaced the more loosely structured GATT (General Agreement on Trade and Tariffs) with the WTO, which has the status of an international organization rather than a treaty (Ellwood 2007: 35).

17. It is important to note that the mining unions were the backbone of the labor movement in Bolivia. As June Nash once noted, "The Bolivian miners have the reputation of being the most revolutionary segment of the Bolivian working class" (1979: 2). In many ways, neoliberal reforms sought to break up these strong unions in distinct parts of the country, with the hope that displacement and fragmentation would demobilize their activities. However, such displacements only reorganized and respatialized their struggles to new locales.

18. The ruptures wrought by neoliberalism displaced whole communities and uprooted them from rural to urban environments. Yet their very organizational structures and political ideology have focused on a concept of reclaiming space and territory in both urban squatter settlements and rural peripheries. These movements begin with the idea that identity, indigeneity, and service delivery is deeply territorial (Gustafson and Fabricant 2011).

19. The Boli-Bras scandal involved Education Minister Hedim Céspedes and his Brazilian associates who had fraudulently received the land, but that was only a symptom of the corruption to which the reform process had fallen victim under postrevolutionary governments, particularly the military dictatorships of 1962–82 (Assies 2006).

20. This was the second of a series of lowland indigenous marches to La Paz. In August of 1990, CIDOB organized the March for Territory and Dignity from Trinidad, Beni, to La Paz in order to recognize four indigenous territories and the government's 1991 ratification of the ILO Indigenous and Tribal Peoples Convention. The second such march was the March for Territory, Land, Political Participation, and Development, which was held in 1996. It began with over 2,000 marchers in Santa Cruz and was joined by the CSUTCB (Confederation of Rural Workers of Bolivia) and the CSCB (Bolivian Syndicalist Confederation of Colonizers). The mobilization coincided with the 1996 passing of the INRA Law. In 2000, CPESC (the regional federation of Santa Cruz), the Mojeño people of Beni, and several Amazonian peoples carried out the March for the Earth, Territory, and Natural Resources from Santa Cruz to La Paz in order to push for changes to the Agrarian Reform Law and officially recognize their indigenous lowland languages. In 2002, indigenous groups from Santa Cruz marched for Popular Sovereignty, Territory, and National Resources. Most recently, in October and November 2006, CIDOB and MST, along with other highland indigenous groups, launched the National March for Land and Territory, where they pushed for the New Agrarian Reform Law.

21. The INRA Law recognized the preexisting claims of *originarios* (highland Indians) and *indígenas* (lowland Indians) through communal landholdings and the application of customary law through the Law of Popular Participation (PPL), which established the legal precedent based on continuity with the past (Albro 2005). In the highlands, the CSUTCB condemned the INRA Law as one of those "damned laws," along with the capitalization and Popular Participation Law. Rival organizations emerged in the region, seeking to reconstitute the ayllu, while in the lowlands, indigenous groups like CIDOB initially supported the new law, which included the legal figure of protection of the TCO, or the habitat of indigenous or originary peoples and communities. For the first time, the lands occupied by indigenous peoples could be legalized as collective property (Assies 2006).

22. The major problem with the World Bank's approach is that it has exacerbated inequality by imposing a burden of debt upon the supposed beneficiaries and by paying inflated prices to large landholders or speculators who obtained land at low prices. By contrast, state-led reforms defined types of landholding and labor systems that were not in the public interest and set rules about which types of land could be expropriated for redistribution (Hertzler 2008).

23. The Chaco War was fought in 1932–35 between Bolivia and Paraguay over the Gran Chaco region of South America, which was incorrectly thought to be rich in oil. The treaty of 1938 ended the war, and a major portion of the disputed desert area was awarded to Paraguay.

24. Agrarian union structures could not withstand the forces of neoliberal globalization in the 1980s. Several decades of Andean migration to Santa Cruz generated colonist unions that together were called the Syndicalist Confederation of Colonizers of Bolivia. As Gill (1987) notes, these colonist unions played an important role in the social organization of frontier settlements and were synonymous with small-scale agricultural communities. Syndicates also directed and participated in a wide range

of activities, including the distribution of land, initiation of infrastructural development, and resolution of internal debates. However, as market forces shifted toward investment in large-scale and export-oriented agriculture, peasants could not make the transition and were forced to sell their lands. Such a process of mercantilizing lands led to the dissolution of union structures.

25. At this meeting, Angel Durán became the first president of the organization. Distinct groups from Oruro, Potosí, La Paz, Cochabamba, Santa Cruz, and Tarija came together to share experiences and political strategies.

26. Beyond creating an alternative socioeconomic model, MST has also struggled to rethink the relationship between humans and the environment. Members have been encamped in areas where land, soil, and forests have been decimated by regional entrepreneurs, who have turned all environmental resources into commodities. MST implemented agroecological zoning and has worked toward the recuperation of degraded land and reforestation in certain areas.

27. Coca attracted the inward migration from other parts of the country that the 1960s colonization schemes had been designed to foster. Between 1967 and 1987, the population of the Chapare expanded nearly tenfold from 24,000 inhabitants to nearly a quarter of a million, including seasonal workers. The increase in coca production was also directly related to the boom in demand for coca, mainly coming from the United States and Europe, which pushed up the price of the leaf. Coca was attractive because it grew alongside other sources of sustenance, so when coca prices were low, farmers could always fall back on other food crops for survival (Crabtree 2005).

CHAPTER TWO

1. Branko Marinkovic, son of the late Silvo Marinkovic, uses his soy power to advance the agenda of the new regional movement calling for a form of decentralized departmental governance or autonomy. From 2006 to 2009, he served as the president of the Civic Committee of Santa Cruz—a regional conglomeration of self-elected agribusiness elites who run citywide politics—and launched a powerful counter-movement to the Morales administration until he was accused of participating in an assassination plot, offering a Hungarian hit man $200,000 to buy weapons "and finish the job we started" (Stapff 2009). Marinkovic's whereabouts are unknown—activists speculate that he might have fled to Brazil or to the United States seeking political asylum—but his sister and other family members continue to run the lucrative business.

2. The demands for departmental autonomy emerged several years before the rise of Morales. Gustafson (2006) claims that the impetus for this new movement really began in the 1990s, as elites saw their grip on power dissolve in the face of powerful social movements that were articulating opposition to the privatization of resources and demanding a new constitution. Elites then began retreating from the centralized state and voicing demands for decentralization whereby they would have complete control over resource wealth.

3. Many Latin Americanists have written about the ways in which indigenous peoples and rural-to-urban migratory patterns disrupt social categories of race and space that have long organized both the urban and national landscape (Weismantel

2001; Goldstein 2004; Guss 2006). Poor and rural citizens transgressing city spaces are often described by elites as "matter out of place" (Douglas 1966), and their bodies are subjected to surveillance and policing (see Kirshner 2010, 2011). As Radcliffe and Westwood (1996) have termed it, these "racialized imaginative geographies" not only organize urban space but also have a temporal element. The countryside stands for the national past, whereas the urban cities are about progress, movement forward, modernity, etc.

4. This resembles Saskia Sassen's (2001) *Global City*, in which she argues that key cities like New York and Los Angeles, which are home to specialized financial and marketing firms with global links, have become critical nodes of commerce, culture, and ideas.

5. Cruceños and Cambas often speak of themselves as mestizos who share the heritage of lowland native peoples of Santa Cruz. Nonindigenous Cruceños view these peoples as "our ethnics," integrating them within a distinct history of mestizaje that they conceptualize as culturally and racially superior to Andean mestizaje. Cruceños, by and large, see themselves as representing a modern, European-looking mestizo. Regionalized discourses and discussions of citizenship writ small become racialized as well in these constructions of Andean Indian versus lowland Camba.

6. As Suzana Sawyer (2004) describes it, the politics of roadblocks worked such that indigenous bodies halted vehicular traffic and flows of products and commercial goods to the markets.

7. See Martínez-Torres and Rosset (2010) for a history of the evolution of this organization—from autonomous organizations, first in Latin America, and then on a global scale during the 1980s and 1990s. The reconstruction of a shared peasant identity serves as a powerful glue that holds their struggle together despite widely different internal differences, creating this idea of a true peasant internationalism.

8. The MAS headquarters in Santa Cruz has become a safe place for many MST workers to receive food and shelter as they conduct their NGO business in the city. There are cots or beds set up for organizers who might not be able to afford to rent a room on the outskirts of the city.

9. If someone is classified as a small-scale producer, he is considered a greater risk for private banking lending practices. Therefore, he must pay high insurance on his loan in order to secure it.

10. Chicha is a fermented drink made of maize, popular in the highlands of Bolivia. For more on the cultural, social, and political significance of chicha, see Weismantel 2001, 2009.

11. Many houses are made of branches from the motacu tree, which is native to lowland Bolivia.

12. This discourse of the poor as lazy and the rich as hard-working citizen is a globalized frame or rationale for neoliberal reforms extending way beyond the industry of agriculture (see Collins, di Leonardo, and Williams 2008).

13. He was hung by his feet with a cord and his head was covered with a nylon bag soaked in insecticide, and then he was repeatedly beaten and threatened with death unless he confessed to "disappearing" the *sicario*. He was harassed and tortured until finally he confessed and signed the confession, without being allowed to consult his

defense attorney. Several days after the arrest, the public was advised that Luis Salvatierra had confessed.

14. With the growing immiseration that accompanies neoliberalism, it is becoming harder for Bolivians to ignore the political movements taking hold at the top and the bottom of the class hierarchy. Those who are just simply interested in surviving must find and identify with either of these movements. Those who are living on the rural peripheries are finding that MST is becoming more about economic necessity; however, many are quite critical of the organization. In this particular case, Salvatierra spoke frequently about how he felt set up by MST and eventually betrayed, as they abandoned him in his most vulnerable moments.

15. All the mainstream media channels are owned by latifundistas in Santa Cruz. Red 1 is controlled by Ivo Kuljis, a member of a powerful landowning family, who originally emigrated to Bolivia in 1938 from the former Yugoslavia. Unitel is owned by Ernesto Monasterios, who has been on a list for years for illegally acquiring a great amount of land during the Banzer dictatorship.

CHAPTER THREE

1. In the municipality, 75 percent of the land is in the hands of large-scale farmers and 25 percent is in the hands of small-scale farmers, so MST still continues to work with landlords.

2. Ponciano Sulca was arrested in his home shortly after the displacement of MST members from the Yuquises hacienda. He was found guilty of participating in the defense of Pueblos Unidos during the period of May 7–9, 2005. Based on fabricated testimony, he was held in preventive detention for more than six months and denied medical treatment for a severe urinary infection caused by bladder cancer.

3. Revilla (2011) discusses this kind of leadership as "the leader who walks alone" in El Alto. He argues that neoliberal reforms greatly influenced leadership, and community representatives became self-interested, technocratic, and at times, selfish. This model, however, can be debated and is contested by the *vecinos*.

4. Just as "insecurity" is not new in Andean Bolivia, cultural forms to articulate this kind of insecurity and fear did not surface merely in the neoliberal era. Mary Weismantel (2001) articulates the circulation of "Pishtaco" stories through time and space, which encapsulate native fears of white *gringos* (foreigners) stealing the fat from Indians. Weismantel embeds such creative processes within a broader structure of economic interdependency, highlighting the racialized, gendered, and sexualized dynamics of such market-based and commoditized interactions.

5. Ideas about security and development are also often shaped and nurtured on a global level: international agencies and NGOs have increasingly come to define security politics and enhance "safety" through multinational "democratic institutions" (see Albro 2010b; Goldstein 2010). Yet, MST is concerned with a very different notion of security that focuses on collective models of land tenure, governance, and food production in order to bring about a form of control and grassroots autonomy. Citizenship, then, does not become a top-down model of rebuilding democracy through the mechanisms of the market, but rather, citizens must return to pre-Colombian ideals

and values, which often occur outside the realm of the state or "on the margins of the state" (Das and Poole 2004).

6. The concept of "buen vivir" includes the ability to maintain a reciprocal relationship with the parts of the holistic world through ethically and spiritually appropriate practices for an intercultural engagement with society and nature. Further, buen vivir has incorporated an understanding of biocultural diversity through continued local interaction with ecosystems and, critically, through acknowledging and respecting different ways of knowing in the world through collective processes. *Sumak kawsay*, or buen vivir, has now also become a framework of political, legal, and natural governance.

7. These commissions are decentralized organic structures that allow the organization to function in a cohesive but flexible manner. The same structure of "collective" governance maps onto MST local politics, in which regional teams represent, for example, the Ichilo province or the Obispo Santiesteban province, and come together to make decisions. Regional commissions, then, fold into broader decision-making bodies at the departmental and national level.

8. Highland Aymara organizations such as CONAMAQ and the Taller de Historia Oral Andina (Andean Oral History Workshop, THOA) have focused on the revival of the ayllu as a space of political-territorial autonomy (Rivera Cusicanqui 1987, 1990). They have greatly influenced migrant political organizations such as MST-Bolivia by employing a discourse of shared "indigenous history as a key to building broad-based coalitions across national territory." THOA has hosted several conferences in the lowlands in which organizations such as the Bolivian Syndicalist Confederation of Colonizers and MST have borrowed from highland political strategies of resistance.

9. Speed (2007a) argues that these dialogic engagements may be influenced by globalized discourses, but indigenous peoples and social movements bring to bear their own particular understandings and goals in ways that shape, reshape, and contest such dominant framings.

10. These councils oversee local programs on food, health, education, etc. The juntas have created their own laws and enforce them, applying punishment when deemed necessary, under a community-based system. This system is built upon a rotational dynamic, such that a community member serves on the council for a short period of time and then a new council is put into power, thus avoiding corruption and the influence of outside structures.

11. The spectacular nature of such punishments is intended to teach community residents a lesson and enforce normative behaviors for the entire community. For example, as Risor explains, "Lynchings may be seen as a sovereign practice and a means by which notions of proper behavior and social order are communicated internally, within a community" (2010b: 466). She describes the hanged effigies as the social and collective production of warning signs, whereby neighbors situate lynching as a collective self-defense in reaction to criminal subjects.

12. Contrary to my practice of giving real names elsewhere, I have changed the name of this CEJIS representative.

13. MST leaders and members describe this horizontal structure as an indigenous, highland form of organizing in which the bases are more important than the leaders.

One leader said, "Many of the unions have become disorganized because leaders assume too much responsibility and they have made decisions for their entire community. But in our case, the bases are the protagonists, they define everything" (MST-Bolivia representative, personal communication, July 2006).

14. Stephenson (2000) and others have distinguished between union-style politics and ayllu movements. Union-style is Western-centric, denying all that is native and isolating gender, while the ayllu structure is more collective, embracing forms of gender complementarity. It is important to demystify such dichotomous comparisons because there is no purity to either model—union-style is infused with collectivism, and ayllu politics with certain forms of individualism.

CHAPTER FOUR

1. In 2005 and 2006, there were several meetings in the northern region about how the members would reconstruct community and work the land and about what kinds of projects they would undertake in order to promote an agroecological model. This montage of voices represents one such meeting, which took place in San Pedro, in the Obispo Santiesteban region of Santa Cruz, in April 2006.

2. The economic success of the ayllu was in the efficient management of labor and the administration of resources they collected as tribute. Collective labor was the base for economic productivity and for the creation of social wealth in Pre-Columbian society. By working together, people in the ayllu created such social wealth. The first efficient management of labor was the *ayni*, which was a form of reciprocity, or helping a community member in need. The second was *minka*, or teamwork for the benefit of the whole community. Examples of the latter include building agricultural terraces or irrigation systems.

3. It is important to note that governments and agribusiness have managed to contain proposals for food security by promoting increased agricultural trade liberation. This practice has had devastating effects on local, domestic agricultural systems, which cannot compete with the influx of cheap and subsidized commodities flooding local markets. "Food security," then, did not offer a real possibility for change, but rather, more of the same policies (see Wittman, Desmarais, and Wiebe 2010).

4. This phenomenon has also become apparent in resource battles, such as the ones Suzana Sawyer (2004) describes in the Ecuadorian Amazon, where leaders transgressed international borders in order to draw attention to the tragedy of oil spills in their communities.

5. Conklin and Graham (1995) argue that Indian-environmentalist alliances in Brazil, which have centered on Westerners' ideas about Indians as eco-friendly, have contributed to indigenous goals of self-determination. At the same time, this new "political ideological middle ground is rooted in contradictions between the realities of Amazonian Indians and the ideas about Indians that have inspired support within a broad public beyond the Amazon" (696).

6. Marc Edelman has extensively written on the possibilities and the challenges of transnational forms of peasant organizing in Central America. For more on transnational peasant organizing, see Edelman 2008, 2009; Edelman and James 2011.

7. Many scholars have written about mobility as a world in a grain of sand, in which ideas and discourses about how people move hold deeply entrenched ideas about race and class (see Henderson 2009; Roy 2009; Monroe 2011). In urban Santa Cruz, for instance, ideas about rural Indians are embedded in discourses of how people move. On many occasions, I heard middle-class Cambas screaming, "Colla de mierda!" from their windows as someone cut them off of the road. Middle-class and elite Cambas will often describe the indigenous bus drivers as occupying too much space on the roads, cutting people off, and not obeying the flows of traffic. They have somehow disrupted the racialized or spatialized logic of nation-state, region, and even cityscape, where poor Indians should remain "submissive, subservient" and on the boundaries or peripheries, not in the center of the roads.

8. Many political economic scholars (McMichael 2005; Patel 2007) have written about this form of alienation as the end result of a globalized industrial system that separates consumers from producers.

9. Commercial speculation in agriculture has traditionally been used by traders and processors to protect against short-term price volatility, acting as a sort of price insurance while helping to set a benchmark price in the cash market. However, today's speculation has become excessive relative to the value of the commodity as determined by supply and demand and other fundamental factors. For example, as of April 2008, corn volatility was 30 percent and soybean volatility 40 percent beyond what could be accounted for by market fundamentals. Price volatility has become so extreme that by July, some commercial or "traditional" speculators could no longer afford to use the market to hedge risks effectively. This, in combination with a deregulated market, will further make it difficult to internalize the costs of agriculture, natural resource re-mediation, and climate change effects in commodity prices. For these and other reasons, governments and regulators must assert control over the futures markets to prevent destabilizing excessive speculation in commodities.

10. First, the tortilla crisis was due to hoarding and speculation by the agroindustrial monopolies. Second, the rising costs of gasoline, diesel, and electricity have affected production, transport, and processing costs. And third, the international price of corn increased due to its use in ethanol production.

11. MST cooperatives in Brazil bring pesticide-free fruits, vegetables, and dairy products to the tables of public schools and social agencies in the region. The cooperative approach not only ensures the subsistence of individuals, but also makes possible investments to expand the cooperative itself, as much of their revenues are funneled back into the business.

12. Pueblos Unidos has had a hard time making ends meet. Due to its large debt, originating from the purchase of two trucks to transport crops to the market and a huge agricultural machine, the village faces financial problems. Unfortunately, despite its commitment to some ecologically sustainable projects, the villagers have had to depend upon large-scale agriculture, a theme to which I will return at the end.

13. Ideas like minka were also politicized and mobilized in MST settlements to build schools and health care systems. They utilized a concept called *mit'a*, Quechua for "turn," but actually, this translates directly to "assigned tasks" in order to reclaim services. Activists asserted that in ancient Andean communities, men from each of

the four communities of an ayllu would work one day a week for two years to provide a steady supply of rotating labor. Each household, they said, was notified as to what day a person would show up, where, and with what implements to comply with that household's mit'a. In the context of the Andes, John Murra (1975, 1978) argues that the very notion of service to the community was fundamentally understood as a contribution in labor, skills, or services, rather than the surrender of a portion of one's crops, goods, and money. This fragmented understanding of the mit'a served as a basis for enforcing the importance of serving the community.

14. They were practicing agroecology, a form of agriculture that presents an alternative to the industrial and global-trade-based model. Agroecology is the technological flag of counter or resistance movements and involves designating and testing systems for small farmers, using a blend of traditional and localized knowledge and modern agricultural science in order to maintain food security and genetic and cultural diversity (see Altieri 1995; Wittman 2010). It emphasizes environmental sustainability and working with nature rather than overcoming it to increase yields in particular environments, while conserving soil fertility and biodiversity (see Wittman 2010). MST-Bolivia has developed, along with the help of international and national NGOs, a form of agroecology that relies upon its members' indigenous practices and cultural frames.

15. Never one-sided performances, these shows are also a way for MST members to obtain international funding and support for their agroecological projects. This need to show, illustrate, and perform is part and parcel of the complicated NGO world, where environmentalists, land reform agents, and others evaluate these spaces in order to continue to support such projects.

16. Oxfam provided technical support to various communities in the lowlands to construct these elevated seedbeds, known locally as *camellones*, to prevent seasonal floodwater washing away seeds and plants.

17. For more on their work with MST, see http://www.veterinariossinfronteras.org/es/PROYECTOS/modelobolivia.html.

18. Alpah Shah (2010) discusses how the looming threat of climate change has made conservation a major global business. The Discovery Channel and National Geographic arrived in India, encouraging particular understandings about what constitutes the natural world and the threat it faces. Shah argues that their global ecological romanticism is underpinned by an evolutionary idea that first there was nature, and then man's technological advances altered and destroyed it.

19. During a conference organized by Johns Hopkins University in the fall of 2010 on rethinking indigeneity, one prominent Latin American scholar told me that in her observations of indigenous organizing, people were not asking for something utopian or ideal; they just wanted to enjoy the benefits of capitalism. They were not trying to overthrow or transform the entire system, but merely to obtain a piece of the pie.

20. Their book explores the sometimes contradictory processes by which questions of indigenous identity and ethnicity have become a part of development thinking over the past two decades. Although they do focus on Bolivia and Ecuador, they mainly concentrate their attention on the role of transnational relations in the production of ethno-development. While they construct a nuanced view of the use of indigeneity for

development projects, the fine-tuned and local details of how indigenous organizers and community residents reappropriate such discourses remain to be seen.

CHAPTER FIVE

1. The columnas organized people in space and created an orderly demonstration. They also served as a human wall, protecting the masses from police brutality, and brought traffic to a standstill. Women used their bodies in imaginative and resourceful ways during the protest marches to form a chain of protection against right-wing groups. The organizational structure of the march also provided opportunities for intercultural and interethnic sharing of problems and struggles associated with land. Stories of hunger, shared in the columna, forged mobile communities of pain (Turner 1969).

2. Elaine Peña (2011) also discusses the critical importance of women's bodies in pain as they make the sacrificial walk to La Virgen de Guadalupe in Tepeyac in Mexico City. She argues that "the moments of pain and discomfort—walking on blistered feet, proceeding with injured knees and cramped legs . . . with too much light and too little sleep—play a comprehensive role in the ritual's development" (89). This physical pain, to a certain extent, draws attention to that which it potentially engenders, envisioning and reinforcing a collective identity.

3. This idea of mobility is very significant here since many of MST's ways of life, livelihoods, and even claims have been circumscribed by elites. Agrarian elites have created their own mechanisms of mobility and control, whereby they have managed to control rural populations through market-based production and control of markets (leaving them with few possibilities for survival). They also control rural bodies by keeping them out of centralized urban spaces of agrarian capitalism through discriminatory practices and violence. These protest marches, then, are very much about placing rural bodies in key strategic sites of commerce and market-based interactions.

4. The reference is to the revolution of 1952, after which the Movimiento Nacionalista Revolucionario (Nationalist Revolutionary Movement, MNR), under pressure from peasant unions, carried out a sweeping land reform in the Andean western part of the country, which had little effect in the east (see Malloy 1970; Grindle and Domingo 2003).

5. *Minifundios* are properties of one or two hectares insufficient for subsistence, as contrasted with latifundios, large-scale holdings of the wealthy, which were maintained in the Oriente, or eastern Bolivia. *Surcofundios*, from the word *surco* (row), is a colloquialism that refers to the fragmentation of land through inheritance, leading to properties of only one or two hand-hoed rows.

6. The Chiriguano statue was actually erected in the mid-1990s by elites of Santa Cruz. It was an effort to illustrate their solidarity and camaraderie with the indigenous peoples of the Oriente. More recently, Evo Morales and the MAS administration have used the statue to gather people in protest—an act of reclaiming this space.

7. I observed this event, which took place in June of 2006, along with MST representatives and tape-recorded the speeches.

8. The legal titles given out by Morales had been dormant in the government offices of INRA for up to ten years, a sign of the snail's pace at which agrarian reform has taken place in Bolivia.

9. As mentioned in previous chapters, land reform has a relatively recent history in Bolivia, beginning with the 1953 Agrarian Reform Law. Many have described this as an incomplete effort because government officials only redistributed land to campesinos in the highlands, while in the lowlands they created a path for export-oriented economic development and large-scale landholding. The 1996 INRA Law, dissatisfaction with the law, and new proposals for an agrarian revolution were the basic grievances expressed through years of grassroots protests between 2000 and 2005 (Assies 2006).

10. Horizontality in such broad-based coalition efforts has become a point of reference for latter-day descriptions of Bolivian social movements in the form of the multitude (Linera 2006) and as standing against the hierarchical arrangements of elite participation in the state that historically characterized Bolivian politics.

11. The marchers used one huge pot, the *olla común*. The common pot has a long history in rural Andean communities, whose members usually prepared a pot during fiestas and collective work projects in order to feed large numbers of people (Harris 1982, 1995). More recently, social movements have utilized the common pot as a kind of moveable feast in order to support striking workers in mines and factories.

12. Domitila Barrios de Chúngara was the leader of the Housewives' Committee of one of Bolivia's militant mining communities. In her famous autobiography, *Let Me Speak* (1978), she details her personal life in the tin mines and the challenges of poverty and inequality in mining towns, while also dealing with the challenges of a broader patriarchal system in Bolivia. Due to her organizing efforts and success in Siglo XX, she became an international symbol of feminist organizing. Yet, she always pointed out on speaking trips and tours, the feminism of the global South was different than white bourgeoisie, middle-class feminism—many of the wives of Bolivian miners were not prepared to reject their compañeros who worked as exploited laborers in the mines, but rather, wanted to work alongside them.

13. Susan Paulson (2006) argues that by looking at the energy invested in ritual meals, we can begin to conceptualize intense corporal experiences and tangible material realities of disenfranchised rural, indigenous communities. She challenges scholarship that focuses solely on multiculturalism and privileges symbols and products of indigenous culture without looking closely at the deep political and economic meaning. Paulson relates such food rituals to other collective bodily practices gaining prominence in Bolivia, like the call for a constituent assembly, pointing toward possibilities of a new kind of civil society grounded in indigenous rights and material needs.

14. MST mystique, or the *místicas* of the movement, emerged directly from Latin American liberation theology, which had a great influence on MST-Brazil. A *mística* can be described as the use of performance, art, and symbolism to preserve historical, cultural, and ideological roots and construct a collective identity (see Issa 2007).

15. The soundscapes we inhabit can be perceived as the daily noises that shape our environmental surrounds.

16. Avelar and Dunn (2011) explore the connections between popular music and citizenship in Brazil, which has served as an effective resource for communities to stake claims to political, social, and cultural rights. Their essays explore music in relation to national identity, social class, racial formations, community organizing, and more. While MST recognizes the importance of various musical forms for rural and indigenous peoples in the Andes and lowlands, its use of music seems to represent something different. A creative improvisational style, the hybridization of cultural and sonoric forms, and its flexible uses for mealtime rituals indicate that this protest or social movement music is pushing the bounds of our classic definitions of citizenship as grounded in national, regional, and ethnic-regional identity.

17. The columnas stayed intact until a few miles from the San Francisco plaza, when everyone suddenly began to run into this historic site. Some MST leaders mentioned that they wanted to arrive before their Aymara brothers and sisters. There was intense competition regarding who would arrive first.

18. Not everyone was thrilled with this massive demonstration. Many *Paceños* (people of La Paz) complained that they could not get to work because the streets were closed off, while others spoke of "*bloqueo* fatigue," the fact that they were tired of daily roadblocks.

19. Oftentimes, mass mobilizations like the most recent march for land and territory prove to be an effective strategy for meeting the demands of the masses and passing critical legislation through the Senate. The attention of mass media and the international press focused not only on Bolivia, but on the pressing problem of land redistribution for poor people. Many of the senators realized that ignoring the demands of the majority indigenous population would only create greater problems, and the pressure from the international community forced swing senators to vote in favor of the New Agrarian Reform Law.

CHAPTER SIX

1. The new constitution was supposed to incorporate and embrace basic indigenous values (Buxton 2009), grant extensive indigenous rights (Bevins 2009; Van Schaick 2009), and empower the native majority (Albro 2010a, 2010b). All of this was part of Morales's broader agenda to lead a cultural and democratic revolution and to decolonize the public administration.

2. Thomas Grisaffi (2009, 2010) notes that while these images of the pure and untouched Indian community might be problematic for anthropologists, they have long been mobilized by political groups with nationalist agendas (Flores-Galindo 1987; Poole 1997). Indigenous culture plays an essential role in the construction of collective identities and in making claims against the state.

3. Performance of Andean indigeneity as a marginalized yet deeply resistant culture, embedded in older ways of being, living, and maintaining territorial connections, holds particular clout now at the grassroots and regional level and has come to inform national agendas. This turn toward the use, mobility, and performance of indigeneity as justification for national change has not always been part of state-making agendas. Indigenous ways, customs, and worldviews have historically been

kept far from spaces of formal governance and places of centralized power, like the Plaza Murillo (Guss 2006). However, with transnational shifts towards incorporating indigenous peoples into nation-states, coupled with a global discursive turn toward indigeneity as the language of rights and legitimization, progressive and left-leaning governments have picked up indigeneity as critical to transforming socioeconomic relations and age-old colonial regimes.

4. At this point, there are many more poor Collas living in Santa Cruz than elite or well-to-do Cambas. The right wing had to make their discourses of indigeneity and regional identity generalizable enough to fit distinct groups of working-class mestizos, poor urban informal workers, and even hard-working Collas into their platform.

5. As mentioned in Chapter 2, historically elite Cruceños identified as direct descendants of Europeans. Ximena Soruco (2011) describes how these groups once referred to themselves as "conquerors" or "colonizers" of the Oriente. This racialized vision of European conquest and dominance over the low-lying plains of the Oriente informed, in the nineteenth and twentieth centuries, their historic right to complete control over regional lands as private property and an economic model of resource extraction. Yet as indigenous peoples became more visible and gained national-level power in the 1990s and 2000s, elites suddenly had to shift discourses and performances and adopt an indigenous identity for their movement.

6. Elites have seized upon mythic tales, initially recorded by Swedish ethnologist Erland Nordenskiöld in 1917, which chronicle the encounter of lowland Guaraní warriors with the Inca empire in the foothills of the Andes during the sixteenth century (Pruden 2003). According to these accounts, the Inca could not overcome the force of the Guaraní militia, which could not or would not give up. Both Pruden (2003) and Lowrey (2006) clarify the actual history behind this tale. In contrast to the elite version, with its imagery of resistance to imperialism, the ethnohistorical documents do not clearly indicate whether Incan imperial ambitions encompassed a desire to expand into Guaraní lands or whether the battle was initiated by the Guaraní during a daring incursion into the far margins of Inca-held territory in search of access to the mines.

7. Allyn Stearman (1985) notes that a prominent joke in the 1970s was that this Christ statue, with its outstretched arms, was saying, "Stop! No more Collas" (75) It is no coincidence that this statue has become the landmark for elite battles against the centralized government, just as the Chiriguano statue has become the sign and symbol of indigenous resistance.

8. For other, more recent, rightist tactics, see Fabricant 2011.

9. The green stands for the limitless natural beauty and abundance of Santa Cruz and the riches of the frontier, while the white symbolizes the pure Spanish lineage and nobility inherited from the colonial period (Gustafson 2006; Fabricant 2009).

10. This was the Right's first attempt to reestablish itself on the national state, through a recall referendum that called for a vote of confidence in the president, vice president, and departmental prefects. They lost decisively; support for the government increased from 54 percent in 2005 to 67 percent in 2008.

11. This *golpe cívico* attempted to weaken the Morales government by borrowing tactics from the CIA-backed coup against democratically elected Chilean president

Salvador Allende in the early 1980s, in which business elites launched civic strikes. For more on the civic coup, see Fabricant 2011.

12. Initially, Morales was trying to pass legislation allowing for unlimited terms for the president. However, due to sustained right-wing resistance—they described Morales's MAS administration as a totalitarian regime, similar to Chávez's, and even went so far as to compare Morales to Hitler and Stalin—he had to make several concessions in order to reach some kind of reconciliation. Future presidents will be allowed to run for office on a two-term limit.

13. While the limitations of this chapter do not allow me to develop the tensions inherent in indigenous self-rule and governance and regionalist ideas of autonomy, several scholars have written about autonomy (see Cameron 2010; Gustafson 2009a). The final version of the constitution recognizes four types of autonomies: departmental, regional, municipal, and indigenous. In June and July 2010, MAS's opposition to indigenous autonomy became more explicit, as they accused lowland indigenous organizations, who had organized a 1,500-kilometer protest march from Trinidad to La Paz, of being financed by USAID, and referred to CIDOB as traitors. Further, they mobilized their forces in the Chapare—the Six Federations of Coca Growers—to block the CIDOB march. In the end, the government and CIDOB came to a negotiated settlement that resulted in several changes to the Framework Law on Autonomy and Decentralization (see Cameron 2010).

CONCLUSION

1. The "resource curse," or dynamic pressure from outside forces in search of critical resources and mineral wealth—like silver from the highlands of Bolivia to fuel the colonial empire, or, more recently, commodities like gas, oil, and soy—has caused much displacement and disruption of native peoples and communities and has led to distinctive forms of indigenous organizing throughout history. This quest for resource wealth has led to much movement (rural to urban, west to east) and the creative mixing and melding of distinct ethnic groups, traditions, rituals, and ways of governance. In short, this hybridity is not new—it has a long history in Bolivia.

2. Hyperindustrialized countries in the global North have greatly contributed to global warming, thereby altering the environments of indigenous populations and rural communities, and damaging productive ecosystems. The United States alone contributes 25 percent of all carbon emissions, while developing countries like China and India have also begun to spew large amounts of carbon dioxide (N. Klein 2009). This, then, is the latest phase of uneven geographical development and expansive capitalism, and debt-strapped and dependent nations in the global South will be some of the first to deal with this problem.

3. The *New York Times*, December 14, 2009, featured a front-page article about the water problems in the highlands of Bolivia due to global warming. The report stated that if water problems are not solved, El Alto could perhaps be the first large urban casualty of climate change. It further reported that climate change would eliminate many glaciers in the Andes within twenty years, threatening the existence of nearly 100 million people.

4. In part, Bolivia is already feeling the effects of climate change because of uneven geographical development and distribution of resources, and increasing poverty and vulnerability. Five of the main impacts of climate change are food insecurity, glacial retreat and water availability, natural disasters, disease, and forest fires. Rises in near-surface temperatures have tripled since the 1970s, which has led to a major retreat in available glacier water. This has created significant effects on the water supply as well as on electricity produced by hydropower. The Tuni Condoriri glacier, which provides the majority of the water supply to La Paz and El Alto, is expected to disappear by 2025. Climate change has also affected the frequency and severity of flooding, and forest fires caused by drought have been more common in the lowlands. Flooding between 2006 and 2008 affected over one million people in a region where 32 percent of people live in poverty and are particularly vulnerable to natural hazards. For more on climate change in Bolivia, see http://www.boliviainfoforum.org.uk.

5. Climate debt (Klein 2009) is about who will pick up the bill. The grassroots movements behind the proposal argue that all the costs associated with adapting to a more hostile ecology—everything from building stronger sea walls to switching to cleaner, more expensive technologies—are the responsibility of the countries that created the crisis.

6. CONAMAQ is a Bolivian confederation of traditional governing bodies of Quechua-speaking highland indigenous communities in the Departments of La Paz, Oruro, Potosí, Cochabamba, Chuquisaca, and Tarija. Specifically, it represents the following sixteen *suyus* (regions or districts): Jacha Carangas, Jatun Quillacas, Asamajaquis, Charcas Qara Qara, Council of Ayllus of Potosí, Qara Qara Suyu, Sora, Kallawaya, Leco, Larecaja, Colla, Chui, Paca Jake, Ayllus of Cochabamba, Kapaj Omasuyus, and Yapacaní. CONAMAQ was founded on March 22, 1997, with the purpose of restoring the self-governance of "original nations," including "collective rights to land and natural resources, re-definition of administrative units and self-determination exercised through indigenous autonomies and direct representation in state institutions."

7. The gas protests in December 2010 are, perhaps, the most recent example of pushback against Morales. The Morales government removed a national gas subsidy, causing transport fuel costs to rise more than 80 percent overnight, from $1.97 per gallon to $3.42 per gallon, and Bolivian popular movements became vocal and militant. The media called the policy change the "*Gasolinazo*," or "The Big Gasoline Hit," and the Gasolinazo led to an immediate mobilization by the country's social movements. This was the first massive protest in opposition to the Morales administration's policies concerning natural resource pricing and distribution. These protests demanded rapid response on his part because they threatened to topple his administration. Thus, in a New Year's Eve message to the nation, Morales said that he had listened to the unions and social organizations, and had decided to rescind the decree, winning support from the movements once again.

8. The Building Bridges Collective (2010) argues that these contradictions are exemplified by the proposed Trans-Oceanic Highway, a project jointly undertaken by the Bolivian, Brazilian, and Peruvian governments to connect their markets to seaports that, if constructed, would destroy ecologically sensitive areas in the Chapare and Beni region. Another example is the $2 billion hydroelectric dam to be built on

the Beni River. This was probably one of the first and the most visible public expressions of wariness toward the Morales administration from his social movement base.

9. In his chapter on the co-option of indigenous autonomies by the state, Fernando Garcés (2011) poses similar kinds of questions: Can the state be changed? Can it be decolonized? Can its practices and routines and its subjection to the constitutive efforts of the powerful be changed?

10. In 2011–12, we have seen the unraveling of this neoliberal structure or order as workers' rights have come under violent attack. From Wisconsin to a slew of European cities in Greece, Spain, and England, sporadic protests have brought people together to stand against such conservative-led austerity plans. Yet, these are all still very sporadic resistance movements without a clear and coherent long-term agenda or a plan for an alternative economic and political model to neoliberalism. Bolivia, however, is a very different case. There, workers' sporadic resistance led to massive movements that linked distinct interest groups—workers, laborers, environmentalists, and indigenous-rights groups—and provided a platform for scaling demands up and reconstructing the state. Still, Bolivians have a long way to go before some of the proposals born on the streets actually transform the economic and political model.

BIBLIOGRAPHY

Abercrombie, Thomas. 1998. *Pathways of Memory and Power: Ethnography and History among an Andean People*. Madison: University of Wisconsin Press.

Albó, Xavier. 1977. *La paradoja Aymara: Solidaridad y faccionalismo*. Vol 8. La Paz: CIPCA.

———. 1991. "El retorno del Indio." *Revista Andina* 9(2): 209–345.

Albro, Robert. 2005. "'The Water Is Ours, Carajo!': Deep Citizenship in Bolivia's Water Wars." In *Social Movements: An Anthropological Reader*, edited by June Nash, 249–71. Malden: Blackwell.

———. 2006. "The Culture of Democracy and Bolivia's Indigenous Movements." *Critique of Anthropology* 26(4): 387–410.

———. 2010a. "Confounding Cultural Citizenship and Constitutional Reform in Bolivia." *Latin American Perspectives* 37(3): 71–90.

———. 2010b. *Roosters at Midnight: Indigenous Signs and Stigma in Local Bolivian Politics*. Santa Fe: School of American Research Press.

Allen, Catherine J. 1997. "When Pebbles Move Mountains: Iconicity and Symbolism in Quechua Ritual." In *Creating Context in Andean Cultures*, edited by Rosaleen Howard-Malverde, 73–84. Oxford: Oxford University Press.

———, 1998. *The Hold Life Has: Coca and Cultural Identity in an Andean Community*. Washington, D.C.: Smithsonian Institute Press.

Altieri, Miguel A. 1995. *Agroecology: The Science of Sustainable Agriculture*. Boulder: Westview.

Andean Information Network. 2011. "Bolivia: New TIPNIS Law Fails to Mollify Protestors and Reflects MAS Divisions." http://ain-bolivia.org/2011/10/bolivia-new-tipnis-law-fails-to-mollify-protestors-and-reflects-mas-divisions/. November 30, 2011.

Anderson, Benedict. 1983. *Imagined Communities: Reflections on the Origins and Spread of Nationalism*. Rev. ed. New York: Verso.

Andolina, Robert J. 1999. "Colonial Legacies and Plurinational Imaginaries: Indigenous Movement Politics in Ecuador and Bolivia." Ph.D. diss., University of Minnesota.

———. 2001. "Between Local Authenticity and Global Accountability: The Ayllu Movement in Contemporary Bolivia." Paper presented at Beyond the Lost Decade: Indigenous Movements and the Transformation of Development and Democracy in Latin America Conference, Princeton, N.J., March 2–3.

Andolina, Robert, Nina Laurie, and Sarah A. Radcliffe. 2009. *Indigenous Development in the Andes: Culture, Power, and Transnationalism*. Durham: Duke University Press.

Appadurai, Arjun. 2002. "Deep Democracy: Urban Governmentality and the Horizon of Politics." *Public Culture* 14(1): 21–47.

Arbona, Juan M. 2008. "'Sangre de minero, semilla de guerrillero': Histories and Memories in the Organization and Struggles of the Santiago II Neighborhood of El Alto, Bolivia." *Bulletin of Latin American Research* 27(1): 24–42.

Arbona, Juan M., and Benjamin Kohl. 2003. "City Profile: La Paz–El Alto." *Cities* 21(3): 255–65.

Arsenault, Chris. 2011. "Zapatistas War with No Breath." http://english.aljazeera.net/indepth/features/2011/01/20111183946608868.html. June 6, 2011.

Assies, Willem. 2002. "From Rubber Estate to Simple Commodity Production: Agrarian Struggles in the Northern Bolivian Amazon." *Journal of Peasant Studies* 29(3): 83–130.

———. 2006. "La 'Media Luna' sobre Bolivia: Nación, región, etnia y clase social." *América Latina Hoy* 43 (August): 87–105.

Avelar, Idelber, and Christopher Dunn. 2011. *Brazilian Popular Music and Citizenship*. Durham: Duke University Press.

Barragán Romano, Rossana. 1999. *Indios, mujeres y ciudadanos: Legislación y ejercicio de la ciudadanía en Bolivia (Siglo XIX)*. La Paz: Fundación Diálogo.

Barrios de Chúngara, Domitila, with Moema Viezzer. 1978. *Let Me Speak!: Testimony of Domitila, a Woman of the Bolivian Mines*. New York: Monthly Review.

Bastien, Joseph W. 1978. *Mountain of the Condor: Metaphor and Ritual in an Andean Ayllu*. St. Paul: West.

Bebbington, Anthony. 2009. "The New Extraction: Rewriting Political Ecology in the Andes." *NACLA Report on the Americas* 42(5): 12–20.

Bellamy Foster, John. 2000. *Marx's Ecology: Materialism and Nature*. New York: Monthly Review.

Bellamy Foster, John, Brett Clark, and Richard York. 2010. *The Ecological Rift: Capitalism's War with the Earth*. New York: Monthly Review.

Bevins, Vincent. 2009. "A New Dawn for Bolivia?" *New Statesman*, January 26. http://www.newstatesman.com/south-america/2009/01/indigenous-rights-constitution. July 6, 2011.

Bigenho, Michelle. 2002. *Sounding Indigenous: Authenticity in Bolivian Music Performance*. New York: Palgrave.

Bjork-James, Carwil. 2011. "Indigenous March in Defense of Isiboro Sécure Arrives in La Paz, Challenges Evo Morales Government." Background briefing, 16 October 2011 (copy provided in personal communiction).

Boal, Augusto. 1979. *Theater of the Oppressed*. New York: Urzien Books.

Branford, Susan, and J. Rocha. 2002. *Cutting the Wire: The Story of the Landless Movement in Brazil*. London: Latin American Bureau.

Brenner, Neil. 2004. *New State Spaces: Urban Governance and the Rescaling of Statehood*. Oxford: Oxford University Press.

Brush, Stephen B. 1977. *Mountain, Field and Family: The Economy and Human Ecology of an Andean Village*. Philadelphia: University of Pennsylvania Press.

Bueno, Rafael Loayza, and Ajoy Datta. 2011. "The Politics of Evo Morales's Rise to Power." Overseas Development Institute. http://www.odi.org.uk/resources/details.asp?id=5674&title=evo-morales-think-tanks-social-movements-mas. July 1, 2011.

Building Bridges Collective. 2010. *A Space for Movement: Reflections from Bolivia on Climate Justice, Social Movements, and the State*. Leeds, U.K.: Footprint Workers Coop.

Burbach, Roger. 2008. "The Rise of Food Fascism: Allied to Global Agribusiness, Agrarian Elites Foment Coup in Bolivia." http://www.counterpunch.org/burbach07012008.html. November 10, 2010.

Buxton, Nick. 2009. "Bolivia's New Constitution." *Transnational Institute*, February 5. http://www.tni.org//archives/act/19180. July 6, 2011.

———. 2011. "The Law of Mother Earth: Behind Bolivia's Historic Bill." http://therightsofnature.org/bolivia-law-of-mother-earth/. July 15, 2011.

Cajías de la Vega, Magdalena. 2004. "El poder de la memoria: Articulaciones ideológicas-culturales en los movimientos sociales bolivianos." *Barataria* 1(1): 18–28.

Calla, Pamela. 2010. "Legal Struggles, Public Policy Narratives and Street Politics in Bolivia: Constitutional Challenges to the Construction of an Intercultural and Non-Patriarchal State." Paper presented at the 'Off Centered States: Political Formation and Deformation in the Andes' SARR Conference, May 27–29, Quito, Ecuador.

Cameron, John D. 2010. "Is This What Autonomy Looks Like?: Tensions and Challenges in the Construction of Indigenous Autonomy in Bolivia." Paper prepared for the Annual Meeting of the Latin American Studies Association, Toronto, October 6–9, 2010.

Canessa, Andrew. 2000. "Contesting Hybridity: Evangelistas and Kataristas in Highland Bolivia." *Journal of Latin American Studies* 32 (1): 55–84.

———. 2005. "The Indian Within the Indian Without: Citizenship, Race, and Sex in an Andean Hamlet." In *Natives Making Nation. Gender, Indigeneity and the State in the Andes*, edited by Andrew Canessa, 130–55. Tucson: University of Arizona Press.

———. 2006. "Todos somos indígenas: Towards a New Language of National Political Identity." *Bulletin of Latin American Research* 25(2): 241–63.

———. 2007. "Who Is Indigenous? Self-identification, Indigeneity, and Claims to Justice in Contemporary Bolivia." *Urban Anthropology* 36(3): 14–48.

———. 2012. *Intimate Indigeneities: Exploring Race and Sex in the Small Spaces of Life*. Durham: Duke University Press.

Collins, Jane, Micaela di Leonardo, and Brett Williams. 2008. *New Landscapes of Inequality: Neoliberalism and the Erosion of Democracy in America*. Santa Fe: School of American Research Press.

Colloredo-Mansfeld, Rudi. 1999. *The Native Leisure Class: Consumption and Cultural Creativity in the Andes*. Chicago: University of Chicago Press.

———. 2002. "Don't Be Lazy, Don't Lie, Don't Steal: Community Justice in the Neoliberal Andes." *American Ethnologist* 29(3): 637–62.

Conklin, Beth. 2001. *Consuming Grief: Compassionate Cannibalism in Amazonian Society*. Austin: University of Texas Press.

Conklin, Beth, and Lauren Graham. 1995. "The Shifting Middle Ground: Amazonian Indians and Ecopolitics." *American Anthropologist* 97(4): 695–710.

Connaghan. Catherine, James M. Malloy, and Luis A. Abugattas. 1990. "Business and the Boys: The Politics of Neoliberalism in the Central Andes." *Latin American Research Review* 25(2): 3–30.

Conquergood, Dwight. 2002a. "Lethal Theater: Performance, Punishment, and the Death Penalty." *Theater Journal* 54(3): 339–67.

———. 2002b. "Performance Studies Interventions and Radical Research." *Theater Journal* 54(3): 145–56.

Cosgrove, Denis E. 1998. *Social Formation and Symbolic Landscape*. Madison: University of Wisconsin Press.

Crabtree, John. 2005. *Patterns of Protest: Politics and Social Movements in Bolivia*. London: Latin American Bureau.

Dangl, Benjamin. 2007. *The Price of Fire: Resource Wars and Social Movements in Bolivia*. Edinburgh: AK Press.

———. 2009. "Neoliberalism Ends Here: Bolivia's Bold New Constitution Empowers the Country's Ethnic Communities with Access to Education and Healthcare." *The Guardian*. http://www.guardian.co.uk/commentisfree/cifamerica/2009/jan/27/bolivia-referendum-constitution-evo-morales. July 14, 2011.

Das, Veena, and Deborah Poole. 2004. "State and Its Margins: Comparative Ethnographies." In *Anthropology in the Margins of the State*, edited by Veena Das and Deborah Poole, 3–34. Oxford: James Currey.

Davis, Mike. 2006. *Planet of the Slums*. New York: Verso.

de la Cadena, Marisol, and Orin Starn. 2007. *Indigenous Experience Today*. Oxford: Berg.

Delgado, Guillermo. 1994. "Ethnic Politics and the Popular Movement" In *Latin America Faces the Twenty-first Century: Reconstructing a Social Justice Agenda*, edited by Susanne Jonas and Edward J. McCaughan, 77–88. Boulder: Westview.

Democracy Now. 2010. "Evo Morales Opens Climate Change Conference in Tiquipaya." http://www.democracynow.org/2010/4/21/evo_morales_opens_climate_change_conference. April 25, 2010.

Desmarais, Annette Aurélie. 2002. "The Vía Campesina: Consolidating an International Peasant and Farm Movement." *Journal of Peasant Studies* 29(2): 91–124.

———. 2007. *La vía campesina: Globalization and the Power of Peasants*. Halifax: Fernwood.

Diemel, Jose Alice. 2010. "Grassroots Based Agrarian Reform in Santa Cruz: A Reason to Hope for the End of Land Concentration?" M.A. thesis, Radboud University, Nijmegen, Neth.

di Leonardo, Micaela. 2008. "The Neoliberalization of Minds, Space, and Bodies: Rising Global Inequality and the Shifting American Public Sphere." In *New Landscapes of Inequality*, edited by Jane L. Collins, Micaela di Leonardo, and Brett Williams, 191–208. Santa Fe: School of American Research Press.

Douglas, Mary. 1966. *Purity and Danger: An Analysis of Concepts of Pollution and Taboo*. New York: Praeger.

Dunkerley, James. 1984. *Rebellion in the Veins: Political Struggle in Bolivia, 1952–82*. London: Verso.

Edelman, Marc. 2008. "Transnational Organizing in Agrarian Central America: Histories, Challenges, Prospects." *Journal of Agrarian Change* 8(2–3): 229–57.

————. 2009. "Peasant-Farmer Movements, Third World Peoples, and the Seattle Protests against the World Trade Organization, 1999." *Dialectical Anthropology* 33(2): 109–28.

Edelman, Marc, and Carwil James. 2011. "Peasants' Rights and the UN System: Quixotic Struggle? Or Emancipatory Idea Whose Time Has Come?" *Journal of Peasant Studies* 38(1): 81–108.

Ellwood, Wayne. 2007. *The No-Nonsense Guide to Globalization*. Oxford: New Internationalist.

Escobar, Arturo. 2010. "Latin America at a Crossroads: Alternative Modernizations, Post-Liberalism or Post-Development." *Cultural Studies* 24(1): 1–65.

Fabricant, Nicole. 2009. "Performative Politics: The Camba Countermovement in Eastern Bolivia." *American Ethnologist* 36(4): 768–83.

————. 2010. "Between the Romance of Collectivism and the Reality of Individualism: Ayllu Rhetoric in Bolivia's Landless Movement." *Latin American Perspectives* 37(4): 88–107.

————. 2011. "A Realigned Bolivian Right: New 'Democratic' Destabilizations." *NACLA Report on the Americas* 44(1): 30.

Fabricant, Nicole, and Bret Gustafson. 2011. *Remapping Bolivia: Resources, Territory, and Indigeneity in a Plurinational State*. Santa Fe: School of American Research Press.

Fabricant, Nicole, and Nancy Postero. 2012. "Hasta las últimas consequencias: Bolivian Hunger Strikes from the 1970s Dictatorship to the Autonomy Battles of the 2000s." *Journal of Latin American Anthropology* (forthcoming).

Farthing, Linda. 2009. "Bolivia's Dilemma: Development Confronts the Legacy of Extraction." *NACLA Report on the Americas* 42(5): 25–30.

Farthing, Linda, and Benjamin Kohl. 2007. "Mobilizing Identity and Memory: Social Movements in Bolivia." Paper presented at LASA International Congress, Montreal, September 5–9.

Ferguson, James. 1990. *The Anti-Politics Machine: Development, Depoliticization, and Bureacratic Power in Lesotho*. Cambridge: Cambridge University Press.

Fernandes, Bernardo Mançano. 2001. "The Occupation as a Form of Access to Land." Paper Presented at the Twenty-third International Congress of the Latin American Studies Association, Washington, D.C., September 6–8.

Flores-Galindo, Alberto. 1987. *Buscando un Inca: Identidad y Utopia en los Andes*. Lima: Editorial Horizonte.

Freire, Paulo. 1970. *Pedagogy of the Oppressed*. New York: Continuum.

Friedsky, Jean. 2005. "Land War in Bolivia: Conflict for Power and Territory." *NarcoNews Bulletin* 39, October 13, http://narconews.com/Issue39/article1470.html. September 1, 2007.

Galeano, Eduardo. 1973. *Open Veins of Latin America: Five Centuries of the Pillage of a Continent*. New York: Monthly Review.

Garcés, Fernando. 2011. "The Domestication of Indigenous Autonomies in Bolivia: From the Pact of Unity to the New Constitution." In *Remapping Bolivia: Resources, Territory, and Indigeneity in a Plurinational State*, edited by Nicole Fabricant and Bret Gustafson, 46–67. Santa Fe: School of American Research Press.

Gill, Lesley. 1987. *Peasants, Entrepreneurs, and Social Change: Frontier Development in Lowland Bolivia*. Boulder: Westview.

Gilly, Adolfo. 2003. "Historias desde adentro: La tenaz persistencia de los tiempos." In *Ya es otro tiempo el presente: Cuatro momentos de insurgencia indígena*, edited by Forrest Hylton, Felix Patzi, Sergio Serulnikov, and Sinclair Thompson, 21–41. La Paz: Muela del Diablo Editores.

Gledhill, John. 2005. "Neoliberalism." In *A Companion to the Anthropology of Politics*, edited by David Nugent and Joan Vincent, 332–48. Malden: Blackwell.

Goldstein, Daniel. 2004. *The Spectacular City: Violence and Performance in Urban Bolivia*. Durham: Duke University Press.

———. 2010. "Security and the Culture Expert: Dilemmas of an Engaged Anthropology." *Political and Legal Anthropology Review* 33(1): 126–42.

Goldstein, Daniel, and Fatimah Williams Castro. 2006. "Creative Violence: How Marginal People Make News in Bolivia." *Journal of Latin American Anthropology* 11(2): 380–407.

Goodale, Mark. 2009. *Dilemmas of Modernity: Bolivian Encounters with Law and Liberalism*. Stanford: Stanford University Press.

Gotkowitz, Laura. 2008. *A Revolution for Our Rights: Indigenous Struggles for Land and Justice in Bolivia, 1880–1952*. Durham: Duke University Press.

Gray Molina, George. 2009. "A Deeper Look at Bolivia's Indigenous Constitution." *CRISE Research News*, no. 5:1–2.

Greene, Shane. 2009. *Customizing Indigeneity: Paths to a Visionary Politics in Peru*. Stanford: Stanford University Press.

Grindle, Merilee Serrill, and Pilar Domingo. 2003. *Proclaiming Revolution: Bolivia in Comparative Perspective*. London: Institute for Latin American Studies.

Grisaffi, Thomas. 2009. "Radio Sovereignty: The Sovereign Voice of the Bolivian Coca Growers?" Ph.D. diss., London School of Economics.

———. 2010. "'We Are *Originarios* . . . We Just Aren't from Here': Coca Leaf and Identity Politics in the Chapare, Bolivia." *Bulletin of Latin American Research* 29(4): 425–39.

Guss, David. 2006. The Gran Poder and the Reconquest of La Paz. *Journal of Latin American Studies* 11(2): 294–328.

Gustafson, Bret. 2002. "Paradoxes of Liberal Indigenism: Indigenous Movements, State Processes, and Intercultural Reform in Bolivia." In *The Politics of Ethnicity: Indigenous Peoples in Latin American States*, edited by David Maybury-Lewis, 266–306. Cambridge: Harvard University Press.

———. 2006. "Spectacles of Autonomy and Crisis: Or, What Bulls and Beauty Queens Have to Do with Regionalism in Eastern Bolivia." *Journal of Latin American and Caribbean Anthropology* 11(2): 351–79.

———. 2008. "By Means Legal and Otherwise: The Bolivian Right Regroups." *NACLA Report on the Americas* 20(7): 1–7.

———. 2009a. "Manipulating Cartographies: Plurinationalism, Autonomy, and Indigenous Resurgence in Bolivia." *Anthropological Quarterly* 82(4): 985–1016.

———. 2009b. *New Languages of the State: Indigenous Resurgence and the Politics of Knowledge in Bolivia*. Durham: Duke University Press.

———. 2010. "When States Act like Movements: Dismantling Local Power and 'Seating' Sovereignty in Post-Neoliberal Bolivia." *Latin American Perspectives* 37(4): 48–66.

———. 2011. "Flashpoints of Sovereignty, Natural Gas, and Territorial Conflict in Bolivia." In *Crude Domination: An Anthropology of Oil*, edited by Andrea Behrends, Stephen Reyna, and Günther Schlee. Oxford: Berghahn Books.

Gustafson, Bret, and Nicole Fabricant. 2011. "Introduction: New Cartographies of Knowledge and Struggle." In *Remapping Bolivia: Resources, Territory, and Indigeneity in a Plurinational State*, edited by Nicole Fabricant and Bret Gustafson, 1–33. Santa Fe: School of American Research Press.

Hale, Charles. 2002. "Does Multiculturalism Menace?: Governance, Cultural Rights and the Politics of Identity in Guatemala." *Journal of Latin American Studies* 34(2): 485–525.

———. 2004. "Rethinking Indigenous Politics in the Era of the Indio Permitido." *NACLA Report on the Americas* 38(2): 16–20.

———. 2006. *Más que un indio: Racial Ambivalence and the Paradox of Neoliberal Multiculturalism in Guatemala*. Santa Fe: School of American Research Press.

Harris, Olivia. 1982. "Labour and Produce in an Ethnic Economy, Northern Potosí." In *Ecology and Exchange*, edited by David Lehmann, 70–96. Cambridge: Cambridge University Press.

———. 1995. "Ethnic Identity and Market Relations: Indians and Mestizos in the Andes." In *Ethnicity, Markets, and Migration in the Andes: At the Crossroads of History and Anthropology*, edited by Olivia Harris and Brooke Larson, 351–90. Durham: Duke University Press.

Harvey, David. 1990. *The Condition of Postmodernity: An Inquiry into the Origins of Cultural Change*. Cambridge: Blackwell.

———. 1998. "Marxism, Metaphors, and Ecological Politics." *Monthly Review* 49(11): 1–7.

———. 2003. *The New Imperialism*. Oxford: Oxford University Press.

———. 2005. *A Brief History of Neoliberalism*. Oxford: Oxford University Press.

———. 2006. *Spaces of Global Capitalism: Towards a Theory of Uneven Geographical Development*. New York: Verso.

———. 2010. *The Enigma of Capital and the Crisis of Capitalism*. Oxford: Oxford University Press.

Harvey, Neil. 1998. *The Chiapas Rebellion: The Struggle for Land and Democracy*. Durham: Duke University Press.

Henderson, Jason. 2009. "The Spaces of Parking: Mapping the Politics of Mobility in San Francisco." *Antipode* 41(1): 70–91.

Hertzler, Douglas. 2008. "From Washington, D.C., to Alto Parapetí: The International Context of Agrarian Reform in Bolivia." Paper presented at Decolonizing the Nation, (Re)Imagining the City (Conference), Evanston, Ill., May 8–9.

Hobsbawm, Eric, and Terence Ranger, eds. 1983. *The Invention of Tradition*. Cambridge: Cambridge University Press.

Holston, James. 1999. "Spaces of Insurgent Citizenship." In *Cities and Citizenship*, edited by James Holston, 155–76. Durham: Duke University Press.

———. 2008. *Insurgent Citizenship: Disjunctions of Democracy and Modernity in Brazil.* Princeton: Princeton University Press.

Holt-Giménez, Eric, and Raj Patel. 2009. *Food Rebellions!: Crisis and the Hunger for Justice.* Oakland: Food First Books.

Humphreys, Macartan, Jeffrey D. Sachs, and Joseph E. Stiglitz. 2007. *Escaping the Resource Curse.* New York: Columbia University Press.

INE (Instituto Nacional de Estadística). 2001a. *Censo nacional de población y vivienda.* La Paz: Instituto Nacional de Estadística.

———. 2001b. "Santa Cruz: Proyecciones de población, por sexo, según municipio, 2000–2010." http://www.ine.gov.bo/indice/visualizador.aspx?ah=PC20407.htm February 9, 2010.

Isbell, Billie Jean. 1978. *To Defend Ourselves: Ecology and Ritual in an Andean Village.* Austin: University of Texas Press.

Issa, Daniela. 2007. "Praxis of Empowerment: *Mística* and Mobilization in Brazil's Landless Rural Workers' Movement." *Latin American Perspectives* 34(2): 124–38.

Kaimowitz, David, Graham Thiele, and Pablo Pacheco. 1999. "The Effects of Structural Adjustment on Deforestation and Forest Degradation in Lowland Bolivia." *World Development* 27(3): 505–20.

Kenner, Dario. 2011a. "Conflict over TIPNIS Road Continues." http://boliviadiary. wordpress.com/2001/11/24/conflict-over-tipnis-road-project-continues/. November 23, 2011.

———. 2011b. "Controversial Highway Plan Resisted by Bolivia's Indigenous Peoples." http://boliviadiary.wordpress.com/2011/09/21/controversial-highway-plan-resisted-by-bolivia's-indigenous-peoples/. September 21, 2011.

Kirshner, Joshua. 2010. "Migrants' Voices: Negotiating Autonomy in Santa Cruz." *Latin American Perspectives* 37(4): 108–24.

———. 2011. "Migrants and Citizens: Hygiene Panic and Urban Space in Santa Cruz." In *Remapping Bolivia: Resources, Territory, and Indigeneity in a Plurinational State*, edited by Nicole Fabricant and Bret Gustafson, 96–115. Santa Fe: School of American Research Press.

Klein, Herbert. 1969. *Parties and Political Change in Bolivia, 1880–1952.* Cambridge: Oxford University Press.

———. 1982. *Bolivia: The Evolution of a Multi-Ethnic Society.* New York: Oxford University Press.

———. 2003. *A Concise History of Bolivia.* Cambridge: Cambridge University Press.

Klein, Naomi. 2009. "Climate Rage." *Rolling Stone*, November 11. http://www.naomi klein.org/articles/2009/11/climate-rage. July 14, 2011.

Kohl, Benjamin. 2003. "Restructuring Citizenship in Bolivia: El plan de todos." *International Journal of Urban and Regional Research* 27(2): 337–51.

———. 2010. "Bolivia under Morales: A Work in Progress." *Latin American Perspectives* 37(3): 107–22.

Kohl, Benjamin, and Rosalind Bresnahan. 2010. "Bolivia under Morales: Consolidating Power, Initiating Decolonization." *Latin American Perspectives* 37(3): 5–17.

Kozloff, Nikolas. 2008. *Revolution!: South America and the Rise of the New Left*. New York: Palgrave Macmillan.

Krupa, Christopher. 2010. "State by Proxy: Privatized Government in the Andes." *Comparative Studies in Society and History* 52(2): 319–50.

Langer, Erick D. 2009. "Bringing the Economic Back In: Andean Indians and the Construction of the Nation-State in Nineteenth-Century Bolivia." *Journal of Latin American Studies* 41(3): 527–51.

Larson, Brooke. 2004. *Trials of Nation Making: Liberalism, Race, and Ethnicity in the Andes, 1810–1910*. Cambridge: Cambridge University Press.

———. 2005. "Capturing Indian Bodies, Hearts, and Minds: The Gendered Politics of Rural School Reform in Bolivia, 1920s–1940s." In *Natives Making Nation: Gender, Indigeneity and the State in the Andes*, edited by Andrew Canessa, 32–59. Tucson: University of Arizona Press.

Lazar, Sian. 2008. *El Alto, Rebel City: Self and Citizenship in Andean Bolivia*. Durham: Duke University Press.

Li, Tania Murray. 2007. *The Will to Improve: Governmentality, Development, and the Practice of Politics*. Durham: Duke University Press.

Linera, Alvaro García. 2006. "State Crisis and Popular Power." *New Left Review* 37 (January–February): 73–85.

Lowrey, Kathleen. 2006. "Bolivia multiétnico y pluricultural, Ten Years Later: White Separatism in the Bolivian Lowlands." *Latin American and Caribbean Ethnic Studies* 1(1): 63–84.

Lucero, Jose Antonio. 2006. "Representing 'Real Indians': The Challenges of Indigenous Authenticity and Strategic Constructivism in Ecuador and Bolivia." *Latin American Research Review* 41(2): 31–56.

Luykx, Aurolyn. 1999. *The Citizen Factory: Schooling and Cultural Production in Bolivia*. Albany: SUNY Press.

Madison, Soyini. 2007. "Co-performative Witnessing." *Cultural Studies* 21(6): 826–31.

Malloy, James. 1970. *Bolivia: The Uncompleted Revolution*. Pittsburgh: University of Pittsburgh Press.

Martínez, Carmen. 2010. "Post-Neoliberal Multiculturalism?: The Backlash against Indigenous Rights in Ecuador's Citizen's Revolution." Paper presented at Repositioning Indigeneity Conference, Johns Hopkins University, Baltimore, November 4–6.

Martínez-Alier, Joan. 2002. *El ecologismo de los pobres: Conflictos ambientales y lenguajes de valoración*. Barcelona: Icaria.

Martínez-Torres, Elena, and Peter Rosset. 2010. "The Vía Campesina: The Evolution of a Transnational Movement." *Journal of Peasant Studies* 37(1): 149–75.

Maybury Lewis, David. 2002. *The Politics of Ethnicity: Indigenous Peoples in Latin American States*. Cambridge, Mass.: Harvard University Press.

McMichael, Philip. 2000. *Hungry for Profit: The Agribusiness Threat to Farmers, Food, and the Environment*. New York: Monthly Review.

———. 2005. "Global Development and the Corporate Food Regime." In *New Directions in the Sociology of Global Development*, edited by Frederick H. Buttel and Philip McMichael, 269–303. New York: Elsevier.

————. 2007. *Development and Social Change: A Global Perspective*. Thousand Oaks: Pine Forge.

————. 2008. "Food Sovereignty, Social Reproduction, and the Agrarian Question." In *Peasants and Globalization: Political Economy, Rural Transformation, and the Agrarian Question*, edited by A. Haroon Akram-Lodhi and Cristobal Kay, 288–311. London: Routledge.

Mendoza, Omar. 2003. *La lucha por la tierra en el gran chaco tarijeño*. La Paz: PIEB.

Monroe, Kristin. 2011. "Being Mobile in Beirut." *City and Society* 23(1): 91–111.

Montoya, Ricardo. 2010. "Cuando la cultura se convierte en política." Paper presented at the Repositioning Indigeneity in Latin America Conference, Johns Hopkins University, Baltimore, November 4–6.

Murra, John V. 1975. *Formaciones económicas y políticas del mundo andino*. Lima: Instituto de Estudios Peruanos.

————. 1978. *La organización económica y política del estado Inca*. Mexico City: Siglo XXI.

Nash, June. 1979. *We Eat the Mines and the Mines Eat Us: Dependency and Exploitation in Bolivian Tin Mines*. New York: Columbia University Press.

Nordenskiöld, Erland. 2001. *Exploraciones y aventuras en Sudamérica*. La Paz: APCOB/Plural. Originally published in 1917.

Ong, Aihwa. 1999. *Flexible Citizenship: The Cultural Logics of Transnationality*. Durham: Duke University Press.

————. 2006. *Neoliberalism as Exception: Mutations in Citizenship and Sovereignty*. Durham: Duke University Press.

Orgaz García, Mirko. 2002. *La guerra del gas: Nación versus transnacionales en Bolivia*. La Paz: OFAVIN.

Orta, Andrew. 2001. "Remembering the Ayllu, Remaking the Nation: Indigenous Scholarship and Activism in the Bolivian Andes." *Journal of Latin American Anthropology* 6(1): 198–201.

————. 2004. *Catechizing Culture: Missionaries, Aymara, and the "New Evangelization."* New York: Columbia University Press.

Paley, Julia. 2001. *Marketing Democracy: Power and Social Movements in Post-Dictatorship Chile*. Berkeley: University of California Press.

Patel, Raj. 2007. *Stuffed and Starved: Markets, Power, and the Hidden Battle for the World Food System*. London: Portobello Books.

Paulson, Susan. 2006. "Body, Nation, and Consubstantiation in Bolivian Ritual Meals." *American Ethnologist* 33(4): 650–64.

Peebles, Gustav. 2010. "The Anthropology of Credit and Debt." *Annual Review of Anthropology* 39(1): 225–40.

Peña, Elaine. 2011. *Performing Piety: Making Space Sacred with the Virgin of Guadalupe*. Berkeley: University of California Press.

Pérez, Gina. 2004. *The Near Northwest Side Story: Migration, Displacement, and Puerto Rican Families*. Berkeley: University of California Press.

Perreault, Thomas. 2008. *Natural Gas, Indigenous Mobilization, and the Bolivian State: Identities, Conflict and Cohesion Programme Paper No. 12*. Geneva: United Nations Research Institute for Social Development (UNRISD).

————. 2011. "Nature and Nation: Hydrocarbons Governance and the Territorial Logics of Resource Nationalism in Bolivia." Unpublished paper.

Petras, James F., and Henry Vetmeyer. 2009. *What's Left in Latin America?: Regime Change in New Times*. Farnham, U.K.: Ashgate.

Platt, Tristan. 1982. *Estado boliviano y ayllu andino: Tierra y tributo en el norte de Potosi*. Lima: IEP.

————. 1993. "Simón Bolívar, the Sun of Justice and the Amerindian Virgin: Andean Conceptions of the Patria in Nineteenth-Century Potosí." *Journal of Latin American Studies* 25(1): 159–85.

PNUD (Programa de las Naciones Unidas para el Desarrollo). 2004. *Informe de Desarrollo Humano Regional Santa Cruz*. La Paz: PNUD/Plural.

Poole, Deborah. 1997. *Vision, Race, and Modernity: A Visual Economy of the Andean Image World*. Princeton: Princeton University Press.

Postero, Nancy. 2007a. "Andean Utopias in Evo Morales's Bolivia." *Latin American and Caribbean Ethnic Studies* 2(1): 1–28.

————. 2007b. *Now We Are Citizens: Indigenous Politics in Post-Multicultural Bolivia*. Stanford: Stanford University Press.

————. 2010. "The Struggle to Create a Radical Democracy in Bolivia." *Latin American Research Review* 45(4): 59–78.

Postero, Nancy, and León Zamosc. 2004. *The Struggle for Indigenous Rights in Latin America*. Brighton, U.K.: Sussex Academic Press.

Pribilisky, Jason. 2007. *La Chulla Vida: Gender, Migration and the Family in Andean Ecuador and New York City*. Syracuse: Syracuse University Press.

Pruden, Hernán. 2003. "Santa Cruz entre la post-guerra del chaco y las postrimerías de la revolución nacional: Cruceños y cambas." *Historias: Revista de la Coordinadora de Historia* 6(1): 41–61.

Quiroga, Omar, and Eulogio Núñez. 2005. *Estudios de impacto en políticas de tierra y territorio: Estudio de caso "Los Yuquises."* Santa Cruz: CIPCA.

Radcliffe, Sarah, and Sallie Westwood. 1996. *Remaking the Nation: Place, Identity and Politics in Latin America*. London: Routledge.

Rappaport, Joanne. 1990. *The Politics of Memory: Native Historical Interpretation in the Colombian Andes*. Cambridge: Cambridge University Press.

————. 1994. *Cumbe Reborn: An Andean Ethnography of History*. Chicago: University of Chicago Press.

————. 2005. *Intercultural Utopias: Public Intellectuals, Cultural Experimentation and Ethnic Pluralism in Colombia*. Durham: Duke University Press.

Regalsky, Pablo. 2010. *Ethnicity and Class: The Bolivian State and Andean Space Management*. Saarbrücken, Ger.: Lambert Academic.

Revilla, Carlos. 2011. "Understanding the Mobilizations of *Octubre*, 2003: Dynamic Pressures and Shifting Leadership Practices in El Alto." In *Remapping Bolivia: Resources, Territory, and Indigeneity in a Plurinational State*, edited by Nicole Fabricant and Bret Gustafson, 121–45. Santa Fe: School of American Research Press.

Risor, Helen. 2010a. "Twenty Hanging Dolls and a Lynching: Defacing Dangerousness and Enacting Citizenship in El Alto, Bolivia." *Public Culture* 22(3): 465–85.

————. 2010b. "Violent Closures and New Openings, Civil Insecurity, Citizens, and State in El Alto, Bolivia." Ph.D. diss., University of Copenhagen.

Rivera Cusicanqui, Silvia. 1987. *Oppressed but Not Defeated: Peasant Struggles among the Aymara and Quechua in Bolivia, 1900–1980*. Geneva: United Nations Research Institute for Social Development (UNRISD).

————. 1990. "Liberal Democracy and Ayllu Democracy in Bolivia: The Case of Northern Potosí." *Journal of Development Studies* 26(4): 97–121.

Rockefeller, Stewart. 2010. *Starting from Quirpini: The Travels and Places of a Bolivian People*. Bloomington: University of Indiana Press.

Rosenthal, Elizabeth. 2009. "In Bolivia, Water and Ice Tell of Climate Change." *New York Times*, December 13. http://www.nytimes.com/2009/12/14/science/earth/14bolivia.html?pagewanted=all. August 10, 2011.

Rosset, Peter. 2009. "Fixing Our Global Food System: Food Sovereignty and Redistributive Land Reform." *Monthly Review* 61(3): 114–28.

Rouse, Roger. 1991. "Mexican Migration and the Space of Postmodernism." *Diaspora* 1(1): 8–23.

————. 1995. "Questions of Identity: Personhood and Collectivity in Transnational Migration in the United States." *Critique of Anthropology* 15(4): 351–80.

Roy, Ananya. 2009. "Civic Governmentality: The Politics of Inclusion in Beirut and Mumbai." *Antipode* 41(1): 159–79.

Sassen, Saskia. 2001. *The Global City: New York, London, and Tokyo*. Princeton: Princeton University Press.

Sawyer, Suzana. 2004. *Crude Chronicles: Indigenous Politics, Multinational Oil, and Neoliberalism in Ecuador*. Durham: Duke University Press.

————. 2007. "Empire/Multitude—State/Civil Society: Rethinking Topographies of Power through Transnational Connectivity in Ecuador and Beyond." *Social Analysis* 51 (2): 64–85.

Sawyer, Suzana, and Edmund Terence Gómez. 2008. *Transnational Governmentality and Resource Extraction: Indigenous Peoples, Multinational Corporations, Multilateral Institutions, and the State*. Geneva: United Nations Research Institute for Social Development (UNRISD).

Shah, Alpah. 2010. *In the Shadows of the State: Indigenous Politics, Environmentalism, and Insurgency in Jharkhand, India*. Durham: Duke University Press.

Sieder, Rachel. 1998. *Guatemala after the Peace Accords*. London: Institute of Latin American Studies.

————, ed. 2002. *Multiculturalism in Latin America: Indigenous Rights, Diversity, and Democracy*. London: Palgrave Macmillan/ILAS.

Smith, Neil. 1990. *Uneven Development: Nature, Capital, and the Production of Space*. Athens: University of Georgia Press.

————. 2009. "The Revolutionary Imperative." *Antipode* 41(1): 50–65.

Soruco, Ximena. 2011. "El Porvenir, the Future That Is No Longer Possible: Conquest and Autonomy in the Bolivian Oriente." In *Remapping Bolivia: Resources, Territory, and Indigeneity in a Plurinational State*, edited by Nicole Fabricant and Bret Gustafson, 73–95. Santa Fe: School of American Research Press.

Soruco, Ximena, Wilfredo Plata, and Gustavo Medeiros. 2008. *Los Barones del Oriente: El poder en Santa Cruz ayer y hoy*. La Paz: Fundación Tierra.

Speed, Shannon. 2007a. "Exercising Rights and Reconfiguring Resistance in the Zapatista Juntas de Buen Gobierno." In *The Practice of Human Rights: Tracking Law between the Global and the Local*, edited by Mark Goodale and Sally Engle Merry, 163–92. Cambridge: Cambridge University Press.

———. 2007b. *Rights in Rebellion: Indigenous Struggle and Human Rights in Chiapas*. Stanford: Stanford University Press.

Spronk, Susan. 2007. "Roots of Resistance to Urban Water Privatization in Bolivia: The 'New Working Class,' the Crisis of Neoliberalism, and Public Services." *International Labor and Working-Class History* 71(1): 8–28.

Stahler-Sholk, Richard. 2010. "The Zapatista Social Movement: Innovation and Sustainability." *Alternatives* 35(3): 269–90.

Stapff, Andres. 2009. "Prosecutor Says Bolivian Opposition Backed Plot." http://www .democraticunderground.com/discuss/duboard.php?az=view_all&address=102 x3861649. October 1, 2009.

Starn, Orin. 1992. "Rethinking the Politics of Anthropology: The Case of the Andes." *Current Anthropology* 35(1): 13–28.

Stavenhagen, Rodolfo. 1988. *Derecho indígena y derechos humanos en América Latina*. Mexico: Instituto Interamericano de Derechos Humanos.

Stearman, Allyn Maclean. 1985. *Camba and Kolla: Migration and Development in Santa Cruz, Bolivia*. Gainesville: University Press of Florida.

Stephenson, Marcia. 2000. "The Impact of an Indigenous Counterpublic Sphere on the Practice of Democracy: The Taller de Historia Oral Andina in Bolivia." Helen Kellogg Institute for International Studies, unpublished paper #279.

———. 2002. "Forging an Indigenous Countersphere: The Taller de Historia Oral Andina in Bolivia." *Latin American Research Review* 37(2): 99–118.

Taylor, Diana. 2003. *The Archive and the Repertoire: Performing Cultural Memory in the Americas*. Durham: Duke University Press.

Tellez, Ramiro. 2007. "Why Food Sovereignty in the Bolivian Constitution?" http:// www.viacampesina.org/en/index.php?option=com_content&view=article&id= 316:why-food-sovereignty-in-the-bolivian-constitution&catid=21:food-sovereignty-and-trade&Itemid=38. July 14, 2011.

Thomson, Sinclair. 2002. *We Alone Shall Rule: Native Andean Politics in the Age of Insurgency*. Madison: University of Wisconsin Press.

———. 2009. "Bolivia's Constitution and Land Reform, Part 2." *Real News*, January 31, 2009. http://therealnews.com/t2/index.php?option=com_content&task= view&id=31&Itemid=74&jumival=3221. August 3, 2011.

Tsing, Anna. 2005. *Friction: An Ethnography of Global Connection*. Princeton: Princeton University Press.

———. 2007. "Indigenous Voice." In *Indigenous Experience Today*, edited by Orin Starn and Marisol de La Cadena, 33–68. Oxford: Berg.

Turner, Victor. 1969. *The Ritual Process: Structure and Anti-Structure*. Chicago: Aldine.

Urioste, Miguel. 2003. "The Abandoned Agrarian Reform: Valleys and High Plains." *Fundación Tierra*. http://web.idrc.ca/uploads/userS/10632197691THE_ABANDONED_AGRARIAN_REFORM.pdf. July 1, 2011.

———. 2006. *Community Redirection of the Agrarian Reform in Bolivia: The Outcomes of a Year and Perspectives*. La Paz: Fundación Tierra.

———. 2007. *Community Redirection of the Agrarian Reform in Bolivia: The Outcomes of a Year and Perspectives*. La Paz: Fundación Tierra.

———. 2010. "Land Governance in Bolivia." La Paz: Fundación Tierra.

Valdivia, Gabriela. 2010. "Agrarian Capitalism and Struggles over Hegemony in the Bolivian Lowlands." *Latin American Perspectives* 37(4): 67–87.

———. 2011. "Coca's Haunting Presence in the Agrarian Politics of the Bolivian Lowlands." *Geojournal*, March 9, 2011, 1–17.

Van Cott, Donna Lee. 2003. "Legal Pluralism and Informal Community Justice Administration in Latin America." Paper presented at Informal Institutions and Latin American Politics Conference, University of Notre Dame, South Bend, Ind., April 24–25.

Van Schaick, Alex. 2009. "Bolivia's New Constitution." *NACLA Report on the Americas*, January 21, https://nacla.org/node/5437. July 1, 2011.

Verdery, Katherine. 1999. *The Political Lives of Dead Bodies: Reburial and Postsocialist Change*. New York: Columbia University Press.

Walsh, Catherine. 2010. "Development as Buen Vivir: Institutional Arrangements and (De)Colonial Entanglements." *Development* 53(1): 15–21.

Watts, Michael. 2004. "Resource Curse?: Governmentality, Oil and Power in the Niger Delta." *Geopolitics* 9(1): 50–80.

Watts, Michael, and Richard Peet. 1996. *Liberation Ecologies*. London: Routledge.

Webber, Jeff. 2011. *From Rebellion to Reform in Bolivia: Class Struggle, Indigenous Liberation, and the Politics of Evo Morales*. Chicago: Haymarket.

Weinberg, Bill. 2010. "Bolivia's New Water Wars: Climate Change and Indigenous Struggle." *NACLA Report on the Americas* 43(5): 19–24.

Weismantel, Mary. 1988. *Food, Gender, and Poverty in the Ecuadorian Andes*. Prospect Heights: Waveland.

———. 2001. *Cholas and Pishtacos: Stories of Race and Sex in the Andes*. Chicago: University of Chicago Press.

———. 2009. "Have a Drink: Chicha, Performance, and Politics." In *Drink, Power, and Society in the Andes*, edited by Justin Jennings and Brenda J. Bowser, 257–80. Gainesville: University Press of Florida.

Williams, Brett. 2004. *Debt for Sale: On the Social History of the Credit Trap*. Philadelphia: University of Pennsylvania Press.

Wittman, Hannah K. 2005. "The Social Ecology of Agrarian Reform: The Landless Rural Worker's Movement and Agrarian Citizenship in Mato Grosso, Brazil." Ph.D. diss., Cornell University.

———. 2009. "Reframing Agrarian Citizenship: Land, Life, and Power in Brazil." *Journal of Rural Studies* 25(1): 120–30.

———. 2010. "Reconnecting Agriculture and the Environment: Food Sovereignty and the Agrarian Basis of Ecological Citizenship." In *Food Sovereignty: Reconnecting*

Food, Nature, and Community, edited by Hannah K. Wittman, Annete Aurélie Desmarais, and Nettie Wiebe, 91–105. Oakland: Food First.

Wittman, Hannah K., Annete Aurélie Desmarais, and Nettie Wiebe. 2010. *Food Sovereignty: Reconnecting Food, Nature, and Community*. Oakland: Food First.

Wolf, Eric. 1969. *Peasant Wars of the 21st Century*. Norman: University of Oklahoma Press.

Wolford, Wendy. 2011. *This Land Is Ours Now: Social Mobilization and the Meaning of Land in Brazil*. Durham: Duke University Press.

Zermeño, Sergio. 2008. "Desolation: Mexican Campesinos and Agriculture in the 21st Century." *NACLA Report on the Americas* 14(5): 28–33.

INDEX

Accumulation by dispossession, 24, 33, 35–36, 39, 58, 175

Agrarian reform: and land redistribution, 3–5, 203 (n. 3); and neoliberalism, 37; symbols of, 171. *See also* Land issues

Agrarian Reform Law (1953), 3–4, 155, 207 (n. 20), 216 (n. 9). *See also* New Agrarian Reform Law

Agrarian syndicates, 35

Agribusiness: and land issues, 3, 35, 196; and power relations, 14, 185; and population shifts, 22; international investments in, 34, 60; in lowlands, 35, 53; and modernity, 49, 59, 70, 73–74, 126; and transnational corporations, 49, 80, 176, 177–78; neoliberal model of, 55, 56, 57–58, 105, 109, 112, 114; and displacement, 55, 66, 196; and rice production, 60, 61; laws supporting, 65; and soy production, 66, 68, 103; and Paz Hurtado, 69; MST as disruptive to, 73; political influence in region, 80, 82; expansion of, 96, 107; and citizenship, 102; and alternative modes of production, 125; and Morales, 164, 176; and right-wing elites, 165; and trade, 212 (n. 3)

Agricultural and Rural Bank (BDP), 138

Agricultural Congress of the East (CAO), 53, 55, 56, 70, 71, 141

Agriculture: international investments in, 3, 5; shifts in, 5, 26–27; redistribution of land for, 38, 49; and unions, 40, 43, 207–8 (n. 24); output of, 52; rescaling to local level, 102; commercial speculation in, 213 (n. 9). *See also* Agribusiness; Large-scale farming; Small-scale farming

Agroecological model: and MST, 66, 71, 74, 103, 104–5, 107, 114, 121, 123–25, 126, 161, 180, 181, 188, 208 (n. 26), 212 (n. 1), 214 (n. 15); and organic farming, 103, 119, 121, 122, 124, 125, 157, 193; and Pueblos Unidos, 104, 117, 120, 123, 125, 126, 214 (n. 14); and ayllu democracy, 106–8, 117–20, 123, 124; in Itapeva, 115–18; and nongovernmental organizations, 123–24, 214 (nn. 14, 15); and ecotourism, 126–27; and Fifth National March for Land and Territory, 148

Albó, Xavier, 29, 99

Albro, Robert, 97

Allen, Catherine, 147

Allende, Salvador, 172, 219 (n. 11)

Alternative modes of production: and communal landholding, 10; viability of, 12–13; and environmental issues, 13, 107, 123, 129, 185; and ayllu democracy, 85, 102–3, 106–7, 118–20, 185; and food sovereignty, 102, 105, 106, 107, 120–22; and MST, 104–5, 108, 187, 194, 196, 197; and small-scale farmers, 105, 106–7, 118, 123, 124, 151; and collaboration, 107–8, 116, 117–18, 119, 212 (n. 2); and displacement, 128–29; and marches, 137. *See also* Agroecological model

Amboró National Park, 59

Andean Oral History Workshop (THOA), 29, 30, 84, 205 (n. 8), 211 (n. 8)

Andolina, Robert, 127

Appadurai, Arjun, 142

Arbona, Juan, 204 (n. 4)

Archer Daniels Midland (ADM), 164, 178

Argentina, 19, 39, 204 (n. 3)

Assies, Willem, 32

Avelar, Idelber, 217 (n. 16)

Cambas, 20–21, 56, 164, 165–68, 169, 170, 204 (n. 3), 209 (n. 5), 218 (n. 4)
CAO (Cámara Agropecuaria del Oriente), 53, 55, 56, 70, 71, 141
Capitalism: globalized, 12, 34, 35, 52, 57, 92, 179; and power relations, 12, 35; and citizenship, 108; and alternative modes of production, 125, 126, 129; indigenous-based model of, 126–27, 128, 180, 214 (n. 19); and food sovereignty, 146–47, 179; resistance to, 155, 184; highland migration as threat to, 168; and climate change, 191, 219 (n. 2); and Morales, 192; and environmental issues, 194–95; and resource distribution, 198; and speculative unproductive landholding, 203 (n. 3); and indigenous mobility, 215 (n. 3)
Cárdenas, Víctor Hugo, 30
Cargill, 164, 178
Cattle ranching, 31, 32, 39, 41, 70, 105
CEJIS (Centro de Estudios Jurídicos e Investigación Social), 17, 65, 73, 88, 94, 96, 120, 124, 205 (n. 8)
Céspedes, Hedim, 206 (n. 19)
Chaco War, 39, 163, 207 (n. 23)
Chamber of Industry, Commerce, Services, and Tourism of Santa Cruz (CAINCO), 55, 70
Chané, 47, 48
Chavez, Adolfo, 10
Chicha, 61, 209 (n. 10)
Chile, 172, 219 (n. 11)
Chimán peoples, 10
China, 219 (n. 2)
Chiquitano Indians, 22
Chiriguano monument, 139, 140, 215 (n. 6), 218 (n. 7)
Choque, Delia, 61–62
Choque, Wilford, 61–62
Christ the Redeemer statue, 159, 169, 218 (n. 7)
Chúngara, Domitilia Barrios de, 146, 216 (n. 12)

CIDOB (La Confederación de Pueblos Indígenas de Bolivia), 10, 207 (nn. 20, 21), 219 (n. 13)
Citizenship: regional, 26; and regional elites, 56, 58, 70, 73, 74, 184; and MST, 58, 101, 102, 103, 108, 110, 128, 129–30, 184, 210–11 (n. 5); land occupation as alternative mode of, 65, 186; agrarian, 67, 82, 102, 108, 122, 123–30, 136; and grassroots strategies, 74; basis of, 82–84, 85, 102, 103, 183, 210–11 (n. 5); and ayllu democracy, 85, 86–87, 101, 136, 183; liberal model of, 108; hybridized models of, 128–30; and indigeneity as political tool, 183. See also Indigenous citizenship
Class: and labor code, 3; and anillos, 17; ethnic identity connected to, 30; and state-led capitalism, 35; and indigeneity as political tool, 42, 110–11, 167; and miners' unions, 43, 197; and neoliberalism, 57–58; and violence, 84; and forms of collectivity, 101; and mobility, 112; and environmental issues, 196, 197. See also Elites; Poverty and the poor
Climate change: and MST, 181, 188; and social movement strategies, 181, 188–92, 193, 194; and water scarcity, 188, 189, 219 (n. 3), 220 (n. 4); effects of, 188, 220 (n. 4); causes of, 189, 219 (n. 2); and climate debt, 189, 220 (n. 5); and Morales, 189–91, 220 (n. 5); and indigeneity as political tool, 190
Climate Summit, 191
COAPRI, 116
Coca: right to cultivate, 1, 161; and War on Drugs, 37, 43, 185; ethnicization of, 43; use of, 104, 154; receiving offerings, 147; demand for, 208 (n. 27)
Cocaleros (coca growers): and indigeneity as political tool, 1, 44, 165; and MAS party, 1, 203 (n. 1); as social movement, 2, 43, 161; and

pre-Columbian cultural forms, 31, 43–44, 161; as migrants, 43, 208 (n. 27); and highland to lowland migration, 53

Cochabamba department: decentralized governing structures in, 82; and Fifth National March for Land and Territory, 133–35, 145, 154; indigenous peasant movement of, 203 (n. 1)

Colla: defined, 19, 204 (n. 3)

Collas, 49, 70, 164, 166–67, 218 (n. 4)

Colloredo-Mansfeld, Rudi, 90

Colonial policies: and inequality, 1, 27, 204–5 (n. 7); and historical memory, 24, 25; effects of, 27, 32, 70, 83, 128–29, 139, 155, 156, 157, 162–63, 176, 198; indigenous resistance to, 28, 31, 32, 44, 161; and violence, 33, 44, 70, 74, 90, 128, 129; and extractive industries, 74; and Katari, 158

Colonization programs of 1950s, 60

Colonization programs of 1960s, 34–35, 208 (n. 27)

Colque, Wilford, 63–64, 91, 94

Columnas, 133, 134, 144, 151, 154, 215 (n. 1), 217 (n. 17)

Comité Cívico Femenino (Feminine Civic Committee), 55, 166

Community Redirection Law, 138

Comunidad Campesina Agroecológica Pueblos Unidos (PU), 73

CONAMAQ (Consejo Nacional de Ayllus y Marcas del Qullasuyu), 10, 191, 192, 211 (n. 8), 220 (n. 6)

Conklin Graham, 212 (n. 5)

Conquergood, Dwight, 92, 150

Constitution of Bolivia: and indigeneity as political tool, 1–2, 11, 186; and social function of property, 4, 6, 40, 65, 138, 173; rewriting of, 6, 13–14, 160–64, 168; compromises of, 13, 156, 172, 173–76; and neoliberalism, 37; and agricultural function of property, 38, 41; and pluriethnic and multicultural state, 88; and Constituent Assembly,

90, 92–93, 160, 171–72, 177, 190, 192, 198; right-wing opposition to, 160, 164, 169, 172, 173, 179, 218 (n. 4); and land issues, 160–64, 172, 173–74, 186–87, 203 (n. 4); and food sovereignty, 176–77, 186; and departmental decentralization and autonomy, 219 (n. 13)

Cortés Arauz, Eulogio, 19–21, 60, 91–92, 96

Cosgrove, Denis E., 123

Costas, Rubén, 71, 167, 169, 170, 172

CPESC (regional federation of Santa Cruz), 207 (n. 20)

Creative destruction, 26, 204 (n. 5)

Cruceño identity, 31, 56, 58, 164, 205 (n. 10), 209 (n. 5), 218 (n. 5)

CSCB (Bolivian Syndicalist Confederation of Colonizers), 207 (nn. 20, 24)

CSUTCB (Confederation of Rural Workers of Bolivia), 207 (nn. 20, 21)

Cusipuma, Braulio, 118

Dangl, Banjamin, 160

Davis, Mike, 5

Decolonization, 8, 162, 163, 164

Deforestation: and soy production, 5, 63; and TIPNIS highway project, 10; and nongovernmental organizations, 54; and air transportation, 112; and ecotourism, 127; and alternative energy sources, 175

Departmental decentralization and autonomy: and neoliberalism, 37; and regional elites, 49, 52, 55, 70, 74, 164, 165, 166–72, 208 (nn. 1, 2); and EXPOCRUZ, 57; and Morales, 187; and constitution of Bolivia, 219 (n. 13)

Dialogic engagements, 86, 211 (n. 9)

Direct foreign investment, 36

Displacement: and consolidation of productive resources, 5; and MST, 22, 67, 196; effect of Spanish conquest on, 27; and neighborhood organizations, 37; and territorial claims, 51, 52; and agribusiness, 55, 66, 196; as side effect of production, 57; and soy production, 68; and ayllu democracy, 85, 96; and alternative modes of production, 128–29; and transnational corporations, 179; and neoliberalism, 183, 184, 206 (nn. 17, 18); and resource curse, 219 (n. 1)

Dispossession: socioeconomic, 5; and grassroots strategies, 13, 85; accumulation by, 24, 33, 35–36, 39, 58, 175; and small-scale farmers, 39, 55; as side effect of production, 57; and indigeneity as political tool, 197

Dunn, Christopher, 217 (n. 16)

Durán, Angel, 17, 40, 208 (n. 25)

Economics: past struggles linked to present, 7; and pre-Columbian cultural forms, 9, 107; and legislation, 12; global, 22, 35, 206 (n. 16); and New Economic Policy, 36; regional, 82; and globalization, 184, and environmental issues, 194–97; and social movements, 200–201; "Western" ideas regarding, 203 (n. 2); Marxist economic theory, 204 (n. 5)

Ecuador, 125–26, 128, 156

Edeman, Marc, 212 (n. 6)

Educational reforms, 37

El Alto: and indigenous resistance, 28, 168; Neighborhood Boards in, 37; miners relocating to, 37, 43, 204 (n. 4); violence of, 81, 83; decentralizing governing structures in, 82; and individualism, 100; and Fifth National March for Land and Territory, 152–53; Ceja sector of, 158–59; and signing of revised constitution, 160–61; and climate change, 219 (n. 3), 220 (n. 4)

El Cuchirón, occupation of land, 50, 60, 63–64

Elites: mestizo, 3, 60, 82, 166, 203 (n. 2), 209 (n. 5); and land distribution, 4, 38, 39, 44, 173–76; and MST, 41, 44, 185;

attitude toward highlanders, 55, 65, 68, 69, 70–71, 164, 165, 166, 167, 168; and Civic Committee of Santa Cruz, 55, 208 (n. 1); and agribusiness, 68; and multinational conglomerates, 156; and right-wing opposition, 160, 164, 165–72, 186–87, 218 (n. 4); collective identity of, 164, 218 (n. 4); and indigeneity as political tool, 165–72, 181, 218 (nn. 5, 6); and direct democracy, 169, 171; and food sovereignty, 179; economic power of, 187. See also Regional elites

Ellwood, Wayne, 24, 35

El Plan Tres Mil, 20, 166

Embodied performance: of indigeneity, 8, 9, 12, 13, 136–37, 141–42, 161–62, 217–18 (n. 3); and social movements, 24, 25–26, 204 (n. 4)

Encomiendas, 26

Energy sources, alternative sources of, 5, 117, 175, 193, 200–201

Enganche system, 21, 32

Environmental imaginary, 123, 124

Environmental issues: and Morales, 9, 176; legal protection of environment, 12; and alternative modes of production, 13, 107, 123, 129, 185; and lowlands, 22, 31; and neoliberalism, 36, 194; and transnational groups, 51; and pesticide use, 54, 71, 103, 112, 121, 125; and soy production, 68; and agrarian citizenship, 102, 128; and indigeneity as political tool, 110–11, 168, 190, 195, 212 (n. 5); and transnational corporations, 179; and climate change, 181–82, 188–94, 219 (nn. 2, 3), 220 (nn. 4, 5); and pre-Columbian cultural forms, 188; and social movement strategies, 188–92; and Law of Mother Earth, 192–94; and economic crisis, 194–97; and MST, 196–97, 208 (n. 26). See also Agroecological model

Escobar, Arturo, 129

Ethnicity: and indigeneity as political tool, 42–43, 51, 181; fluidity of, 68; and development, 127, 214 (n. 20)

Europe: and mining in Latin America, 26; and rubber era, 69, 205 (n. 11); and demand for coca, 208 (n. 27)

Experiential authenticity, 149

EXPOCRUZ (Feria Inernacional de Santa Cruz), 56–58, 73, 139

Export-oriented production: and grass-roots strategies, 13; and lowland areas, 35; and soy production, 39, 47, 52, 54, 68, 103, 110, 177–78; and coca production, 43; and land allocation policies, 60; and timber resources, 63; and rubber era, 69, 205 (n. 11); and elites, 173, 184; and transnational corporations, 203 (n. 3); and agricultural unions, 208 (n. 24)

Extractive industries: model of, 13, 26, 49, 50, 51, 52, 56, 198–99; and modernity, 58; and illegal sale of land, 64; and Ichilo, 66; and colonial policies, 74; and divide between rural peripheries and urban centers, 82; and alternative modes of production, 125, 129, 182; and mining, 156; and right-wing elites, 168; and Morales, 176, 191, 192; and transnational corporations, 179; and climate change, 193; and neoliberalism, 194

FAO (Food and Agriculture Organization), 177

Farthing, Linda, 51, 127

Federation of Cane Producers, 53

Fernández, Ermelinda, 41

Fifth National March for Land and Territory (2006): and food sovereignty, 130, 137, 144–48; and columnas, 133, 134, 144, 151, 154, 215 (n. 1), 217 (n. 17); performative nature of, 135, 136, 139–42, 144, 148–52, 154–56; and ayllu democracy, 137; and Morales, 138; structure of, 142–44; and power

relations, 152–57; purpose of, 207 (n. 20)

Food Acquisition Program (EAP), 117

Food sovereignty: proposals for, 9, 13, 156; and trade, 9, 109, 212 (n. 3); and MNR, 53; and citizenship, 58, 108, 128, 137; definition of, 58–59; and gender, 99; and alternative modes of production, 102, 105, 106, 107, 120–22; and MST, 103, 142, 176–79, 196; global discourse on, 109–11, 113–14, 115, 121, 123, 130; and ayllu democracy, 109–11, 117–18, 185; and Fifth National March for Land and Territory, 130, 137, 144–48; and domestic food markets, 176–80; and climate change, 181, 189, 193, 220 (n. 4)

Food Sovereignty Conference, 109

Framework Law on Autonomy and Decentralization, 219 (n. 13)

Fraser, Nancy, 155

Freire, Paulo, 144

Frictions: in social movement state, 8, 173–76; and food sovereignty, 9; in social movements, 10–14, 86–87, 102; and ayllu democracy, 87, 93, 148; and agrarian citizenship, 125–26, 127, 128; and climate change, 190, 191

Garcés, Fernando, 174, 187, 221 (n. 9)

Gas and oil industry: nationalization of, 6, 162, 163; and Gran Chaco Region, 39; conflicts over, 39–40; as nonrenewable resource, 51; and Ogoni people, 67–68; and transnational corporations, 125–26, 156; and Morales, 162, 163, 191, 220 (n. 7); and privatization, 197–98

Gas Wars of 2003, 163, 198

GATT (General Agreement on Trade and Tariffs), 206 (n. 16)

Gender: and inequality, 57, 146; and peripheries and urban centers, 82; and ayllu democracy, 85, 92, 93, 97–99, 102; and pre-Columbian cultural forms, 97–98; and food preparation, 145–47, 216 (n. 13); and environmental issues, 196. *See also* Women

Genetically modified organisms (GMOs), 74, 125, 176, 177–79

Gill, Lesley, 69, 205 (n. 11), 207 (n. 24)

Gilly, Adolfo, 198, 204–5 (n. 7)

Gledhill, John, 30, 205–6 (n. 14)

Global interconnectedness: and economic transformations, 2; and MST, 22; and resistance in highland rural areas, 26–27, 42, 48; and resistance in lowland areas, 30–32, 42, 48

Globalized capitalism: and power relations, 12; and neoliberal multiculturalism, 29; and agribusiness, 34, 35; and reterritorialization of state, 52; and EXPOCRUZ, 57; and territorial autonomy, 179

Goldberg, Philip, 172

Goldstein, Daniel, 82, 119, 136

Golpe cívico, 172, 218–19 (n. 11)

Governance: social and reciprocal models of, 1; rebuilding of local governance, 7; Morales's reclaiming of, 8; indigenous forms of, 12, 13, 28, 29, 51, 67, 74–75; and mestizo elites, 82; and MST, 83, 84, 96–97, 194, 196; of Pueblos Unidos, 84–85, 89, 96; and indigeneity as political tool, 162; "Western" ideas regarding, 203 (n. 2)

Gran Chaco region, 39–40, 42, 51, 163, 207 (n. 23)

Grassroots strategies: Morales's use of, 7–8; and power relations, 8, 155, 187, 201; and citizenship, 13, 41, 74, 83–84, 101, 108, 122, 127; and historical memory, 25; and ayllu democracy, 30, 93, 101; and pre-Columbian cultural forms, 84; and global indigenous framework, 86; and food sovereignty, 114, 176–77, 179; and alternative modes of production, 122; mobility of, 161–62; and indigeneity as political

tool, 179–81, 185, 187, 217–18 (n. 3); and climate change, 191, 194, 220 (n. 5); and economics, 197; and transnational corporations, 198

Greenpeace, 51

Grisaffi, Thomas, 43, 217 (n. 2)

Guabira, 34

Guaraní Indians: and lowland areas, 21; population of, 22; rebellion of 1892, 30, 32–33; territory of, 39; and right-wing elites, 165–66, 167, 168, 169, 218 (n. 6); and Morales, 191

Guarayo Indians, 21

Guarayos province, 68

Guayocho, Andres, 32

Guevara, Che, 159

Guillén, Juan, 68

Gustafson, Bret, 8, 32–33, 124, 162, 203 (n. 3), 204 (n. 2), 208 (n. 2)

Habilitación, 32

Hale, Charles, 29

Harderman, 47, 48

Harvey, David, 24, 57, 195–97, 200

Highland rural areas: indigenous people of, 1, 21; and social movements, 3, 26; and labor code, 3, 27; lowlands compared to, 21–22, 24, 209 (n. 5); and population shifts, 22; and global interconnectedness, 26–27, 42, 48; and pre-Columbian cultural forms, 28–31; and migration to lowlands, 33, 34–35, 50, 51, 53, 55, 69, 166; agrarian reform in, 34; and MST membership, 67; and water scarcity, 188, 219 (n. 3); and INRA Law, 207 (n. 21); and land redistribution, 216 (n. 9)

Historical memory: contemporary movement organizing defined by, 6–7, 21, 23, 24–25, 29, 44, 161, 185, 204 (n. 4); and coca production, 43; and citizenship, 58; and agroecological model, 119–20; and indigeneity as political tool, 168; and right-wing elites, 171; and Morales, 186

Holston, James, 65
Humphreys, Macartan, 51

Ichilo province, Santa Cruz: and MST, 6, 63–66, 124–25; agribusiness in, 44, 53; regional history of, 48–49; occupation of land in, 50; timber resources of, 50, 63–64; colonization in, 53; rice production in, 60–61, 66; and ayllu democracy, 93–94, 211 (n. 7)
ILO Indigenous and Tribal Peoples Convention, 207 (n. 20)
INC (Instituto Nacional de Colonización), 53
Inca empire, 21, 30, 84, 154, 166, 218 (n. 6)
India, 142, 214 (n. 18), 219 (n. 2)
Indigeneity, performances of, 8, 9, 12, 13, 136–37, 141–42, 161–62, 217–18 (n. 3)
Indigeneity as political tool: and Cocaleros, 1, 44, 165; and constitution of Bolivia, 1–2, 11, 186; and MST, 2, 6, 44, 110, 181–82, 196, 197; and mobilization, 6–10, 12, 33, 42–43, 44, 49, 168, 186; complicated nature of, 9, 75; and consultation, 11, 12, 203 (nn. 4, 5); and territorial autonomy, 42, 51, 67, 74; and class, 42, 110–11, 167; and reclamation, 51, 52, 75, 184, 186, 198; and alternative modes of production, 107, 120, 181; and environmental issues, 110–11, 168, 190, 195, 212 (n. 5); and legitimacy, 161; and Morales, 162, 163–64, 168, 180, 186, 189, 190; and right-wing elites, 165–72, 181, 218 (nn. 5, 6); and alliances, 179–80, 183–84; and grassroots strategies, 179–81, 185, 187, 217–18 (n. 3); and resistance, 184, 217 (n. 3); limits of, 200–201
Indigenous citizenship: and grassroots strategies, 13, 41, 74, 83–84, 101, 108, 122, 127; and international organizations, 30; battles over, 49–50; and reterritorializing power, 67; flexibility of, 110–11, 151; mobility of, 136–38, 139, 149, 151, 156; defining of, 157; and identity, 217 (n. 16)
Indigenous identity: as language of protest, 43, 185; fluidity of, 68; and territorial autonomy, 86; shared identity through dance, 149, 155; and claims against the state, 162, 217 (n. 2); and CEJIS, 205 (n. 8); and development, 214–15 (n. 20)
Indigenous languages, recognition of, 207 (n. 20)
Indigenous law: and communal decision-making, 87–88; and usos y costumbres, 88–97
Indigenous peoples: subjugation of, 1, 13, 26, 27, 32, 156, 183, 184, 204–5 (n. 7); rights to ancestral lands, 4, 5, 11; and Morales, 6, 11, 154, 203 (nn. 4, 5); relationship with state, 9–10, 11, 183, 186; community political power of, 28; dress of, 48; mobility of, 49, 136, 215 (n. 3); and violence in urban areas, 50, 141; and land allocation policies, 60; dual identity of, 205 (n. 8)
Individualism: and citizenship, 83–84, 108, 128, 151; and ayllu democracy, 94–96; within group structure, 99–100; and economic models, 101, 102, 106; and unions, 212 (n. 14)
Indonesia, 8
Inequality: and colonial and neocolonial policies, 1, 27, 204–5 (n. 7); new forms resembling old forms of, 24, 26; and resource extractivism, 52; gendered, 57, 146; and insurgent citizenship, 65; and neoliberalism, 83, 183–84; and constitution of Bolivia, 88; inverting historic spaces of, 130; healing scars of, 157; and capitalism, 180; and climate change, 188. See also Landed inequality
Informal economy, employment in, 5, 22, 36–37, 47, 55, 62, 180, 196
Inkarrí myth, 159

movement state, 8, 173–76; retreat of, 82–83, 85, 86, 101, 106, 173–74; democratic structures independent of, 84; and citizenship, 108, 128; and right-wing elites, 171–72, 187, 218 (n. 10); and international investment, 175; and food sovereignty, 176–80; and power relations, 187; and climate change, 188

Natural resources: and neoliberalism, 37, 194; and MST, 41, 84; protection from exploitation, 49; and resource curse, 51–52, 219 (n. 1); depletion of, 59, 197, 198–99; and power relations, 70; and ayllu democracy, 85; redistribution of, 86, 145; reclamation of, 153; state's management of, 160, 162; and indigeneity as political tool, 168, 183, 219 (n. 1); and Morales, 176; and food sovereignty, 177; distribution of, 220 (n. 4). *See also* Extractive industries

Navarro, Angélica, 189

Neocolonial policies: and inequality, 1, 27, 204–5 (n. 7); relationship with colonial policies, 24; effects of, 27, 128–29, 157, 198; indigenous resistance to, 44; and violence, 90

Neoliberalism: and land legislation, 5, 37, 38–39; culture-centered challenges to, 13; exacerbation of global antipathies, 24; and multiculturalism, 29, 184; and rights-based approach, 30; shifts in approach, 33, 35; and trade, 35, 36, 86; and poverty discourses, 35, 83, 183, 184, 209 (n. 12); and market liberalization, 35–36, 38, 39; and classic liberalism, 35–36, 205–6 (n. 14); and environmental issues, 36, 194; in Bolivia, 36–39; and unions, 37, 187, 206 (n. 17); corruption in reforms, 38, 206 (n. 19); and relocation of miners, 43, 204 (n. 4); and soy production, 54; and agribusiness, 55, 56, 57–58, 105, 109, 112, 114; and identity, 56; and class, 57–58; and decentralized

governing structures, 82, 86; and insecurity, 85, 106; structural adjustments of, 90; and ayllu democracy, 101, 119, 198; MST proposals compared to, 104–5; social, 127; resistance to, 155, 161; and Morales, 176, 191–92; and environmental spending, 206 (n. 15); and leadership, 210 (n. 3)

New Agrarian Reform Law (2006): inauguration of, 6, 74, 165; and neoliberalism, 37; and Morales, 74, 154, 155, 156; marches for, 135–36, 141–43, 207 (n. 20), 217 (n. 19); right-wing opposition to, 140, 164, 165; and land redistribution, 173

New Economic Policy (NEP), 36

Nongovernmental organizations (NGOs): and Cortés Arauz, 21; and ayllu system, 29–30, 120, 205 (n. 9); and narratives of indigenous resistance, 33; and March for Territory and Dignity to La Paz, 38; and economic development, 51; and MST, 96; and indigeneity as political tool, 110, 185; and agroecological model, 123–24, 214 (nn. 14, 15); and Morales, 138; and Fifth National March for Land and Territory, 145; and social movements, 151; and climate change, 189, 190; and security, 210 (n. 5)

Nordenskiöld, Erland, 32, 218 (n. 6)

North-South Highway, 47, 48

Obispo Santiesteban province, Santa Cruz: and MST, 6, 100, 104, 143; agribusiness in, 44, 53; regional history of, 48–49; soy production in, 50–51, 54; colonization in, 53; and ayllu democracy, 211 (n. 7)

Ogoni people, 51, 67–68

Olla común, 145, 147, 153, 216 (n. 11)

Ong, Aihwa, 56

Orgaz García, Mirko, 162

Oriente region, 32, 33, 205 (n. 12)

Orta, Andrew, 29

118–19; and violence, 82; governance of, 84–85, 89, 96; and agroecological model, 104, 117, 120, 123, 125, 126, 214 (n. 14); and ayllu democracy, 118–20; and alternative modes of production, 120–22; financial problems of, 125, 213 (n. 12); and Fifth National March for Land and Territory, 143; and food preparation, 145; infrastructure of, 175; and indigeneity as political tool, 185

Puerta del Sol, Tiwanaku, 9

Quechua Indians: as contract laborers, 3; and highland rural areas, 21; population of, 22; and migration to lowlands, 34; and Morales, 192

Quechua language, 139

Quince de Agosto, 66

Quispe, Felipe, 30

Quispe, Rafael, 192

Race and racism: and labor code, 3, and legislation, 12; and *anillos*, 17; and indigeneity as political tool, 42, 181; and land allocation policies, 60; and violence, 82; history of, 156; and right-wing elites, 165, 218 (n. 5); and migrants, 167, 208–9 (n. 3); and food sovereignty, 179; and climate change, 189; and environmental issues, 196; and biological model of race, 203 (n. 2); regional elites, 209 (n. 5)

Radcliffe, Sarah, 127, 209 (n. 3)

Rappaport, Joanne, 7, 86

Reforestation, and MST, 208 (n. 26)

Regional elites: resistance of, 13; and power relations, 14, 184; and land issues, 33, 44, 184; and departmental decentralization, 49, 52, 55, 70, 74, 164, 165, 166–72, 208 (nn. 1, 2); and borders between sites of production and sites of consumption, 49–50, 208–9 (n. 3); and highland migrants, 53, 55; and modernity, 56, 57, 58, 209

(n. 5); and citizenship, 56, 58, 70, 73, 74, 184; and soy production, 68; and hybrid models, 129; and right-wing opposition, 165; and Morales, 172; and INRA, 175

Resistance: and MST, 22–23, 211 (n. 8); forms of, 27–28, 90; and Guaraní rebellion of 1892, 30, 32–33; and Mojeño rebellion of 1887, 32; narratives of, 33, 42; and alternative modes of production, 107; and indigeneity as political tool, 184, 217 (n. 3)

Resource-based movements: and Cocaleros, 1; history of, 13; and indigeneity as political tool, 42–43, 44, 51, 74, 212 (n. 4). *See also* Land issues; MST

Revilla, Carlos, 119, 210 (n. 3)

Revolutionary Nationalist Movement (MNR), 34, 53, 138, 163, 215 (n. 4)

Revolution of 1952: and peasant uprising, 3, 163; and *sindicalista* tradition, 203–4 (n. 1)

Rice production: in Ichilo, 60–61, 66; and small-scale farming, 60–63; wage laborers in, 67

Risor, Helen, 81, 83, 211 (n. 11)

Rivera Cusicanqui, Silvia, 29

Rocha, J., 116

Rodriguez, Eduardo, 73

Rosset, Peter, 209 (n. 7)

Rubber era, 32, 69–70, 205 (n. 11)

Saavedra, Ruceno, 32

Sachs, Jeffrey D., 51

Saisari, Silvestre: as MST leader, 17, 91; background of, 18–19, 20, 21; and historical memory, 24–25; and Yuquises occupation, 72–73; and ayllu democracy, 89, 106, 119; and air transportation, 111, 112; and agroecological model, 117; and land redistribution, 140

Sala Sala, Juan, 40

Salvatierra, Hugo, 139

Salvatierra, José, 105

Salvatierra, Luis, 72, 209–10 (n. 13), 210 (n. 14)

San Aurelio sugar mill, 53

San Cayetano region, 68

Sánchez de Lozada, Gonzalo, 2, 37, 38, 88, 198

San Cristobal Mining Company, 191

San Pedro, 47, 48, 79–80

Santa Cruz (city): elites of, 3, 5, 35, 49, 53, 61, 69, 203 (n. 2), 204 (nn. 2, 3), 205 (n. 11), 218 (nn. 4, 5); sugarcane plantations of, 3, 20–21, 31, 32; growth of, 3, 56; rebuilding of local governance, 7; modernization in, 13; *anillos* of, 17, 204 (n. 2); and Cruceño identity, 31, 205 (n. 10); international investment in, 34, 52; and agricultural output, 52, 54, 56; Civic Committee of, 55, 57, 170, 208 (n. 1); and globalized agrarian identity, 56–58; MAS headquarters in, 59, 80, 209 (n. 8); and marches, 139, 140; and *casco viejo*, 204 (n. 2); mobility in, 213 (n. 7)

Santa Cruz (department): and MST occupation, 45; and Bolivia's GDP, 52; and deforestation, 63; Departmental Agrarian Commission, 73; and soy production, 79; and Collas, 166–67; flag of, 170, 218 (n. 9); and citizenship, 184

Santa Cruz Youth Union. *See* UJC

Santa Fe, 59–60

Santos Vargas, Paulina, 166–67

Saro-Wiwa, Ken, 67

Sassen, Saskia, 209 (n. 4)

Sawyer, Suzana, 75, 125, 156, 209 (n. 6), 212 (n. 4)

Schumpeter, Joseph, 204 (n. 5)

Second International Conference of Vía Campesina, 109, 115

Self-determination: and Aymara Indians, 30; legitimacy of, 33; and environmental issues, 51; of Ogoni people, 67; and governance, 74–75; and ayllu system, 85; and Zapatistas, 86; and indigenous

law, 88, 90; and alternative modes of production, 124

Self-help justice, 83

Self-sufficiency: effect of Spanish conquest on, 27; and neoliberalism, 37; and pre-Columbian cultural forms, 42; and alternative modes of production, 106

Shah, Alpah, 110, 214 (n. 18)

Sieder, Rachel, 88

Sindicalista tradition: and MST, 17, 143; and highland migrants, 53; history of, 203–4 (n. 1)

Six Federations of Coca Growers, 219 (n. 13)

Slave labor: and subjugation of indigenous people, 1, 31, 32, 168, 197; and sugar plantations of Santa Cruz, 20–21, 31, 32, 42; and historical memory, 24

Small-scale farming: and loss of landholdings, 5, 39, 196; and transformation of land use, 5, 184; MAS's proposals for revival of, 9; and debt, 35, 39, 55, 59, 60–62, 66; and market liberalization, 36; and neoliberalism, 37, 39; and *sindicalista* tradition, 53; and large competitors, 54–55, 187; and citizenship, 58; and rice production, 60–62; and indigeneity as political tool, 75; and alternative modes of production, 105, 106–7, 118, 123, 124, 151; and food sovereignty, 110, 115, 177; and loans, 138, 209 (n. 9); structural support for, 156, 157; and Morales, 176, 179; and transnational corporations, 179; relationship with state, 187

Smith, Adam, 35

Smith, Neil, 199, 200

Social movement strategies: and indigeneity, 1, 2; capacity of, 2; and pre-Columbian cultural forms, 6–10, 161, 187; and role of state, 8, 12, 13–14, 107, 173–76, 181–82, 187–88, 197–201;

White elites, 3, 60

Wiebe, Nettie, 114

Wind turbines, 117

Wittman, Hannah, 108

Wolford, Wendy, 67, 116

Women: political disenfranchisement of, 97–99; religious pilgrimages of Mexican, 136, 215 (n. 2); household duties of, 145–46; and dancing, 150; and columnas, 215 (n. 1). *See also* Gender

Workers' rights, 199, 221 (n. 10)

World Bank, 38, 54, 125, 206 (n. 16), 207 (n. 22)

World Food Summit, 110

World People's Conference on Climate Change and the Rights of Mother Earth, 189–92

World Social Forum, 109

World Trade Organization, 206 (n. 16)

YPFB (Yacimientos Petrolíferos Fiscales Bolivianos), 162

Yuquises hacienda, occupation of, 45, 48, 50, 66–68, 70–72, 73, 79, 80, 91, 104, 149

Yuracaré peoples, 10

Zapatistas, 86, 211 (nn. 9, 10)

Zero-coca policies, 43